ISSUES IN THERAPY WITH LESBIAN, GAY, BISEXUAL AND TRANSGENDER CLIENTS

Edited by
CHARLES NEAL
and
DOMINIC DAVIES

OPEN UNIVERSITY PRESS
Buckingham · Philadelphia

Open University Press
Celtic Court
22 Ballmoor
Buckingham
MK18 1XW

email: enquiries@openup.co.uk
world wide web: www.openup.co.uk

and
325 Chestnut Street
Philadelphia, PA 19106, USA

First Published 2000

A catalogue record of this book is available from the British Library

ISBN   0 335 20331 0 (pb)   0 335 20332 9 (hb)

Library of Congress Cataloging-in-Publication Data
Issues in therapy with lesbian, gay, bisexual and transgender clients / edited by
    Charles Neal and Dominic Davies.
        p.   cm.
    Includes bibliographical references and index.
    ISBN 0-335-20332-9 (hb) — ISBN 0-335-20331-0 (pbk.)
    1. Gays—Mental health.   2. Bisexuals—Mental health.
3. Gays—Counseling of.   4. Bisexuals—Counseling of.
I. Neal, Charles, 1948–   II. Davies, Dominic, 1959–
RC451.4.G39 I87   2000
616.89′0086′64—dc21   99–056819

Typeset by Graphicraft Limited, Hong Kong
Printed in Great Britain by Biddles Limited, Guildford and Kings Lynn

This book is dedicated to Jeremy Cole and Lee Adams, our partners, who so beautifully demonstrate love in action and special ways of being men.

Contents

Notes on contributors   ix

Acknowledgements   xiii

Foreword   xv
Moira Walker

Introduction   1
Charles Neal and Dominic Davies

1   Embracing difference: addressing race, culture and sexuality   7
    Rita Brauner

2   Kink therapy: SM and sexual minorities   22
    Denis Bridoux

3   The management of ethical dilemmas associated with dual
    relationships   35
    Lynne Gabriel and Dominic Davies

4   Issues in HIV/AIDS counselling   55
    Pavlo Kanellakis

5   Expressive therapy: freeing the creative self   68
    Timothy McMichael

6   Psychosexual issues   83
    Ian McNally and Naomi Adams

7   We are family: working with gay men in groups   102
    Charles Neal

8   Looking both ways: bisexuality and therapy   115
    Elizabeth Oxley and Claire A. Lucius

9   Working with people who have been sexually abused
    in childhood   128
    Fiona Purdie

10 Long-term consequences of bullying   146
    Ian Rivers

11 Gay men and sex: clinical issues   160
    Jan Schippers

12 Transgender issues in therapy   176
    Tony Zandvliet

Index   190

Notes on contributors

Naomi Adams qualified as a clinical psychologist in 1997 and has been working in sexual health in East London since that time. She is a committee member of the British Psychological Society Special Interest Group in HIV and Sexual Health. Naomi's current research interests include psychosexual difficulties and related issues in lesbians. Her clinical work includes therapy with psychosexual problems in lesbians, gay men and bisexuals.

Rita Brauner is a UKCP registered psychotherapist and a human rights activist. She is a white. British bicultural lesbian woman with German roots. She works part-time as a health adviser in the NHS, provides training around the multifaceted issues of oppression and has a private therapy practice. She has worked for over ten years in the HIV/AIDS and sexual health fields and has many years of experience working with gay and bisexual men, other sexual minorities and black people. Rita's therapy training background includes HIV/AIDS counselling, psychosexual, gay affirmative, time limited and intergrative therapy. Rita has a diploma and an MSc in transactional analysis psychotherapy and a diploma in intercultural therapy.

Denis Bridoux is a counsellor, a wellness coach and a licensed NLP trainer based in Yorkshire. He is a member of *Kink Aware Professionals*, an international body supporting the needs of the SM and sexual edge communities. Secretary of Halifax Area Gay Group from 1982 to 1992, he was involved with the establishment and running of HIV voluntary organisations in Yorkshire in both voluntary and management capacities from the mid-1980s and AIDS/HIV coordinator for South Humberside Health Authorities from 1991 to 1995. Denis runs licensed NLP courses for health-related professions with *Post-Graduate Professional Education*, for gay men as

Outcome, and business coaching on the telephone as *EnVision*. He was recently made Honorary Fellow of the international *Institute for Neuro-Semantics®* for his contributions to the expansion of the field.

Dominic Davies is a BAC accredited and UKRC registered independent counsellor and therapist who has been practising in the person-centred approach for 20 years. He was co-chair of the Association for Lesbian, Gay and Bisexual Psychologies UK, and co-editor with Charles Neal of *Pink Therapy* and *Therapeutic Perspectives on Working with Lesbian, Gay and Bisexual Clients* (Open University Press 1996 and 2000 respectively). Dominic runs an international consultancy developing sexuality training for therapists and other helping professionals in Europe and Australasia. He is a Visiting Fellow of Nottingham Trent University.

Lynne Gabriel, MEd Counselling and the Management of Human Resources; Diploma Counselling; ITD Certificate in Training and Development. Lynne works in private practice as a counselling therapist and supervisor and is currently a doctoral student at the University College of Ripon and York St John, York. Her research area is duality phenomena in counselling and psychotherapy. She has served on BAC's Standards and Ethics Committee and is a member of their Professional Conduct Committee.

Pavlo Kanellakis is a chartered counselling psychologist, BAC accredited counsellor trainer, chartered health psychologist and organisational consultant. His work experience includes being an HIV counselling officer and clinical supervisor. He has also worked for major HIV, AIDS and lesbian and gay organisations.

Claire A. Lucius has worked as a counsellor in both university and health settings since 1991. She currently works in London and Brighton as a counsellor and supervisor in primary care and in private practice. She is a UKRC registered independent counsellor and a BAC accredited counsellor.

Timothy McMichael is a therapist, supervisor and trainer from the person-centred tradition. Using expressive therapy in differing forms for nine years, he passionately believes it helps in unlocking repressed gay identity. Away from counselling he's a family mediator and sometimes works in finance. Home is West London where he's 'married' to Glen who, along with his dearest friend and colleague Amanda Davidson, provides so much inspiration and encouragement to work and play expressively.

Ian McNally works as a clinical psychologist at the Royal London Hospital in Whitechapel and in private practice. He specialises in sexual health and HIV-related problems and is conducting research into transcultural aspects of male sexual problems. He is currently completing training as a cognitive analytic therapy (CAT) practitioner.

Charles Neal is a UKCP accredited humanistic and integrative psycho-therapist and a supervisor and trainer in private practice. He is founder and former chair of the Association for Lesbian, Gay and Bisexual Psychologies UK and co-editor (with Dominic Davies) of *Pink Therapy* and *Therapeutic Perspectives on Working with Lesbian, Gay and Bisexual Clients* (Open University Press 1996 and 2000 respectively). Charles is also a director of *Transform Consultancy* – 'an agency for change', and has special interests in creativity, intimate relationships and sexualities.

Elizabeth Oxley qualified as a clinical psychologist 20 years ago. She has worked in a number of specialisms including adult mental health, substance misuse and sexual health. She established and managed a successful drugs team and has conducted research into service delivery and quality in drugs and HIV services. More recently she has worked extensively with people who have experienced serious sexual abuse or trauma. She favours an integrative, questioning approach.

Fiona Purdie is a BAC accredited counsellor who has been trained in both the person-centred approach and as a Gestalt psychotherapist (Metanoia). She has worked with survivors of childhood sexual abuse for over two decades, first as a social worker and founder member of ChildLine and latterly as a therapist and supervisor in private practice. She has extensive experience of training counsellors and therapists and taught at Metanoia in London for five years before moving to the East Midlands. Fiona currently works as Senior Lecturer in Counselling and Psychotherapy at Nottingham Trent University and also trains counsellors at Temenos in Sheffield.

Ian Rivers is currently Senior Lecturer in social psychology at the University College of Ripon and York St John. He is an active researcher in the field of human development and his previous work has included a study of the nature and long-term implications of bullying at school for lesbians, gay men and bisexual men and women, partly funded by the Froebel Educational Institute and the University of Luton. His current research interests surround the social implications and development of sexual orientation, and in particular bisexuality.

Jan Schippers studied clinical psychology at the Vrije Universiteit in Amsterdam. For 14 years he worked at the SAD-Schorerfoundation, the Dutch national agency for homosexuality, specialising in psychotherapy and psychosocial care for gay men. During this period he wrote several books and many articles on these issues. In 1996 he published his doctoral thesis, *Gay Identities* at the medical faculty of the University of Amsterdam. Since 1996 Jan has worked as a psychologist-sexologist at the Leijenburg Hospital in The Hague.

Tony Zandvliet studied social sciences at the University of Amsterdam, majoring in psychology, sociology and political science and training in psychotherapy. Since 1987 she has specialised in gender identity development and has an independent practice as a gender therapist in Amsterdam and London. Tony also lectures and is a consultant for individuals and groups concerned with the social and political implications of transgender and sexuality, including relatives, partners and children of trans people.

Acknowledgements

Dominic wishes to thank all his close friends and colleagues for their support and encouragement to undertake and pursue this project. He is also grateful for the expert consultation of Mani Bruce Mitchell on aspects of the book.

Charles offers loving thanks to Rex Bradley, Terry Cooper and Jenner Roth, for so many years as wonderful teachers, and Dominic Davies, for doing more than his fair share of this work, when life was difficult for me, with such good grace. Without the love of my sons, my sister, my mother and my dear friends, I would not be able to sustain my work.

The editors would like to thank Michael Jacobs for his valuable feedback and editorial support and all our contributors for their patience and commitment over a long period. We also thank Natalie Rogers and Science and Behavior Books for permission to use her illustration in Chapter 5.

MOIRA WALKER

Foreword

I am delighted to write this brief introduction to what promises to be a further valuable addition to the literature on gay affirmative therapy, following the first two volumes in this trilogy. This has been an area previously consistently neglected in the therapeutic literature and often sidelined, misunderstood, or avoided in both therapeutic practice and training. As a result, counsellors and therapists have been misinformed or uninformed: inevitably this has resulted in clients not always receiving a sufficiently sensitive, knowledgeable and respectful response. Prejudices, stereotypes and oppression have been rife both in a wider society and within some 'therapeutic' circles.

This book marks a significant step forward in informing and challenging. It puts firmly on the therapeutic map an area that should have been there long ago. The rapid success of the first volume has demonstrated that the demand for good literature, in what has previously been marginalised and invalidated as supposedly an area of minority interest only, is very considerable. This success reflects the growing awareness among counsellors and therapists, both those who would identify themselves as members of sexual minorities and those who do not, of the need for a greater knowledge base, a greater skill base, and far more awareness of the complexity of issues that can be presented. This volume and the others in this trilogy also succeed in making this complexity of ideas, subjects and material accessible to a wide range of readers working across a variety of helping contexts. It brings together an impressive array of authors representing a range of theoretical approaches and key areas.

The subjects covered in this volume are crucial to effective practice. It offers therapists, counsellors and others insights and information into aspects of their work with lesbian, gay, bisexual and transgender people that they will not find elsewhere. Some of the material will be challenging to some readers in terms of their existing knowledge and pre-conceptions. Stereotypes are recognised and described, questioned and challenged; myths and prejudices are explored; and areas of particular concern and relevance are highlighted and analysed in terms of their origins and their ongoing impact. Such challenges and questions are essential if counsellors and therapists are to offer a service to clients that is relevant to their experiences of themselves and their world, and that recognises the impact of a wider culture.

The book is particularly valuable in that the authors and editors have a wealth of practical experience that is effectively communicated to the reader. Practitioners will benefit greatly from the suggestions for good practice that are a theme running throughout these chapters. Clinical practice and clinical issues are emphasised and explored sensitively and creatively. Through this book, readers will find access to both an increased theoretical awareness and an important contribution to the range of their therapeutic skills.

Finally, as a trainer and a practitioner myself, I would like to thank the editors and all the authors for the contributions they make in this volume. It poses both a crucial challenge to many existing ideas and, perhaps most importantly, thereby contributes to improving the therapeutic responses to our clients.

Moira Walker
Leicester

CHARLES NEAL AND
DOMINIC DAVIES

Introduction

Welcome to the last in our trilogy of independent, closely related texts on what is currently known as 'gay affirmative therapy'. It has been vital to address issues for clients and practitioners about counselling and therapy with people from sexual minorities: there had been a dearth of constructive European material for clinicians, trainers, researchers and supervisors in this expanding field. In this volume we seek to further challenge prejudices and misconceptions about various aspects of living as lesbian, bisexual, transgender or gay people.

How healthy is gay affirmative therapy for the new millennium? We have now demonstrated that gay affirmative therapy is basically *person* affirmative and that therapists do not use a separate body of techniques and skills, but instead need a level of self-awareness and comfort with sexuality *per se*, and homosexuality in particular. Most practitioners like to claim an ease with sexuality and many claim expertise in working with clients from sexual minorities. Few UK therapy and supervision training programmes, however, include much in the way of personal development on human sexuality: even more rarely do their curricula include working with clients from sexual minorities. We know of no courses teaching 'gay positive' theories of child development or human relationships. Many therapists seem to feel that a common sexual orientation is by itself a qualification for working with clients from these minorities. We do not agree!

We are saddened by dwindling support for the Association for Lesbian, Gay and Bisexual Psychologies UK which one of us founded, both have chaired, and of which most of our contributors have been members, and the corresponding decline in the European network. Our training conferences and seminars were precious opportunities for practitioners to share queer issues safely. Judging by advertisements in the gay press, plenty of therapists want to work with homosexual and bisexual clients. What a pity so few treat their responsibilities seriously enough to contribute to a healthy national professional association! There remains so much to do.

It is also lamentable that the British Association for Counselling and the United Kingdom Council for Psychotherapy have yet to develop lesbian or gay sections equivalent to those long established in the USA. Such a section was finally established at the end of 1999, after a lengthy struggle by the British Psychological Society to resist: congratulations! As we write the Labour government, upon which many pinned high hopes of legislative change against homophobic discrimination and injustice, has failed to deliver substantive change.

Some chapters here reveal the grim consequences for young people. For example, Ian Rivers, an academic psychologist, discusses the lifelong effects of a widespread form of abuse: bullying. His groundbreaking research at the University of Luton horrifyingly reveals children's daily experiences of homophobia in action and the long-term consequences for self-esteem, intimacy, trust and depression in adulthood. His work is invaluable to clinicians and educators and demands addressing in our schools and wider communities. How can we protect our children and young people when educators remain afraid to be seen as 'promoting' homosexuality?

Abuse continues in other forms. Fiona Purdie writes from extensive clinical experience with 'survivors' of sexual abuse. Many practice issues are shared with other survivors, yet inadequate attention has been paid to the specific contexts, power dynamics and issues for children from sexual minorities who are abused, in spite of their over-representation in both sexually abused, and client, populations. Purdie examines some underlying myths and suggests ways of working ethically.

The need to heal the wounds of homophobic oppression also continues. Pavlo Kanellakis explores the impact of HIV not only for those who are infected, but also for others who are affected – partners, friends, families, practitioners and gay, lesbian and bisexual communities as a whole. He explores the traumatic effects of adjusting to multiple cumulative losses and the relevance of psychosocial factors, particularly social support, in maintaining wellness. Kanellakis importantly highlights the effects of working with these client groups on the therapist's own well-being.

Timothy McMichael shows how creative techniques help clients rediscover their creativity and self-awareness when so many queer people have learned to repress these parts of themselves, and this has stunted their fuller growth. He offers numerous practical methods for working creatively at the client's pace towards self-actualisation. Some practitioners will find these techniques especially challenging and others will be inspired.

Charles Neal shares his experience, methodology and influences in working with gay men in groups through explorations of being male, gay and in groups. He discusses what seems important about these identities, and how vital the healing of group work can be. He describes the styles, exercises and foci which have proved valuable and what emerges from group members' own feedback.

European Association for Lesbian, Gay and Bisexual Psychologists' founder, Jan Schippers, has considerable experience demystifying issues of gay male sex and sexuality. Here he explores the awkward relationship between intimacy and sex in male subcultures and advances a theory about 'sexual lovestyles'. Other issues illustrated through his case examples include body image, identity development and aversion to anal sex.

Exclusion continues and the ostracism of minorities is not just by majority cultural groups. In this volume we learn about the particular issues faced by people frequently excluded by homosexual and bisexual communities and practitioners. Rita Brauner, for instance, stresses the importance of practitioners processing their own history around culture, race and ethnicity and of clearly addressing differences between client and therapist, not ignoring these. She explores racism and heterosexism in therapy and the dangers of holding a solely 'White' perspective.

Elizabeth Oxley and Claire A. Lucius believe distinctly bisexual experience remains underrepresented in traditional or 'gay affirmative' psychology. They look at definitions of bisexuality and some consequences of embracing such an identity and outline issues clients may bring and what therapists need to address themselves, as well as giving examples of helpful and unhelpful practice.

Tony Zandvliet challenges us to reconsider gender and sexuality through some experiences and issues for transgender people. In her critique of clinical assumptions she argues that, while changing gender has implications for sexual orientation, the concepts of gay, lesbian, straight and bisexual imply dichotomies that are undermined by transgender. Her case studies, discussion and practical guidelines increase our awareness and the sensitivity of our responses to clients.

And there are still taboo subjects. Denis Bridoux addresses working with clients interested in SM sexual practices and 'kink' lifestyles. Despite a rapidly expanding 'kink' community in the UK, clients are wary of discussing their issues because of ignorance and prejudice on the practitioner's part. Bridoux discusses common myths about SM and gives guidelines for working respectfully.

Further taboos are challenged when ethical dilemmas arise from dual relationships between practitioners and clients living in the same or overlapping communities. These are explored by Lynne Gabriel and Dominic Davies. Theoretical and ethical perspectives are related to the management of such dilemmas, including boundary maintenance, and Gabriel's problem-solving models are applied to practical examples.

Ian McNally and Naomi Adams, psychologists in sexual health clinics, challenge heterosexist paradigms of treatment for sexual problems. They root their theoretical and practical experience in a clinical context via case studies which illustrate affirmative, culturally sensitive ways of working with specific issues of sexual functioning which clients from sexual minorities bring.

These texts go some way to providing information about how to work ethically with lesbian, gay, bisexual and transgender clients: they are not a substitute for the deep personal development and training needed to provide a high-quality service. It is not sufficient to read texts. It takes extraordinary hard work in personal therapy and supervision with therapists and supervisors with whom one feels safe enough not to self-censor, or hide one's shame, grief and discomfort with oneself. Too often therapists (queer ones perhaps more than most) are unable to admit failings and lack of knowledge, paying lip-service to political sensibilities instead. We have been trained all our lives to 'pass' and curry favour, to make ourselves acceptable to powerful majority communities. Supervisors and trainers are too frequently identified with those communities.

As editors, practitioners and trainers, we are increasingly developing our own work on gay affirmative issues in Europe and elsewhere.[1] We hear of lesbian and gay therapists who do not 'agree' with bisexuality or transgender and refuse to work with clients who identify thus. We hear of therapists 'disapproving' of SM sex, believing all casual sex is unhealthy, seeking to help clients cure their 'sexual addiction', or believing only long-term single partner relationships are desirable. Such examples of unprofessionalism display a want of experience and training in matters of sexual diversity. Sexual minorities experience the world differently: therapists working with us need training in understanding the resulting differences in psychology.

Irrespective of sexual orientation, therefore, we believe that therapists need to be prepared to work at depth on their attitudes, prejudices, feelings and behaviours about lesbian, gay, transgender and bisexual issues *before* working with people from these communities. We need to find ourselves before we are able to find our clients. We need specific training to do so.

It is our wish that in this trilogy as a whole, those interested in updating their thinking and practice and challenging their own assumptions and prejudices about sex and sexuality, in order to make themselves open to experiences of others, are gifted with a great deal to think and talk about. More than 40 practitioners have shared a mass of positive information and experience with us all in these books: many of them had never written about their work before. We have reason to be grateful and motivated as a result. Good practitioners continually refine their own frames of reference in order to see the world as clients might.

We desperately need more open-minded, open-hearted and culturally sensitive therapists, researchers and trainers so that sexism and homophobia do not continually contaminate our lives and cultures, to say nothing of our psyches. We profoundly hope that this work encourages others to take these issues forward in research and debate, clinical practice and training, in all the many places that need to let in fresh air and daylight to clear away archaic ways of oppressing one another.

Notes on case examples and terminology

'**Case examples**' are used in most chapters. In order to protect confidentiality they are composites which do not refer to specific clients or their work. Exceptions are clearly identified and always have informed permission given.

'**Gay affirmative**' has come to us to mean truly *person affirmative*. Authors in all three volumes argue persuasively that treating *all* people with respect, compassion, equity and as having equal value is fundamental to the work of therapists, counsellors and related occupations, not an additional, special way of being with people from particular groups (See Davies and Neal 1996, 2000).

Defining sexualities: we use terms such as 'gay', 'lesbian', 'queer', 'bisexual', 'transvestite', 'transgender', 'transsexual' and 'straight' to refer to people who describe themselves this way. While the development of distinct identities is important, we increasingly recognise that all categorising of the range of human experience is inadequate and over-defining. Each of us must be allowed to define ourself. People of different sexualities can support each other in fighting oppression, without forcing themselves or others into falsely homogeneous groups.

'**Therapy**' and 'the therapeutic relationship' are used to include the whole range of counselling and psychotherapy approaches as well as closely related encounters. We hope that no terms used have inadvertently excluded or offended readers.

Contributors to this volume do not necessarily share the views expressed by fellow contributors. We are all, however, committed to respecting diversity of opinion.

References

Davies, D. and Neal, C. (eds) (1996) *Pink Therapy: A Guide for Counsellors and Therapists Working with Lesbian, Gay and Bisexual Clients*. Buckingham: Open University Press.

Davies, D. and Neal, C. (eds) (2000) *Therapeutic Perspectives on Working with Lesbian, Gay and Bisexual Clients*. Buckingham: Open University Press.

Note

1 Dominic Davies: tel: +44 (0)20 7739 5542 or email:
pinktherapy@serene.dircon.co.uk
Charles Neal: TRANSFORM Consultancy: tel: +44 (0)20 7387 6758.

| RITA BRAUNER

Embracing difference: addressing race, culture and sexuality

Introduction

I am writing this chapter from my personal perspective as a lesbian psycho-therapist committed to anti-oppressive clinical practice and as a white bicultural practitioner who has made the decision to acknowledge and work with issues related to race, culture and racism. By sharing my cultural background and the influence that shaped me I want to highlight the multitude and complexity of issues related to sexuality, race and culture.

I grew up in Germany in a small, working-class mining town where the dominant society was defined mainly through white, male, middle class and heterosexual values. Like many other lesbian women worldwide, I had no positive role modelling when I was trying to come to terms with my sexuality. As a lesbian I continue to experience discrimination and, despite my British passport, continue to be at the receiving end of xenophobia because of my German background. As a German I have to come to terms with the painful history of my birth country in killing six million Jews and other 'unwanted' persons, some of whom were black or gay. As a British person I have to accept the role Britain had in the history of imperialism, colonialism and slavery. As a white person I learnt to accept that I am privileged in comparison to members of the black communities and that I am, by definition, part of the racist system that operates in Britain. This meant that I had to take responsibility for the painful truth of being potentially racist myself.

For the last 15 years I have worked through many aspects of my conscious personal racism and my internalised homophobia. For me it was a long way from knowing what the issues were to integrating them into my belief system and professional practice. I believe this is an ongoing lifelong task.

My training background includes humanistic and cognitive as well as psychodynamic approaches and I define myself as an integrative psychotherapist. I work in private practice and in a number of HIV related settings. In my anti-oppressive approach to therapy I am guided first by the concept of gay affirmative therapy, which Maylon (1982: 69) defines as: 'Not an independent system of psychotherapy. Rather it represents a special range of psychological knowledge which challenges the traditional view that homosexual desire and fixed homosexual orientations are pathological'.

Clients who are gay, lesbian or bisexual have different life experiences from those of their heterosexual counterparts. This difference needs to be taken into account rather than pathologised in therapeutic work, just as much as the experience of black clients who live in a white dominant, racist society. As a therapist, guided by gay affirmative principles, I therefore see homosexuality, bisexuality and transgender as 'valid and rich orientations in their own right' (Davies 1996: 40).

Second, as a therapist trained in intercultural therapy, I believe that white therapists can help black clients appropriately if they understand the basic concepts of intercultural therapy, are willing to address their own racism, have understanding of cultural issues relevant to their black clients and have the insight to decide when to refer on to a black therapist if that becomes necessary.

The main concept of intercultural therapy, as I practise it, is based on being comfortable with difference. In the broadest sense this can address all differences between therapist and client (e.g. gender, religion, age, class, disability and sexual orientation). In a more focused sense it means working with difference in the context of race and culture and thereby addressing the issues of racism. The late J. Kareem, co-founder of intercultural therapy as practised by NAFSIYAT, the London-based intercultural therapy centre, describes it as:

> A form of dynamic psychotherapy that takes into account the whole being of the patient – not only the individual concepts and constructs as presented to the therapist, but also the patient's communal life experience in the world – both present and past. The very fact of being from another culture involves conscious and unconscious assumptions, in the patient and in the therapist. I believe that for the successful outcome of therapy, it is essential to address these conscious and unconscious assumptions from the beginning. So this means that when we are treating patients from black and ethnic minority groups we have to take up the issues of their real life experience of racism.
>
> (Kareem 1988: 63).

I am also guided by another important concept of intercultural therapy which assumes that the relationship between a white therapist and a black client started long before the two first met and that this historical relationship has often been based on distorted beliefs and attitudes about each person's race or cultural group. In order to get to a therapeutic relationship and for clients to be able to develop real transference, these issues have to be addressed. Curry (1964) describes this as the concept of 'pre-transference'.

As a white lesbian integrative psychotherapist, committed to the principles of gay affirmative and intercultural therapy, I feel well equipped to work with the multifaceted issues that can arise with black clients who are also gay, lesbian or bisexual. I will use a number of examples and illustrations to demonstrate aspects of my clinical work: these are all fictional in order to prevent identification of my clients.

A word about definitions

The terminology used in the areas of race, culture and sexuality is plentiful and there are many concepts and theories explaining racism, race, culture and blackness. Therefore it is necessary to define my use of the term 'black'. The definition I have found most useful is that of the London Black Lesbian and Gay Centre, quoted in Mason-John and Khambatta (1993: 9): 'Descended (through one or both parents) from Africa, Asia (i.e. the Middle East and China, including the Pacific nations) and Latin America, and lesbians and gay men descended from the original inhabitants of Australasia, North America and the islands of the Atlantic and Indian Ocean'.

Although bisexuality and transgenderation are not stated in this definition I extend it to include black bisexual and transgender people. Mason-John and Khambatta (1993) point out that all these groups have suffered racial discrimination or cultural subjugation in the colonial past and have experienced racism in Britain on a personal or institutional level. I support this point of view because it emphasises the commonality of black people's experience in relation to the European former colonial and imperialistic powers rather than the diversity of their cultural heritages.

Being black

Before I focus on the issues that black clients from sexual minorities have to deal with on a daily basis, it is essential to first draw attention to the impact of what it means to be black in Britain. It is crucial for me to hold an overview of black history and stay informed about current issues affecting the black communities in order to work in a client-centred, intercultural way with these client groups. From my perspective it is vital to integrate discussions about race, gender, sexuality, age and other relevant differences that exist between myself and my black clients into the therapeutic work.

Lago and Thompson (1996) remind us that black clients do not exist in a vacuum but within social systems. Therefore, I need to view my black clients, in the context of these systems and be aware of the influence that environment has on their development, history and identity as well as their thoughts, emotions and actions. This means that I keep in mind that the external and internal worlds of my clients are interrelated. One way of demonstrating my awareness is through the use of empathy in order to attempt to see 'through my client's eyes'. I encourage my black clients to discuss their experience of racism, heterosexism and discrimination during the assessment and in ongoing work. I will acknowledge their experience and help them explore the impact this has on them. For many it is important and healing in itself that I, as a white person, will listen and accept their experience of racism without denial or justification.

Case example 1

Arni is a 29-year-old working-class black British gay man with Caribbean roots. He presented to therapy because he was not succeeding with his career and felt like a failure. He had looked for a gay therapist and been given my number by a former client. That meant he knew I was a lesbian practitioner. He had chosen to contact me as I was close to where he worked. After taking a detailed history and exploration of his presenting concerns and his current situation the conversation continued as follows:

R: Arni, you have now been here for a while. I am wondering how you are getting on with me?

A: Fine.

R: Can you tell me what this means?

A: I guess you are OK.

R: Um, you seemed a little hesitant as you said this? Perhaps part of you feels that I could be OK and another part of you is not so sure if you can trust me?

A: Yeah, well, I think that this is true. You see, I saw a therapist before but I didn't go back after the first meeting. I did not feel she understood me because she kept on telling me that she had no prejudices against black gay people and she treated all people the same anyway when I asked her if she worked with black people before.

R: It sounds like you did not feel seen and acknowledged as the black gay man that you are?

A: Yes that's it.

R: But I guess that this was probably not the first time that you had such an experience?

A: Well, no, no.

R: Yes, I can see that you might be in two minds about me. Will I just be another white person who is racist, even though we are both gay?

A: Yes that's been on my mind. It's very important to me.

R: Of course it is. Are you willing to talk about this further?

Arni agreed. He recalled, over a substantial number of sessions, the impact discrimination, racism and homophobia had on his past and current life. We then went on to issues related to his conflict as a black gay man and his low self-esteem. In therapy Arni was able to link his sense of 'feeling like a failure' to his experiences of being bullied at school for being gay (see also Chapter 10), to issues related to internalised racism and internalised homophobia which were constantly enforced through his father telling him he was stupid, and to racist and homophobic attitudes that he experienced, often on a daily basis, in his interaction with other people. Arni learned to appreciate his coping strategies as strengths that he had developed in dealing with societal racism and homophobia.

In my view, when addressing racism and heterosexism in psychotherapy, practitioners need to re-evaluate the models, concepts and value systems that we use, and understand the potential effects on black clients from sexual minorities. We need to acknowledge that psychotherapists and counsellors in Britain are mostly from the white racial majority, middle class and heterosexual. Furthermore, we white therapists have to remind ourselves that the social, historical, economic and political contexts in which most black clients live are radically different. However, we also have to remember that black people are not a homogeneous group; they arrived in Britain from diverse places, for different reasons and at different points in history. A substantial number of black people are British born and define themselves as black-British or black Asian-British despite the enormous level of racism they have to deal with.

The majority of black people in the UK arrived after World War II but they were not the first. Fryer (1984) reminds us that in the 1770s about 10,000 slaves arrived in Britain. Slavery is a major landmark in black history. Colonialism took over where slavery left off. Some of my black clients have initially been very cautious about my German background as they associate this with Fascism and Nazism. With my encouragement they eventually freely speak of their assumptions in relation to me as a powerful destructive white person. This often uncovers their fears, held consciously as well as unconsciously, of being 'wiped out' and 'killed off': a reality for many of their ancestors. With a few clients this has also led to an understanding of their internalised oppression.

Fatinilehin (1989) draws attention to the effect of having a different culture from the experiences of white Jewish immigrants to Britain who escaped Nazi Germany. He points out that, in the process of acculturation, a white person may lose aspects of their original culture and be given the same treatment as the host population due to lack of observable differences. This does not happen with members of black communities. No matter how much acculturation in terms of accent, language, education and values, black people still form a visible racial minority in British society. White clients can opt in or out of coming out with regard to sexuality in order to protect themselves from discrimination. Although this is also true for our black peers, because of their visual difference they do not have the option of preventing racial discrimination.

It is important not to stereotype black people from the same ethnic group. Although there are similarities there will also be differences due to religion, gender, sexual orientation, social class before and after migration, the length of time in Britain and the degree of acculturation. However, a substantial number of black people are British-born and have grown up living in two cultures. Some of my clients recall that part of their distress is due to being black in Britain rather than being a migrant with a different culture.

Rack (1982) noted cross-cultural differences in manifestations of distress and in the interpretations of these. A good example is the manifestation and diagnosis of depression. Many British-born white clients describe their mood first and corresponding somatic symptoms afterwards. Some of my clients from an Indian or Pakistani background describe their somatic symptoms first. McGovern and Cope (1987) discuss how this can lead to misdiagnosis of depression and underdiagnosis of affective disorders in black clients.

Another factor that, in my experience, can lead to depression and low self-esteem in black clients is the negative images that pervade the media and all aspects of our society. Even everyday language portrays 'white' as good and desirable, and 'black' as bad and undesirable. This is one example of racist language we have learnt to use without reflecting what impact it might have. I remember exploring this with one of my working-class clients. She had internalised that she was worthless as a black person. Her 'sense of worthlessness' was further reinforced through negative messages as a result of homophobic, sexist and classist language. This meant that we had to address all the different layers of her 'worthlessness' in therapy before she was able to resolve this issue for herself.

These are some aspects of the historical, social, political and economic contexts in which many black clients from sexual minorities live in Britain and which have an impact on their mental health. Interactions between white and black people have been shaped by these influences since the days of slavery 400 years ago. They are part of British history which, whether we want it or not, is brought into the therapy room when white therapists and black clients, despite sharing the same sexuality, work together. They have potential impact on the therapeutic relationship.

Lago and Thompson (1996) describe different philosophical assumptions underlying world views. They refer to three sets of hypotheses which I have found helpful in my clinical work. These describe the differences between

European, Asian and African conceptual systems. Below are brief descriptions of these concepts as I understand and use them.

European cultures place high values on the owning of objects. External knowledge is assumed to be the basis of all knowledge. The outcome of this cultural assumption is a view of the world based on science, technology and dualism – the split between mind and body. The consequence of this belief system is an identity based on body image, wealth, prestige and status symbols.

Asian cultures promote the concept of cosmic unity with the highest value placed on cohesiveness of the community. Internal and external knowledge is assumed to be the basis of all knowledge. This focuses on an integration of mind, body and spirit. The logic of the cultural assumption is defined as unity of thought and mind which ultimately leads to the concept of universal harmony.

African cultures promote both spiritual and material value systems with the highest value placed on interpersonal relationships between the sexes. Self-knowledge is seen to be the basis of all knowledge that one is assumed to access through symbolic imagery. This cultural assumption emphasises co-unity between and through humans and spiritual networks. The consequence of this belief system is an identity and sense of self-worth that are intrinsic.

Lago and Thompson (1996) suggest that these cultural assumptions inform different concepts of healing and influence black people's perceptions and expectations of therapy and, indeed, access to therapy. This is also my experience. A number of my black lesbian, gay and bisexual clients describe initial reluctance to seek outside help with mental and emotional problems. This is because mental distress or illness is associated with shame and stigma and there is an expectation that these problems should only be solved within the family system.

Case example 2

Bena is a 29-year-old who defines herself as working class and from mixed racial heritage (Asian-Malaysian). She heard from a friend about my intercultural background. She did not know about my sexuality. She had been in heterosexual relationships all her adult life and had recently felt more and more in doubt about her sexual identity, especially since the break up with her last boyfriend. She came to therapy feeling very confused. She felt there was something wrong with her as she was sexually attracted to women. She felt she needed to find a clearer way of expressing her feelings in general, not just in relation to her sexuality. Bena also felt very confused as to whether she was black or white as she had light skin, had lived in England for most of her life and saw this as home in contrast to her parents, who planned to return to Malaysia when they reached retirement.

Bena was initially hesitant to engage in therapy. The Asian part of her felt that therapy was not an acceptable way to solve personal conflicts and the western part believed that she would be able to find a solution. She also felt that, by entering therapy, she was betraying the value system of her family, which was to sort out problems among themselves. It took about four months before she felt comfortable with coming to therapy and taking space for herself. During that time we explored the different cultural aspect of herself, her identity confusion and her attachment to her family and culture. After that we worked on her racial, cultural and sexual identity. Had I stayed within a Eurocentric framework I would probably have misinterpreted her reluctance to engage with therapy and pathologised her ambivalence rather than respected and explored it.

Being black and gay, lesbian, bisexual or transgender

In Britain there has recently been an increased publication of psychological literature that explores gay and lesbian issues and, to a lesser extent, bisexual issues, from an affirmative perspective. Similarly there has been a significant growth in researching the roles of culture, race and ethnicity in psychological development and therapeutic work. I refer to some of these writings and research findings in this chapter. However, very little attention has been paid to gay men, lesbians and bisexuals who are also members of black communities. Research into gay and lesbian issues mostly involves white middle-class people and such research rarely addresses differences in sexual orientation among members of black communities. Greene (1997: 217) concludes that: 'There has been little exploration of the complex interaction between sexual orientation and ethnic identity development, nor have the realistic social tasks and stressors that are a component of gay and lesbian identity formation in conjunction with ethnic identity formation been taken into account'.

Black gay men, lesbian women, bisexual or transgender people, men who have sex with men and women who have sex with women are minority groups within their communities. As black people they already face multiple levels of discrimination and have to come to terms with the additional task of integrating two major aspects of their identity which are generally devalued by society: race and sexuality. For a significant number of clients with whom I have worked, their families and friends also devalued their sexual orientation as a 'white disease'.

Many black people grow up with strong ties to their birth and extended families, and are socialised into their communities and their racial and cultural identities long before they become aware that they have a different sexual orientation. Many black lesbian, gay, bisexual and transgender people identify very strongly with their communities. This helps to deal with the racism of the dominant culture they confront, often on a daily basis. Like their white counterparts, black people are exposed to, and subsequently internalise, a range of negative stereotypes about minority sexualities. Hence they must not only manage the heterosexism and racism of the dominant society but also the heterosexism and internalised racism of their own communities.

There are several problems that face the majority of my black clients:

- Concerns about 'coming out' to their families. Several fear bringing shame and dishonour to their families and being ostracised if they disclose their sexual orientation.
- Difficulties in identifying as black as well as gay, lesbian, bisexual or transgender. Many feel a sense of selfhatred because they have internalised negative stereotypes related to homophobia, biphobia and racism. I have worked with several black lesbians who felt torn between challenging racism, issues of sexuality and women's oppression.
- Difficulties in finding places as black people in the gay, lesbian, bisexual or transgender communities due to the discrimination and racism of their white peers. Some of my male clients especially have spoken of being seen as 'exotic' or 'a nice piece of black meat' by white gay men.

Additional problems arise for black gay and bisexual men living with HIV or AIDS because of the stigma still associated with these illnesses. I have worked with a number of black HIV positive, gay and bisexual male clients who presented with the issues described above. The stress of having to constantly keep aspects of themselves hidden or separate, depending on who they are with, is enormous and poses a great risk to their health (see also Chapter 4). This needs to be taken seriously by therapists. For quite a few of my clients I was the first person who acknowledged the enormity of the multifaceted issues they have to deal with. Our therapy time became a safe space where they could work towards a more integrated self, without being pathologised, and eventually also address issues of internalised oppression.

Case example 3

Ciso is a 28-year-old middle-class gay man of mixed race. His mother is white and English and his father is African American with roots from Haiti. He also has an AIDS diagnosis. One year ago he nearly died and was put on combination drug therapy. Then his health rapidly improved, which was perceived by everyone around him as a miracle. Ciso himself did not share this point of view. He presented with depression: he felt lost and confused and struggled to find his place in the world. He was unemployed and received benefits. We slowly discovered that his 'sense of being worthless' had many layers. We worked on the multifaceted issues that HIV and

AIDS brought up for Ciso: living with uncertainty and fear of his future, of a further illness and the enormous task of coming to terms with living on a daily basis in the face of death. Ciso disclosed that he felt ambivalent about his mixed-race heritage and his sexual orientation. After detailed exploration he realised that he actually felt confused about his racial identity and was acting out his social marginalisation further through his sexual ambivalence. This facilitated work around his internalised oppressions. Ciso associated white and heterosexual as good and black and gay as bad. These aspects had been in constant struggle with each other: he was eventually able to integrate them. At the end of therapy Ciso felt more comfortable with being a mixed-race gay man living with AIDS.

Being black, gay, lesbian or bisexual and coming out

'Coming out' and 'being out' are seen in the white gay, lesbian and bisexual communities as an acknowledgement of one's sexual identity to oneself and others. They are usually related to positive self-acceptance and self-esteem and are often seen to be an important political statement in the context of living in a heterosexist society. Not 'coming or being out', is described by Smith (1997: 279) 'as presumed to be negative and less healthy psychologically and is characterised by negative terms such as being *in the closet*' (original emphasis). This is often associated with shame and denial about one's sexual identity.

From an intercultural perspective the above values and assumptions are Eurocentric. Chan (1997: 240) points out that 'non-Western cultures, such as East Asian cultures, may not have concepts of sexual identity, comparable to the concept found in Western cultures'. Hence there might be several reasons why clients from different cultural and racial communities may not relate to these matters in the same way as their white peers. Concepts such as lesbian, gay and bisexual are predominantly based on the philosophy of the 'individual' in western societies. In many eastern cultures the focus is on the family and community. For example: one of my black Asian clients describes herself as defined by her role and responsibilities in her family as oldest daughter and sister. I've noticed also that some black Asian male clients who were having sex with men defined themselves as married rather than gay or bisexual, their focus being on their role in the family and community. All of these clients reported that the concept of 'coming out' as an individual does not necessarily fit into the value systems of themselves, their families and communities.

Furthermore, in many black communities, expectations of gender roles are strongly embedded and have implications for coming out. Conformity to traditional gender and role expectations, and especially reproductive sexuality, is viewed by many as a means of continuing the community's presence in a racist society. Greene (1997: 218) suggests that the following factors need to be considered:

> The importance of procreation and the continuation of the family line; the nature, degree and intensity of religious values; the importance of ties to the ethnic community; the degree of acculturation or assimilation of the individual or family into the dominant culture; and the history of discrimination or oppression the particular group has experienced from members of the dominant culture.

Coming out may result for a black client in an additional burden to the level of discrimination already dealt with. The social gains and costs are, for example, very different for a white, middle class, affluent man than they are for a black working-class woman. Coming out to their family was, for a number of my white male clients, crucial to their psychological health and, for a number of my black clients it was equally crucial to psychological health *not* to come out to their families. For the latter it was more important to maintain their closeness to their community and racial identity and to continue to fight racism, rather than address homophobia within the community and the wider society. This choice was sometimes linked to negative experiences that some had in trying to find niches in the sexual minority communities. It is important not to pathologise such choices. Our job as therapists is to help support what is important and appropriate for clients even though it may differ from our point of view.

Smith (1997: 295) points out that an Afrocentric way of coming out 'may be better understood in this context as "taking in" a significant other as if they were a member of the biological family' and refers to the fact that 'African American families may display appreciation for the importance of an individual member's partner even in the absence of overt acknowledgement of the label lesbian or gay'. This has been my experience with some clients.

Case example 4

Donny (42 years) and Emir (37 years) are an interracial gay male couple. Donny is a white Scottish man and Emir is black British with Ugandan roots. They have been together for one year. Donny's parents have always been supportive of his gay identity and his family has welcomed Emir as their son's partner. Emir feels that Donny's family treat him like a son. Emir is 'out' to his friends but has never 'come out' to his family. However, over the years his family has stopped commenting on the fact that he mostly has male friends and is not married. Donny was introduced to Emir's family as his friend. Their sexuality was never discussed in Emir's family: discussions about sexuality in general were not encouraged. Yet Emir's family accepted their couplehood in the same way as all the other family member's marriages. Donny appreciated this, yet he was becoming more and more resentful about the fact that he was not able to be 'openly gay'. On the other hand, Emir felt fine about his family's approach and found it hard to understand why Donny was angry. This had recently become the reason for several arguments between the couple. When they came to me for couple's therapy, they had reached an impasse in communication. Detailed exploration of the problem revealed that they had never been able to discuss their racial and cultural differences and the different value systems and approaches to being gay men. This became the focus of the therapeutic work. At the end of the therapy they were able to understand, accept and acknowledge their differences.

Implications for clinical practice

So far I have considered several issues that are relevant for black clients from sexual minorities in relation to sexual, racial or cultural identity and the multidimensional aspects of coming out. I will now focus on some implications that I consider relevant for clinical practice when working with these client groups.

Berman (1979) stressed the importance of the personal influence of the therapist in psychotherapy. He indicates that the therapist's ability to communicate to the client that they are understood and can be helped is crucial to the development of the therapeutic relationship. To Carl Rogers (1962) the relationship which the therapist forms with clients is the most significant aspect of the therapy process. In my experience there are several factors that may influence the development of the therapeutic relationship negatively when the therapist is white and the client is black, despite sharing sexual orientation. The client will have had previous experience with white people who were racist, homophobic or biphobic. This will undoubtedly influence their attitudes towards the therapist.

Barbarin (1984) points out that the therapist can be experienced by clients as holding power compounded by whiteness. This may lead to an attitude of caution or suspicion in the client that can initially hinder the establishment of the therapeutic bond between them. The views that some white gay, lesbian and bisexual therapists may hold in terms of racial or sexual stereotypes can also have an effect on the therapeutic relationship.

A mistake, which I made in the early days of my clinical work, was overidentification with black lesbian, gay, bisexual and transgender clients. This hindered the development of our therapeutic relationship as I oversimplified client problems by accounting for everything through race or sexuality issues. I had, in good faith, focused too much on the external process of oppression at the expense of attention to intra-psychic processes.

In order for white therapists to deal effectively with the issues of racism and heterosexism in black clients' lives they have to be aware of their own attitudes, assumptions and behaviours. Green (1987) suggested that white therapists and white people in general could be helped to deal with their feelings of and about racism by investigating their own experiences of oppression. I think this is equally true in relation to heterosexism. This has helped me very much in understanding some aspects of my racism and internalised homophobia, and especially how much oppression hurts.

It is necessary for white therapists to explore and work through their guilt and defensiveness with regard to racism and internalised homophobia or biphobia. Turner and Armstrong (1981) found that white therapists who reported distress around race issues were less able to confront and work through client's negative attitudes about therapy. I was only able to address issues of racism and heterosexism with black clients from sexual minorities once I had acknowledged and worked with these issues myself.

Challenging racist and heterosexist assumptions in our theoretical orientations is another important issue. Rack (1982) maintains that therapists encountering a different and unfamiliar culture will encounter difficulties in distinguishing what is 'normal' and what is 'pathological' behaviour. He argues that cultural differences in behaviour are those determined by beliefs and values of an individual culture – any dysfunction, therefore, needs to be seen in relation to that culture. We have to remember that white therapists are also influenced by biased attitudes from their own cultures towards members of black communities. These biases can become the basis of prejudice when working with black clients. It is the task of every therapist to take responsibility for cultural, racial and sexual biases, which may have impact on their therapeutic work.

The perception of black people merely as subjects of racism or heterosexism has resulted in their being seen as victims, who are disadvantaged, underprivileged and oppressed. It is essential to acknowledge the reality of racism and heterosexism and insufficient to do so in isolation from the systems and structures which surround black clients, including an acknowledgement of the strength of their families and communities. Failure to take account of this can result in an approach which operates within a framework of cultural deficit, excluding the possibility of empowerment, community resources, self-help strategies and self-determination. It is important to assist clients to develop positive self-concepts, followed by strategies to safeguard self-esteem. This involves facilitating client's work around internalised oppression. I recall a woman client who was in a positive transference with me. When I carefully named and explored this with her she was eventually able to talk about her negative self-image as a black lesbian woman.

Finally I want to focus on the issue of self-disclosure. Depending on the different settings I am working in, my clients may or may not be aware of my sexual orientation. I do not routinely disclose my sexual orientation but believe that appropriate self-disclosure is important after an exploration of my client's fantasies and assumptions about me. I have found that appropriate self-disclosure has been of therapeutic value for most of my gay and lesbian clients and helped to alleviate concerns and fears of being pathologised. My experience with bisexual clients has been that it was more therapeutic to explore our sexual differences, and for me to openly share my non-discriminatory value system in terms of a bisexual lifestyle. Where clients present with sexuality conflicts, early self-disclosure is not helpful as it can be experienced as threatening or an expectation to conform to the therapist's sexuality.

Conclusion

To conclude this chapter I suggest that white gay affirmative therapists, besides having a clear and explicit knowledge and understanding of the generic characteristics of therapy, need to have additional skills in order to operate from an intercultural, anti-racist and therapeutic frame of reference. These skills are:

- to be aware of their own cultural and racial heritage in order to be able to value and respect differences within the areas of race, culture and sexuality;
- to be aware of their own racial, cultural and sexual values and biases and how these may affect black clients;
- to have a good understanding of the social-political systems operating with respect to the treatment of black people, who are also members of sexual minorities;
- to take responsibility for having access to relevant knowledge about the particular group worked with in terms of race, culture and sexuality;
- to be aware of institutional barriers which prevent black clients from sexual minorities from using mental health and therapy services.

Acknowledgements

I would like to thank my friends Mita Hiremath and Linda Brown for their support and contributions to this chapter.

References

Barbarin, D.A. (1984) Racial themes in psychotherapy with blacks. *American Journal of Social Psychiatry*, 4(1): 1–2.

Berman, J. (1979) Counselling skills used by black and white male and female counsellors. *American Journal of Counseling Psychology*, 26(1): 81–4.

Chan, C. (1997) Asian lesbians: psychological issues in the coming out process, in B. Greene (ed.) *Ethnic and Cultural Diversity Among Lesbians and Gay Men.* Thousand Oaks, CA: Sage.

Curry, A.E. (1964) Myth, transference and the black psychotherapist. *Psychoanalytic Review*, 51(1): 7–14.

Davies, D. (1996) Towards a model of gay affirmative therapy, in D. Davies and C. Neal (eds) *Pink Therapy: A Guide for Counsellors and Therapists Working with Lesbian, Gay and Bisexual Clients.* Buckingham: Open University Press.

Fatinilehin, I. (1989) Psychotherapy for blacks. *Changes*, 7(2): 52–7.

Fryer, P. (1984) *Staying Power: The History of Black People in Britain.* London: Pluto Press.

Green, M. (1987) Women in the oppressor role: white racism, in S. Burns and M. Maguire (eds) *Living with the Sphinx: Papers from the Women's Press.* London: The Women's Press.

Greene, B. (1997) Ethnic minority lesbians and gay men: mental health and treatment issues, in B. Greene (ed.) *Ethnic and Cultural Diversity Among Lesbians and Gay Men.* Thousand Oaks, CA: Sage.

Kareem, J. (1988) Outside in . . . inside out: some considerations in intercultural psychotherapy. *Journal of Social Work Practice*, 3(3): 57–71.

Lago, C. and Thompson, J. (1996) *Race, Culture and Counselling.* Buckingham: Open University Press.

Mason-John, V. and Khambatta, A. (1993) *Lesbian Talk: Making Black Waves.* London: Scarlett Press.

Maylon, A. (1982) Psychotherapeutic implications of internalised homophobia in gay men, in J. Gonsiorek (ed.) *Homosexuality and Psychotherapy.* New York: Haworth Press.

McGovern, D. and Cope, R. (1987) The compulsory detention of males of different ethnic groups with special reference to offender patients. *British Journal of Psychiatry*, 150: 505–12.

Rack, P. (1982) *Race, Culture, and Mental Disorder.* London: Tavistock.

Rogers, C. (1962) *Person to Person, the Problem of Being Human: A New Trend in Psychology.* Lafayette, CA: Real People Press.

Smith, A. (1997) Cultural diversity and the coming-out process: implications for clinical practice, in B. Greene (ed.) *Ethnic and Cultural Diversity Among Lesbians and Gay Men.* Thousand Oaks, CA: Sage.

Turner, S. and Armstrong, S. (1981) Cross-racial psychotherapy: what the therapists say. *Psychotherapy: Theory, Research Practice*, 18(3): 375–8.

Kink therapy: SM and sexual minorities

Introduction

Originally standing for sado-masochism, the initials SM relate to power-play and the polarities of pain and pleasure, dominance-control and sub-mission, and attraction-repulsion, all of which form part of the domain of sexual behaviour known as SM or 'kink' sex, a generic term now used in America to incorporate all sexual practices beyond plain vaginal, oral or anal sex, and standing in opposition to 'vanilla' (non-SM) sex. The term SM itself is now widely used to include relationships and activities which are not necessarily sadistic or masochistic in nature. Some of these may be: bondage, branding, chastity games, corporal punishment, enemas, fantasies, fetishism, fisting, piercing, piss, role-playing games, scat (faeces), shaving, tattooing, tit play. The letters sM are also used to indicate slave/Master relationships – the use of lower case for slave and upper case for Master are conventions within the kink community. As Keith Alcorn (1995: 141) states:

> Pain as pleasure
> People enjoy all kinds of power games involving discipline and domina-tion, role-playing and pleasurable 'torture'. The human body is con-structed in such a way that there is often a very fine dividing line between pain and pleasure. This can be especially the case in sexual activities where only a very slight change in sensation can cross the boundary between pain and pleasure, something perhaps best encapsulated in a phrase such as 'that hurts so good'. The importance of this resides in the intensity and spontaneity of the sensations that arise on the borders of sexual pain. Science tells us that the endorphins released

when the body experiences certain kinds of pain act as a kind of internally produced recreational drug which can give a particular kind of high. The best-known example of this is provided by the intense highs experienced by athletes. Thus, for some people pain-related sexual games can come to be a satisfying (or even preferable) alternative to penetrative sex. SM does not have to involve pain. Since it is more to do with power games and role-playing, pain can often play only a minor role, if any, in an SM scene. The reasons for this confusion over pain and SM are mainly to do with popular myths, and the fact that sadomasochism has been a political battleground for at least the last twenty years.

Ten years ago, incorporating such a chapter in a book on gay affirmative therapy would have been unthinkable in Britain. However, the UK appears to be becoming more tolerant, more hospitable to difference and more accepting of diversity. Though levels of tolerance relating to sexual orientation have increased, making it easier to 'come out' as lesbian, gay or bisexual, many sexual behaviours remain which society has, until the very recent past, considered unacceptable and sought to repress.

Television and radio programmes in the late 1990s demonstrated, however, that 'cool Britannia' was haltingly moving towards the wider tolerance already practised in the rest of Europe, and SM was beginning to become more a matter for curiosity than fear or revulsion. This may ultimately make owning to an interest in SM or kink sexuality – until recently considered a 'closet within a closet' – easier, especially in metropolises. The experience in San Francisco over the past 20 years has shown that this can only be for the good as, among others factors, it has enabled a significant reduction in new cases of HIV.

More people than ever partake of a kink sexual lifestyle, and a significant proportion of these are members of sexual minorities. Compared with heterosexuals, a higher proportion of gay men and lesbians enjoy the practice of SM. Although no formal statistical evidence exists to support this, the abundance of anecdotal qualitative information, such as the multiplication of clubs catering for kink lifestyles, the acreage spent on the subject in gay newspapers and magazines, the increase in popularity of dress, hair, tattoo and piercing styles directly related to kink in the gay community, all point towards this conclusion. As intolerance to different sexual practices gradually dwindles, at least in the gay communities, and venues are being set up where it is possible to meet potential sexual partners, especially in larger cities, many people are expanding their repertoire of sexual activities into SM-related activities, bringing them similar joys and, some say, greater intensity, than vanilla sex. Yet many are still unable to openly admit to their SM practices, even to peers, because of the links people continue to make with sexual violence and abuse. The likelihood is therefore greater than it once was for a therapist to see clients who practise kink sex in one form or another.

Lest their clients suffer a fate similar to those who identified their homosexuality, bisexuality or transgender to their therapists and found themselves 'treated' for it, even though it may have had little to do with their initial reason for seeking help, it is important to fill some gaps in knowledge and to highlight some key issues which the therapist needs to have in mind in order to work effectively.

One purpose of this chapter is, therefore, to dispel myths and confusions and address issues identified within a pragmatic framework. This, in turn, will allow a response which will be appropriate, resourceful, practical and validating.

SM becomes mentally healthy

Many people think that, in order to enjoy receiving or inflicting pain, or putting yourself in a position of vulnerability at the mercy of another's power, you need to have a sick mind, or a 'personality flaw', and this was indeed the belief of the medical professions until recently. As with homosexuality and bisexuality, this is another area where the language was borrowed from the discourse of psychopathology.

The terms 'sadist' and 'masochist' denoted mental health problems which should, at worst, be repressed, and at best, be cured. This labelling itself refers to two figures of the literary world, namely: the Marquis de Sade (1740–1814), French author of *Juliette*, *Justine* and *The 120 Days of Sodom*, whose books depicted the uses of pain, torture and degradation for sexual satisfaction, and Leopold von Sacher-Masoch, the nineteenth-century author of *Venus in Furs*, where a man expresses his desire for domination by a woman and his fetishism for the garments she wears. Many SM relationships and activities involve neither sadism nor masochism.

After decades of stigmatisation the medical profession is revising its outlook on SM practices. Following the low-key campaigning of psychologists and psychiatrists in the USA, the American Psychiatric Association chose to significantly amend its *Diagnostic and Statistical Manual of Mental Disorders IV* (1990), and removed the simple practice of SM from the category of psychopathology. So, whereas:

> previous editions of the DSM categorized both SM practices and SM fantasizing as psychosexual disorders that by their very nature called for treatment, by contrast, the wording in DSM-IV labels masochism a disorder *only when 'fantasies, urges or behaviors cause clinically significant distress or impairment' to the ability to conduct one's business, social or personal life*. The change in the section on sadism is similar.
>
> (*International Drummer* 1995: 59–61, my emphasis)

Basically, whatever you do with your body is your own business, as long as it doesn't have serious negative effects on your life, health and well-being or that of others.

Such a pragmatic approach, long in the coming, is welcome, as it removes many of the stigmas associated with kinky sexual practices. These stigmas have their roots in various social and religious taboos which have also repressed other so-called deviant behaviours, such as masturbation or homosexuality. One hopes that, in the same way that stigmas were lessened from such practices as a result of a redrafting of *DSM-III* (1980 and 1987), the updating of *DSM-IV* will enable people who are into kink not to be perceived as requiring treatment just for what they like doing to others or having done to themselves.

One of the paradoxes of taboos is that behaviour perceived as appropriate in one context may not be so in another. Many people who are seriously into SM follow in the ancient 'ecstatic' or 'dionysiac' tradition, seeking ways of pushing their boundaries, finding fulfilment, or, perhaps, just of achieving an 'endorphin high', in the extremes of physical sensations (from abundance to deprivation), like climbers who take pride in climbing mountains unaided. The Christian tradition, among others, especially in its monastic institutions, abounds with examples where behaviour such as flagellation and self- or other-wounding was encouraged as a means of achieving ecstatic transcendence or demonstrations of religious fervour. For example, a form of blood-letting, called *minution* – a word originally meaning 'reducing' – was used for ritual purposes to weaken the body in such a way as to induce altered states. It was also, and perhaps more significantly, used to ensure passivity in more recalcitrant members of the order. Likewise, many aspirants to religious orders make vows of poverty, chastity and obedience which would not be out of place in a slave-Master contract. However, whereas this behaviour is God- or deity-focused, in SM lifestyle it is, by and large, person-focused, or humanistic.

One of the many ways of asserting ownership of your own body is to do with it things other people might think outlandish. Much of the hostility apportioned to kink practices relates to the transgression of traditional roles they represent. We live in a culture which worships power in all its forms. So, whereas behaviours one might well call 'sadistic' are often condoned, colluded with and even accepted in many quarters where the traditional role of the male is to be masterful and that of the female is to be submissive, masochistic behaviours, especially when expressed by males, are perceived as undermining traditional values. Thus, while it may be perfectly acceptable for a man to seek to assert his power over others, and even to inflict punishment upon them, a man would have to be mentally unbalanced to seek punishment or to be at the receiving end of this power. On the other hand, because a woman asserting her power over another is perceived as reproducing and replicating the traditional cultural pattern, which has oppressed and repressed women for millennia, the issue of SM among lesbians is far more political than among gay men.

The cultural tradition which perpetuated the above stereotypes was successfully challenged in the 1950s and 1960s by feminism and in the 1970s and 1980s by various gay liberation movements and campaigns. Reflecting traditional taboos in our own culture, itself based on transgression, we may in turn stigmatise people using the same yardstick used to stigmatise us with in the first place. SM and kink is indeed the next frontier we need to challenge, so that people can live their lives as they see fit, irrespective of gender, sexual orientation or practices.

SM and the history of health

Some kink practices, though not SM *per se*, involve playing with excretory body fluids, like urine (golden showers/piss), or faeces (scat/shit), through activities like oral-anal contact (rimming), which most cultures consider taboo. There are many reasons why people may want to do this. Some relish the perception that they are transgressing such taboos and find in these activities the means to achieve a sense of greater individuality. Echoing the sensualist, humanistic approach referred to above, they may appreciate that the whole of the human body, and what it has to offer, is to be celebrated, as opposed to the narrow (above the belt) range which tradition allows. Most people know the health implications of practices like scat, such as the transmission of hepatitis B or A, and take these into account. Context is again everything: after all, humans are the only animals who repress their own smells and adorn themselves with the excreta of other animals, which form the basis of many perfumes like musk from the anal glands of the musk ox, civet from the urine of the civet cat, or ambergris from whale glands.

People commonly believe that kink practices are dangerous and indeed some, such as those involving 'fist fucking' (technically known as *brachio-proctal* penetration), breath control or piercing, potentially are. Yet many people have been known to play on those lines for many years with no harmful effects. Obviously they play with due care. Many anxieties were raised when HIV came on the scene. These were dispelled by the realisation that many kink practices which, in earlier days, would have fallen under the category of foreplay by the fact that they are non-penetrative and rarely involve the exchange of body fluids, are safer sex practices. The significant uptake of SM by the gay population, at least in the UK, may be due to the way government-funded gay sexual health projects and health promotion initiatives have been duly promoting this fact since the early 1990s.

The drive to make sweeping generalisations from particular incidents is in our human nature: thus, until recently, many people believed that ALL gay men were child abusers on the basis of a few cases. Individual cases, like that of Mark Dutroux in Belgium, who abducted, raped and tortured young girls, tar all SM practitioners with the same infamous brush, whatever they are involved in.

It is also easy to observe a behaviour and to impugn an intention based on one's own perspective or world view. From an outsider's perspective therefore, people who practice SM abuse their partners – they perpetrate acts of cruelty against unwilling partners who are coerced into submission: in brief, they are 'evil'.

In fact, most kinky sex acts are carried out with the explicit consent of all partners: the more intense the practices, the more they are, or need to be, negotiated. This very consent will be renegotiable throughout the 'scene', depending on its progress. The ground rules of a long-term SM relationship are often written down as a contract, although it may not always be possible to do so for brief encounters. To this effect, the kink scene is replete with signs and signals, such as key and handkerchief locations and colours, which help identify a compatible mate; indeed, the so-called 'Hankie Code' is quite elaborate and currently lists about 50 colours and textures! Likewise, social SM clubs, such as the euphemistically named European Confederation of Motorsport Clubs (ECMC), the UK Federation of United Kingdom Clubs (FUKC), the American Motorsport Clubs Confederation (AMCC) or even commercial kink clubs with strict codes, strive to ensure that potential partners know the 'rules of the game' and abide by them, with the aim of providing an element of security for newcomers.

Thus, as one SMer recently stated in an Internet newsgroup:

My understanding of this is this: the bottom in a sado-sex encounter (i'm not excluding the top – i just don't know) places him/her self in a position of vulnerability emotionally, spiritually, as well as physically. It is done based on an understanding which has been COMMUNIC-ATED and trust . . . Thus: those of us into the S&M practice have developed profound (i think generally) abilities to: KNOW OUR-SELVES; to get to KNOW OTHERS; and to have a commitment to WHOLENESS and COMPLETENESS (integrity) in our dealings . . .

. . . you may not yet understand this about S&M sex, but communication about what you're into and what you're not is PRIMARY. It's blatantly obvious that one reason for this is so that actions, which to others may seem cruel and violent, can be contained within a consensual fantasy-sex environment. (there's a dichotomy here which can lead to confusion, mistreatment, bad sex, and true danger) . . .

. . . Additionally, the S&M sexual encounter is an encounter at a much deeper level than merely a 'bar trick'. In particular, the bottom is open at a level of psyche MUCH MUCH DEEPER (internally, emotionally and spiritually). This openness, which is often the key to a truly profound and personal psycho-sado-sex experience, opens the psyche in ways it is not 'normal' to operate in. (Some compare it to differing states of hypnosis). In this way, the bottom does not have the same access to all of his social skills and protections he has in a normal-walkaday state. Just know this . . . or if you can't know it, understand it . . . and if you can't understand it . . . ACCEPT THAT IT MIGHT BE SO. . . .

(alt.personal.bondage.gay)

This is far from understood, however and, even when explained at length in front of a court of law, as in the Spanner case (see below), the complex equivalence between SM and torture cannot easily be dispelled. Whereas traditional, religious-minded people tend to equate SM with sin, many humanists, who had earlier advocated the liberalisation of sexualities, find themselves on the other side of the fence this time, as many believe SM to amount to no less than abuse, cruelty and torture. Thus do the staunchest allies of yesterday become the fiercest enemies of today.

The 'Spanner' case

In 1987, a group of gay men who had been meeting regularly for SM parties were raided by the police and arrested. One committed suicide and several lost their jobs as a result of this arrest. As adults consenting to these activities in the privacy of their own home, the men sought to demonstrate that, whatever they were involved in doing, they could not have engaged in abusive activities. Ignoring the more ritualistic and role-playing activities they took part in, successive higher courts, including the House of Lords, upheld their convictions. Eventually, they appealed to the European Court of Human Rights in The Hague, Netherlands.

Contrary to expectations, the Court upheld the former House of Lords judgement and decreed, three years after the publication of *DSM-IV* and its revised perspectives on SM, that there could be no consent where 'torture' was involved. Although no bias was expressly professed against homosexuals versus heterosexuals engaged in SM, the Court reviewed a previous case where a husband branded his wife at her request and the House of Lords had judged them not guilty and declared it a strictly private matter: 'Consensual activity between husband and wife, in the privacy of the matrimonial home, is not, in our judgement, a proper matter for criminal investigation, let alone criminal prosecution' (European Court of Human Rights Judgement 1997).

Reading the judgement, it is obvious that the judges, whose opinions may have been fashioned partly in response to Nazi atrocities during World War II, could not conceive of sado-masochistic activities in a context distinct from torture, abuse and violence. Their model of the world could not contemplate allowing such an expansion, and the ramifications of the judgement are quite considerable, especially for a therapist, as we will see below.

SM as shared joy

Although I am currently aware of no research investigating this subject, it is my belief that there may be a significant percentage of people from sexual minorities who began their SM sexual career consciously or unconsciously reliving instances of physical, psychological or sexual abuse. Some of them may in turn replicate this pattern with other partners, or even themselves, and may indeed be in need of help. Enabling therapists to work with them more effectively is one of the aims of this chapter. But, in the weird and wonderful way that a problem also has the potential of being a solution, others have found ways of exorcising these early traumas, learning from experience and transcending them. Such survivors of abuse may, and usually do, have a lot to contribute to the developing healthy kink community. Yet others may come to SM without any identified background of abuse or trauma, although Stanislaw Grof (1990), one of the developers of transpersonal psychology, believes that they may have had such experiences through before-birth or birth traumas. They may simply have started on this journey from a desire for wider or deeper, more intense experiences, richer sensations and the promise of rapture. Whichever way people have set out on this road, to the beat of a 'different drum', what matters ultimately is that they can live and share their experiences positively.

Pointers for the counsellor/therapist

Although there may be a number of people who live a kink lifestyle who were abused in one way or another in childhood, it is a tribute to the flexibility and ingenuity of the human mind to state that the majority have developed coping mechanisms to make this a learning experience, enabling each to move on, in their own way. Only a minority seek help, either in direct relation to this early trauma, or in an indirect way, because of behaviours which may be a consequence. Only a minority of these latter's issues may directly pertain to their lifestyle. The affirmative model, presented by Davies (1996), based on tolerance and pragmatism, should apply to the same extent to clients of any gender and sexual persuasion practising SM. I present below some pointers a therapist may want to consider when working with a client who owns to an SM or kink lifestyle.

There is a long way to go. The gradual acceptance of an SM sexual lifestyle means that psychological difficulties such as those experienced by sexual minorities before our cultural liberalisation and presented, among other places, in *Pink Therapy* (Davies and Neal 1996), may also decrease as a result. However, SMers will and do seek psychological help on a range of matters, few of which may be directly related to their sexual lifestyle.

Model of the world

As therapists our duty is to leave our model of the world on the back burner, so that it doesn't interfere with the client's. It would be inappropriate to allow our model of the world, and the beliefs and values which shape it, to intrude and impinge on a client, either to deter the practice of an SM lifestyle if one disapproved, or to encourage it. It is hoped that the information provided here will begin to help therapists to abstract from their own world view to allow their clients to resolve problems with their support.

Respect

Respect is the core value a therapist should seek to apply: even more than in the case of homosexuality, a client may 'indulge' in practices a therapist may find objectionable, yet they have come for help and support and a therapist owes it to them to do their best. This is, after all, a learning experience for them also.

Relevance

Is the SM lifestyle expressed actually relevant to the problem the client presents? If not, why latch onto it? After all, 'if it ain't broke, don't fix it'. It may be that, contrary to being part of the problem, this lifestyle is part of the solution a client has so far been seeking. Many SM experiences can lead to states of fulfilment which allow clients to cope with problems or to transcend them in some way.

Ecology

This concept, based on systems theory, invites the therapist to consider the implications and consequences of a given behaviour for an individual in all the facets of their personality, as well as for others, directly or indirectly involved, and for the wider communities. Thus a behaviour which may appear harmful to one aspect of a person at a given moment and situation may have positive consequences for the rest of that person, either as it occurs or at a relevant later point or situation. We weigh the consequences of our actions, albeit rarely consciously, and decisions which do not have positive consequences would be unecological.

Like others, SM relationships can be ecological or not, depending on whether all the people involved are happy with the outcome and congruent with what they're getting out of it, and if that relationship and its associated behaviours is regularly renegotiated. On the other hand, as soon as one imposes oneself upon another, sexually or not, without their express permission, it's unecological. Any abusive relationship thus stands out as inherently unecological. Conversely, even an outwardly outrageous SM relationship, involving all sorts of hanky colours, can be ecological if it meets the above criteria.

The issue of ecology has even wider ramifications. Psychological problems are often tied in with creativity or fulfilment. Had van Gogh been successfully treated for his psychological problems, would he have been as creative? Or would he have become even more creative, if perhaps in different directions? It is not because a person may be suffering from some untoward side-effects of their lifestyle that they automatically want to be rid of this lifestyle. The solution for an unhappy masochist may not therefore be to become a happy non-masochist, but simply a happy one. After all, our role is not to change clients, but to enable them to become more themselves than they've ever been. If a client enjoys their kink lifestyle, a satisfactory outcome would be one which can enrich and enhance further all aspects of their life, including that lifestyle.

Legal implications

The 'Spanner' case has left us with a messy legal legacy. On the one hand we know that more and more people practise SM perfectly happily. On the other, 'acts of violence, such as those for which the applicants were convicted, that could not be considered of a trifling or transient nature, *irrespective of the consent of the victim*', are now illegal. (European Court of Human Rights 1997, emphasis added).

All therapists must abide by the rules and regulations of their profession. These explicitly state that, should a therapist be faced with a conflict between the responsibility they owe their client, including confidentiality, and any legal obligations, such as upon the realisation their client is engaged in illegal activities, the therapist must conform to legal requirements.

Conversely, there is considerable anecdotal evidence that the current law is not enforced, is increasingly unlikely to be so, and that, unless discovered or blatant, cases of SM activity between consenting adults will not be prosecuted. Had this been otherwise, many commercial clubs and venues where such activities take place would have been raided and the owners and key participants prosecuted, along with the many publishers of magazines which promote these venues.

Ultimately the therapist will be left to make their own decisions based upon important factors, such as the ecology of their client's SM lifestyle. It may be comforting to know that 'even if an activity is illegal, it is not unlawful to discuss that activity for the purpose of providing information to protect people's health [including mental health] and lives' (Alcorn 1995: 141).

Stress and self-esteem

Like any other behaviour, SM or kink lifestyle is affected by the stress levels of an individual. In stress-free conditions, this lifestyle will tend to be eco-logical, fulfilling and generative. Conversely, in times of stress, this lifestyle can tend to become more extreme and less ecological. The power-based structure of SM sexual interactions means that the therapist may affect sexual partners more deeply perhaps in an unconscious attempt to redress the imbalance stress has caused. Such attempts at re-balancing rarely succeed, and may make the matters worse, leading to more extreme behaviour patterns. A non-informed therapist might be tempted to treat the symptoms rather than addressing the underlying source of stress.

A person may assert their power over another in an unconscious attempt to boost their own level of self-esteem, or push themselves way beyond usual thresholds of pain or pleasure in a sexual 'scene', in order to gain the approval of their partner or to prove to themselves that they can do it. This approach can and has been known to redress poor levels of self-esteem but success is more easily guaranteed when the client is able to identify and address the reason for this low self-esteem, and to increase their self-esteem in a more ecological fashion. They may choose to push their limits after-wards, but from a perspective of safety rather than danger, as is the case with an athlete whose levels of performance are inversely proportional to their stress levels.

Confusing fantasy and reality

Many kink activities involve enacting or re-enacting fantasies. While this may be harmless for most, some may come to perceive their fantasy as the real world they live in (or ought to live in). An example of this might be wanting to be, or to have, a full-time slave: when all the aspects of the relationship have been carefully negotiated even this may actually work. However, when people seek to impose their fantasy world onto others, they suffer themselves or make others suffer when reality does not match the expectations of their fantasy. Finding ways of re-establishing clear bound-aries between the two realms, as well as well-defined means of crossing or stretching these boundaries, as and when appropriate, is effective in enabling the person to function socially again.

Conclusion

In brief, kink activities can be defined as different from others, in that they make explicit those components (such as power and control) which are

Table 2.1

Kink Is not	But is
A sign of mental illness	Just another and no less sane way of enjoying yourself and others
Sinful	One of many practices which glorify humankind and our potential
Immoral	As moral as anything else
Degrading	An expression of a person's individuality
Dangerous to health	Less dangerous than many other things
A consequence of child abuse	About acknowledging that people come to SM from a range of backgrounds: what matters is what they do with it
Abuse/torture	A heightened form of sexual communication, based on interdependence

inherent in any relationship, sexual and otherwise, which other forms of relationship leave unsaid. Making these explicit gives one the choice to act upon them and to play with them, instead of suffering from their side-effects, as may occur if they are unconscious. This desire for openness and explicitness is best demonstrated by the fact that many SMers expressly advertise that they seek partners for 'safe, sane and consensual' encounters and relationships.

The other key difference is that an SM or kink lifestyle offers a wider spectrum of sexual choices, where everything and anything can be construed as a sexual act, if so agreed: this palette does not replace traditional, or vanilla, sex but includes it instead as one of the many options available.

Working with a client who practises an SM or kink lifestyle does not have to be different from working with any other client, but an understanding of the issues which they may raise is essential to place their model of the world and enable them to resolve their issues.

In this brief overview chapter I have sought to raise awareness of these issues in order to dispel individual fears and further nurture a tolerance which counsellors and therapists in sexual minorities communities have been displaying in abundance over the past few years. Building on gay affirmative work it is possible to begin to apply 'kink affirmative' therapy.

By accepting and embracing the diversity of people's lifestyles, therapists can help people to play and interact without fear of judgement and all the possible side-effects this may entail. In so doing, therapists may enrich our culture further by supporting clients and friends and enabling them to accept themselves and others even more fully.

Dedication

To all my friends in the kink community, those living and those who have died, who have enriched my life for the past 25 years: you know who you are.

Resources

Baldwin, G. (1993) *Ties That Bind*. San Francisco, CA: Daedalus Publishing Company. The kink counsellor/therapist's bible.
Jacques, T. (1994) *Leathersex*. San Francisco, CA: Daedalus Publishing Company. An excellent and thoughtful all-round introduction to the SM/kink lifestyle.

References

Alcorn, K. (ed.) (1995) *AIDS Reference Manual*. London: NAM Publications.
American Psychiatric Association (1994) *Diagnostic and Statistical Manual of Mental Disorders*, 4th edn. Washington, DC: American Psychiatric Association.
Davies, D. (1996) Towards a model of gay affirmative therapy, in D. Davies and C. Neal (eds) *Pink Therapy: A Guide for Counsellors and Therapists Working with Lesbian, Gay and Bisexual Clients*. Buckingham: Open University Press.
Davies, D. and Neal, C. (eds) (1996) *Pink Therapy: A Guide for Counsellors and Therapists Working with Lesbian, Gay and Bisexual Clients*. Buckingham: Open University Press.
Grof, S. (1990) *The Holotropic Mind*. San Francisco, CA: Harper & Row.
International Drummer (1995) 186: 59–61.

LYNNE GABRIEL AND
DOMINIC DAVIES

The management of ethical dilemmas associated with dual relationships

Introduction

Dual relationships are defined here as those where a client-therapist relationship extends, intentionally or unintentionally, to include encounters, activities or relationships outside the therapeutic one. This chapter considers ethical dilemmas associated with dual relationships, arising within possibly unique social and cultural contexts of sexual minority communities, for therapists and clients who are members of those communities.

Definitions of 'dilemma', 'dual relationships' and 'boundary' provide a framework for the discussion. Theoretical perspectives are introduced and related to the management of ethical dilemmas, including boundary management and the use of problem solving models. Case studies are presented for discussion. The authors note the limitations of existing theory in relation to therapeutic work in the sexual minority communities and seek to develop ethical practices which strive to honour and respect diverse social, political and relational realities.

This chapter does not claim to be exhaustive. It is offered in the spirit of exploration, for the benefit of the authors as well as the readers; and, ultimately, our clients and communities. We have no intention to prescribe a definitive set of practitioner beliefs and behaviours, but value ongoing debate and development in counselling theory and practice.

The terms 'counsellor' and 'therapist', 'counselling' and 'therapy' are interchanged and used generically to avoid ambiguity regarding their interpretation. The pronouns *he* and *she* will be used as appropriate, and for ease of reference the therapist-client relationship will be referred to as the therapeutic relationship.

Definitions and contexts

Dilemmas associated with therapy with clients from minority sexual communities take us into unexplored territory. Conflicts of relationships are central to human existence, yet conflict resolution and the management of dilemmas are not areas of human expertise. Perhaps this is why we sometimes shy away from difficult situations or lock horns in destructive ways. Dictionary definitions indicate that a dilemma is a situation to be avoided: 'A position that leaves a choice between equally unwelcome possibilities; argument forcing opponent to choose one of two alternatives, both unfavourable; difficult situation.' (*Concise Oxford Dictionary* 1982: 268).

It is hardly surprising that counsellors' dilemmas are not more openly discussed. To do so might make us personally and professionally vulnerable, challenging the profession's image of competency and reliability (Bond 1997). Through avoidance, however, we shun opportunities for personal and professional development, since seeds of growth can be contained in the midst and aftermath of dilemmas.

To see, or seek, the positive in the face of a dilemma is not a typical reaction. It is more likely to generate anxiety, fear or panic. Despite anxiety about overlap between therapy relationships and imagined or actual encounters with clients in our shared communities, the potential exists to deal respectfully with duality, and develop what Clarkson (1995) refers to as 'role fluency'.

Dual relationships have been described as containing the potential for exploitation and the impairment of professional and clinical judgement (Kitchener 1988), and have been the subject of professional contention and dispute as well as the cause of civil litigation (Borys and Pope 1989). Professional opinions range from dual relationships *always* being unethical (Pope 1991) to *sometimes* being unethical (Berman 1985). Perhaps the fears and exhortations to avoid dual relationships are based upon deep-rooted fears about intimacy within the profession. Protest against dual relationships has been based upon their potential for client harm, and it has been suggested that the risk of damage increases with corresponding increases in the level of intimacy and power differential (Pearson and Piazza 1997).

Despite a history of prohibition, perceptions of dual relationships are shifting. There is growing recognition that in some contexts they are unavoidable (see, for example, Anderson and Kitchener 1996; Pearson and Piazza 1997). Whatever the root of past injunctions and judgements, little account has been taken of the culture and context of the communities in which lesbian, gay, transgender and bisexual therapists and their clients exist. It may not be realistic to expect counsellors to divorce themselves from their communities. Importantly, therapy does not exist in a vacuum or hermetically sealed container (Clarkson 1995). Directives against seeing friends or acquaintances as clients have been almost universally accepted, and almost as universally violated (Roll and Millen 1981). A growing number of theorists and practitioners have noted links between bisexual, gay and lesbian therapy and community contexts (see, for example, Brown 1984, 1985, 1989a; Dworkin and Gutierrez 1989; Dworkin 1992; Gartrell 1992; Lyn 1995; Burgess 1997).

The reality of living and practising within ones community can resemble that of a small town, where interconnections and knowledge of the inhabitants are shared. Brown (1984) describes this type of environment as akin to 'life in a fishbowl'. Such a situation demands clarity regarding what is available for the 'public domain' and what must be held in the 'private domain'. Complex boundary situations may arise where non-monogamous relationships are common (Browning *et al.* 1991). There can be overlapping links between clients, ex-lovers, current lovers, friends of ex-lovers, friends of clients and so on. Managing the relationship boundaries in such a matrix may create difficulties for the counsellor who chooses to actively participate in the community and its events. A therapist may have to choose between avoiding events held at the only lesbian or gay social venue, and finding means of dealing with the inevitable overlap. Some avoid participating and this may generate unconscious reactions that have an impact upon the client-counsellor relationship. Evasive action can separate the therapist from the very community in which they choose to live and work.

Boundary dilemmas constitute some of the most anxiety-inducing situations for counsellors (Gabriel 1996), yet limited focus is given to the subject during training; especially to the role that boundaries play in minimising professional mismanagement (Webb 1997). *Boundary* is a concept that is often misunderstood or experienced as difficult to define. Practitioners tend to feel that they understand the concept intuitively, yet often encounter problems in bringing it to life and attempting to explain it (Gutheil and Gabbard 1993). Counsellors' difficulties with boundaries range from confusions and mismanagement, through mild exploitation, to seriously abusive boundary violation (Webb 1997). How then might we define boundary?

The *Concise Oxford Dictionary* (1982) defines 'boundary' as a *limit line*, with a *boundary rider* defined as an individual who rides a perimeter fence, undertaking necessary repairs. The boundary in counselling can be perceived as a limit line, with inherent fluidity and permeability, as well as safety and security. It is a limit that requires the thoughtful actions of the *boundary rider*, the counsellor, to monitor and repair where necessary in order, as far as is possible, to ensure security and safety (Gabriel 1996). This resonates with a definition offered by Peterson (1992) whereby boundaries are viewed as limits for protective and holding purposes. The concept of boundary rider complements Gutheil and Gabbard's (1993) notion of boundary crossings. An example of a boundary crossing might be giving a client a hug. The risk level or capacity for harm inherent in this action will depend upon a complex range of factors including, for example, client and counsellor personality and emotional well-being, the type and context of the hug, the intentions and perceptions of the individuals involved. Appropriate boundary management needs to be contextually based, and operate according to different rules within different roles and relationships (Webb 1997).

Research data and professional literature specific to boundaries in dual relationship situations is minimal and the majority is derived from an analytical, psychodynamic or feminist perspective (see, for example, Langs 1976, 1978, 1979; Brown 1984, 1985, 1989a, 1994; Epstein and Simon 1990; Margolies 1990; Gartrell 1992; Peterson 1992; Milton 1993). From a feminist perspective, theologian Carter Heyward (1993) has offered interesting notions of mutuality within the therapy relationship and suggests that clients can accurately perceive a therapist's struggle with boundary issues. Writing from a client perspective she offers a poignant reminder that the client's experience of the boundaries and frame of therapy is crucial to the process and must not be ignored or undermined. It is significant that counselling research has paid minimal attention to a client's perception of boundaries and, importantly, how they experience boundary issues where dual relationships and overlapping connections occur.

Complex relationship dynamics, including issues of power and trust, are central in dilemmas of dual relationships. For some, meeting outside therapy will engage therapist and client in delicate exploration and reparation of the therapeutic relationship and the dynamics of the duality situation. Indeed for some, duality may lead to the decision to end the therapeutic relationship. Discussion during the contracting phase of counselling helps to clarify and 'rehearse' appropriate actions where overlapping connections might arise. Essentially, we are promoting *anticipation* as a disciplined response where dual relationships are likely, rather than *wisdom* after the event (Jamieson 1998). Facilitating a client's self-empowerment and their capacity for managing duality can become a significant aspect of the work for therapists and clients who share a community.

Mainstream professional influences: attitudes, morals, philosophies and theories

Certain aspects of sexual minority experience, if made central to all psychological enquiry and debate, would influence and expand our ability to further comprehend both the intrapsychic and interpersonal realms of human existence (Brown 1989b). In essence, this is a request for the expansion of the boundaries of therapy and counselling research. However, it will necessitate the willingness of mainstream counselling, psychology and psychotherapy professions to critically appraise the views of Brown and others who strive for theoretical and clinical recognition (see, for example, Kitzinger 1987; Coyle 1993, 1995; Gonsiorek 1994; Davies and Neal 1996, 2000).

Despite homosexuality being declassified as a mental illness by the American Psychiatric Association (APA) in 1973, discrimination and homophobic attitudes continue within the helping professions. Though the APA's watershed decision opened the way to professional developments and a psychology which understood members of sexual minorities within non-pathological frameworks, there remains a long way to go (Coyle 1995). Therapists have tended to remain 'in the closet' and therefore invisible in mainstream professional literature. Very little has been published that is of immediate and practical assistance to the sexual minority therapist, and virtually all of the key historical figures in counselling and therapy have been men (McLeod 1993).

These imbalances have misrepresented and distorted theoretical and clinical approaches. Encouragingly, there are indications of changing perceptions. Anti-discriminatory policy and practice is central to recent National Vocational Qualifications (NVQs) in counselling, and the British Association for Counselling (BAC) have amended their *Codes of Ethics and Practice* to incorporate equal opportunities and anti-discriminatory clauses (BAC 1998). Other publications have addressed the need for anti-oppressive and multicultural practices to be upheld within the helping professions (see, for example, Lago and Thompson 1989; Young 1995).

Recently, greater emphasis has been placed upon moral principles and their relevance to counselling (see Kitchener 1984; Bond 1993; McGrath 1994; Henry 1996). Where the lives of the client and therapist cross, codes of ethics and practice may provide inadequate guides, or prove inappropriate for minority communities, since the codes do not (and cannot) account for the web of complex relationships encountered. The development of ethical boundary management in dual relationships can be informed through knowledge of the moral principles which underpin most codes of conduct within the helping professions. The principles of *autonomy* (maximum degree of choice for all), *justice* (people are treated fairly), *beneficence* (action undertaken for the good of the client), *non-maleficence* (no harm is done to anyone), and *fidelity* (action in good faith) provide additional dimensions through which to explore issues or dilemmas. Fidelity is closely related to issues of trust, power dynamics and informed consent (Meara and Schmidt 1991) and may be significant to therapy in sexual minority communities. For example, where the client and counsellor have a tacit agreement about attending a community event, does the practitioner explicitly seek the client's informed consent on each occasion? How might we know whether a client is merely deferring to the more powerful position of the therapist?

Ethical dilemmas: processing and problem solving

Placing moral problem solving and decision making within the context of the counselling relationship is an important step towards ethical practice.

As stated earlier, there is a perceptible shift in beliefs from 'Dual relationships are never appropriate', to 'Dual relationships are inevitable in some contexts; given this, how can we best manage the situation?' Figures 3.1 and 3.2 are offered as generic models for ethical problem solving and decision making incorporating the five moral principles outlined above.

Figure 3.1 Process model for ethical problem solving and decision making

---

- **Write a brief description of the problem or dilemma**
  This helps to minimise confusion and is particularly helpful where you are discussing the situation with your supervisor or colleague.

- **Whose problem or dilemma is it?**
  - The counsellor's?
  - The client's?
  - Joint problem?
  - Agency/organisation problem?

  Where joint responsibility exists, then clarification, negotiation and issues related to the boundaries within the therapeutic relationship need to be thoroughly discussed between client and counsellor, using the process steps. Supervisor consultation is advised to facilitate this process.

- **Consider ethics, codes and guidelines**
  Consider appropriate sources of guidance, e.g. British Association for Counselling (BAC) codes and guidelines. Consider where appropriate:
  - What actions are prohibited or required according to available ethics codes?
  - What actions are prohibited or required by law?

- **Consider the moral principles underlying counselling**
  - *Beneficence:* what will achieve the greatest good?
  - *Non-maleficence:* what will cause the least harm?
  - *Justice:* what will be fairest for all parties involved?
  - *Respect for autonomy:* what maximises opportunities for choice?
  - *Fidelity:* what actions ensure that the counsellor remains faithful to the therapeutic relationship? This is a *fiduciary* relationship, that is, it is given in trust. Breaking the client's trust in the counsellor constitutes a serious violation of the therapeutic relationship, and reparation and redemption of the alliance may not be possible.

- **Identify possible courses of action**
  Brainstorm all possible courses of action. Depending upon circumstances, this step will be carried out with the support and cooperation of the client, supervisor and counselling colleague.

- **Select the most appropriate course of action**
  Consider the preferred course of action from the following perspectives:
  - *Universality:* could the chosen action be recommended to others? Would I condone it if undertaken by a colleague?

- *Publicity:* could I explain my chosen action to colleagues? Supervisor? Would I be willing to have it exposed to scrutiny in court, to the media or other public forum?
- *Justice:* would I take the same action with other clients? If the client were well-known or influential, would my decision have been the same? Different?

Answering *no* to any of these questions indicates a need to reconsider, preferably with your supervisor.

- **Evaluate the outcome**
  Consider:
  - Was the outcome as you hoped?
  - Had you considered all relevant factors so that no new factors emerged?
  - Would you do the same again in similar circumstances?

If you answered *no* to any of these questions, consider what you would do differently.

Source: Gabriel (1996) adapted from Bond (1993)

Figure 3.1 is not a definitive process model or framework for solving ethical dilemmas but a guide to consideration of appropriate action. The case examples later in this chapter draw upon the model to illustrate how it might work. The case examples offer *interpretations* of the model in action, not definitive solutions. Ethical codes and moral principles provide important background for decision making and can be enhanced through consulting colleagues, supervisors and available literature. Personal and professional morals, beliefs and values will consciously or unconsciously inform principles, decisions and practices. Therapists need to accomplish a balancing act between personal and professional aspects through the ongoing assessment, monitoring and reviewing of competing elements in our boundary management. Where conflict arises during decision making, it may provoke actions that widely divert codes of ethics and have an adverse impact upon client–therapist dynamics. Each dual or multiple role situation requires attention to the psychological, emotional and contextual features unique to that situation (Sim 1997). It is appropriate for practitioners to develop *realistic* and *reasoned* frameworks within which to practise, and from which the dynamics of the therapeutic relationship and community connections can be monitored and managed.

Figure 3.1 offered a framework for problem solving in ethical dilemmas, while Figure 3.2 presents an overview of possible phases involved in working through dilemmas in dual or overlapping relationships. Used in partnership, they provide a perspective for charting routes through a dilemma, beginning with the moment of 'impact' and developing to the longer-term direction that the therapeutic work and relationship may take.

Figure 3.2 Working with dilemmas in dual relationships and overlapping connections

---

Stage 1: impact and containment

Immediate actions	Contain shock and impact of situation
	Invoke stress/crisis management techniques
	Contain any immediate 'fallout'/acting-out impulses
	Invoke an 'internal supervisor'
	Make contact with client, acknowledge situation
	Seek agreement to discuss situation at the next therapy session
	Model healthy, appropriate behaviour

Stage 2: containment and processing

Intermediate actions and interventions	Acknowledge situation at next therapy session
	Discuss with client issues of confidentiality, boundaries, overlapping connections and possible rehearsal of agreed actions should other situations arise
	Address client's reactions/responses to the situation
	Address transference issues
	Provide ongoing containment
	Redeem the therapeutic alliance
	Discuss countertransference reactions in supervision and personal therapy

Stage 3: ongoing processing

Longer term	Explore transference and countertransference in personal therapy and supervision
	Work with issues triggered by or linked to dual or multiple roles and relationships

---

Source: Gabriel (1998)

Invoking these process models requires consideration of professional ethical codes. For example, BAC's *Code of Ethics and Practice for Counsellors* states that: 'Counsellors must establish and maintain appropriate boundaries around the counselling relationship. Counsellors must take into account the effects of any overlapping or pre-existing relationships.' (BAC 1998: Section A.5). This statement implies that where clients and counsellors share communities, the counsellor holds a responsibility to delineate and define overlapping connections and boundaries between therapy and community.

The BAC *Code* also states: 'Counsellors are responsible for setting and monitoring boundaries throughout the counselling sessions and will make explicit to clients that counselling is a formal and contracted relationship and nothing else' (BAC 1998: Section B.5.1). This statement implies a clear role definition between which behaviours and actions belong within the counselling relationship and which remain beyond the realms of the client-therapist dynamic.

In relation to resolving conflicts in our practice, the BAC *Code* offers:

> Counsellors may find themselves caught between conflicting ethical principles, which could involve issues of public interest. In these circumstances, they are urged to consider the particular situation in which they find themselves and to discuss the situation with their counselling supervisor and/or other experienced counsellors. Even after conscientious consideration of the salient issues, some ethical dilemmas cannot be resolved easily or wholly satisfactorily.
>
> (BAC 1998: Section B.1.6.3.)

The horns of ethical and professional dilemmas may be sharp, and undoubtedly possess the potential to inflict damage, yet they can powerfully assist us in excising redundant theoretical debris. We may need to conscientiously discard any concepts that hinder realistic solutions to dual relationships. Imagine a counsellor placing herself between the horns of a dilemma, thus providing a creative conceptual space in which to craft a reasoned exploration of all the salient issues. If the counsellor and one of her clients meet at a social gathering, we can begin to consider some of the possible issues. For example, in not contracting at the outset of therapy for the possibility of overlap between counselling and community, has the counsellor contravened any ethical principles? In aiming to respond in the dual relationship situation in a way that upholds BAC's stated counsellor values of integrity, impartiality and respect (BAC 1998) the counsellor can maintain these notions as a type of mental template or framework, while monitoring and evaluating her decisions and actions. Through empathic and respectful management of the initial impact and subsequent containment phases, the therapy can move on. Reaching mutually agreed strategies for subsequent duality situations will aid redemption and repair of the therapeutic alliance. Not all alliances will be retrievable, however, and termination or referral may be more appropriate.

Clear role definitions and boundary demarcations will be crucial in dual role situations. This can model containment, relationship limits, and the capacity to relate as separate individuals (this supports the moral principle of autonomy) across a range of roles. Ensuring clarity of roles between the therapy relationship and that of being members of a sexual minority, who may meet at social gatherings, will be crucial to 'damage limitation' (this incorporates the principles of non-maleficence and beneficence). The counsellor's theoretical perspective will influence how this process is managed. The process will also be influenced by the emotional and psychological capacity of the client. For example, from a psychodynamic, object-relations position, the therapist may be concerned about the client's stage of ego development and their capacity to withstand the complexities of dual roles.

It is important to remain faithful to the spirit of the relationship through being aware of power dynamics generated by the situation, and striving not to abuse the client's trust (principle of fidelity). Ensuring justice may be especially challenging. For example, is it *just* – that is, *fair* – for counsellors to deny themselves access to community social events, especially where there is one major community meeting place? What type of behaviour is this modelling for clients? Modelling is extremely powerful (Vasquez 1988), and will influence the client's perceptions and beliefs about the counsellor and the therapy. One solution might be a rota system reasoned and agreed between counsellor and client. It is crucial that the client has agreed to any decisions or actions from a position of informed consent. Achieving this can be complex since power is shared unequally in the therapy relationship. The client may defer to the more powerful position of the counsellor, or accede from a transferential position.

The counsellor will benefit from striving towards emotional, intellectual and conceptual literacy in order to feel confident and competent in processing ethical and professional dilemmas. This places responsibility upon the individual to pursue personal and professional development. Of significance in managing dilemmas will be the counsellor's intentionality: the conscious or unconscious forces underpinning their motives and actions. The use of self as a 'therapeutic tool' in decision making invokes our uniquely personal set of ethics and beliefs, informed by our life experiences. Nevertheless, these need to be complemented by other resources such as professional codes and moral principles, since used in isolation they may produce a distorted response to the situation (Kitchener 1984).

Further aspects which will influence how the situation is dealt with include: finding respectful and confidential ways of checking out social situations while withholding client identity; fostering and encouraging, in non-counsellor friends, the need for boundary clarity, containment and confidentiality; considering therapeutic issues and themes relevant to theoretical and clinical frames (for example, working with attachment and loss, intimacy, envy and jealousy); issues of power and control; transference and countertransference; the counsellor's, as well as the client's, capacity to manage and withstand conflict and dissonance.

Ultimately, how we contextualise that which is beneficent, just, or respectful of autonomy, is based upon integrating our professional and personal experience and knowledge with our vision of human life (Betan 1997). Essentially, a holistic approach can be adopted, with the framework for problem solving (Figure 3.1) underpinning choices and actions, and the process model (Figure 3.2) supporting our route through the dilemma.

By exploring challenging, even 'worst case' scenarios, we can rehearse effective ethical behaviour which may help therapists who encounter a dual relationship dilemma and feel unable to work out ethical behaviour in advance or discuss dilemmas in training and supervision.

Case example 1

You are invited to an intimate dinner party in honour of your fortieth birthday. The hostess tells you there will be eight people but is keeping their identities secret! When you arrive you notice Sarah, a current client, deep in conversation with Naomi, recently your lover for three years. The hostess, one of your closest friends, notices the look of shock on your face. She tells you Sarah is Naomi's new lover, present at Naomi's request. You parted amicably six months ago and have had little contact. From the therapy relationship with Sarah, you know that she's recently begun a relationship with a lover, who is unaware that she is seeing a counsellor. Sarah had previously felt socially isolated and found making new relationships and friendships difficult. You are also aware of her developing an erotic transference towards you.

Issues

Personal issues and immediate reactions
Despite my initial shock and wish to leave the party, it would seem ill-mannered to do so, since it was being held in my honour. My friend (unaware that Sarah is a client) is curious about my reaction. I may feel resentful at what feels like an intrusion upon my personal and social space. I might ask myself questions such as: 'Should I leave the party? Will Sarah disclose that I am her therapist or Naomi disclose that I am her ex-lover? Will they discuss me, or share details with other friends? Will Naomi share intimate details of our relationship with her new lover, my client? Now Sarah and Naomi know I have arrived, what are their reactions? Should I immediately approach them or wait for one to approach me? Should I seek a private moment with Sarah to acknowledge the situation?'

Professional issues and responses
Following a few minutes 'thinking, stress management and composure time', I consider next steps and what actions to take. I regret that there has been little rehearsal in the therapy relationship regarding potential social overlap. I feel concern about the effects of the erotic transference and working through this and the client's relational difficulties in a 'healthy' way. I am also concerned about the therapy boundaries, and subsequent redemption and repair. I question the overall impact upon the therapy relationship and decide to explore the dilemma in supervision.

Processing the case: process steps for ethical problem-solving and decision making

What is the dilemma?

My meeting a current client at an intimate party, partnering a recent former lover of mine.

Whose dilemma is it?

It is both the therapist's and client's dilemma. I experience it as a personal as well as a professional dilemma. In both respects I may feel compromised. I may feel it would be untenable to continue work with Sarah. The impact of discovering that her current lover and therapist are ex-lovers presents Sarah with a personal dilemma and raises issues regarding the integrity of the therapy relationship. She may decide that she is unable to continue with the therapy.

Professional codes

As a member of BAC, I scrutinise the *Code* for applicable guidance. The *Code*, however, offers only general information not guidance specific to my situation, so I consider the dilemma against the moral principles in Figure 3.1. I reflect upon my own beliefs, morals and ethics and consider how they might inform decisions and actions. Where 'inner codes' are discordant with BAC's I consult my supervisor and peers for feedback and support in my decision making.

Consider moral principles

I would consider the situation against the moral principles outlined in Figure 3.1. For example, would it be *fair* for Sarah or myself to have to leave the party? – principle of *justice*; would my leaving cause the least harm to all? – principle of *non-maleficence*; should the therapeutic relationship survive and continue, how might I ensure *fidelity* is upheld?

Identify possible courses of action

- Leave the party
- Ignore the situation
- Acknowledge the situation with the client in private and suggest we explore it at our next session
- Remain at the party and consider how my emotional state may influence my behaviour

Select the most appropriate course of action

It is important not to act through fears or anxiety. My immediate action would be to privately acknowledge with the client our both being present and seek agreement to discuss the situation at our next therapy session. I would consider my behaviour and how it might have impact upon the client. Modelling emotional well-being by participating in one's community, and the development and containment of healthy relationships, can trigger responses and issues for therapeutic exploration. Modelling of isolation and estrangement from one's community is questionable, and communicates a way of being that may promote emotional ill-health.

Supervision is important throughout the whole process of dilemma management: it will be especially helpful to me at this stage. I see it as my responsibility, as counsellor, to remain the *boundary rider* – checking and instigating repair of boundaries as well as facilitating ongoing management. While I endeavour to instigate the 'best possible' course of action, I nevertheless recall BAC's comments on resolving ethical conflicts in counselling practice, and their recognition that 'some ethical dilemmas cannot be resolved easily or wholly satisfactorily.' (BAC 1998: Section B.1.6.3).

Evaluate the situation

Evaluation would take place in the therapy relationship and in supervision. There may also be exploration of a more personal nature in my own therapy. Where the counselling continues, it is important that the client has a voice and active presence in monitoring the immediate, intermediate and longer-term working through of the situation.

Case example 2

You are participating in an exciting group sex scene in the dark room of a gay sauna. The lighting is dim, but you can make out details once you get a couple of feet away from someone. You have been kissing one person, another has been fellating you, and your right hand is masturbating someone else. As you look to see who is attached to your hand, your eyes meet a client's.

The client is in ongoing therapy with you. He holds highly ambivalent attitudes to sex – mostly he is fairly sex negative (erotophobic). The roots of this are a strong religious upbringing. He has previously described his encounters with casual sex as 'compulsive', about which he feels he has little control. He usually feels guilty about his experiences with casual sex, but 'finds himself' returning time after time. You didn't know that he used this sauna; he did not know that you did. Your own attitude to saunas and cruising is positive and you see nothing 'pathological' in enjoying or even celebrating casual, uncomplicated sexual expression.

Issues

Personal issues and immediate reactions

- I may feel guilt: buried shame about my sexual needs could have been triggered off as if I am 'caught out'
- Concern about possible psychological damage to the client
- Worry about implications of this event for my career
- I may feel angry that I can't have time 'off-duty'
- I may experience frustration at not being able to remain part of the group scene

Professional issues and responses

After some composure time I can begin to think more clearly. I would consider how best to contain the situation. I would be concerned whether I have irrevocably damaged the client-therapist relationship. I would want to reassure the client that I want to work the implications of this through with him.

I may feel anxious about remembering how well I managed the contracting and negotiation of boundaries at the beginning of the relationship. I would resolve to check my notes and ensure in future that I am clear with clients when exploring the likelihood of all social contact.

I would be concerned about whether I breached ethical codes and how many codes I breached. I would need to review the codes and discuss the situation with my supervisor. I may worry about the client making a complaint. Since this is a possibility, I would take advice from BAC, and inform my professional indemnity insurers about a possible risk, as well as seek advice from them.

Processing the case

What is the dilemma?

I have been having sex with a client. This is a clear breach of the *Code of Ethics*. Contact outside of the therapeutic relationship should be explored at the contracting stage. It is important to monitor boundaries, dual roles and relationships, and minimise them where possible. I recognise that this isn't always possible and that there can be positive outcomes to dual roles and relationships.

Whose dilemma is it?

It is my dilemma, in that I am engaged in sexual activity with a client. My face would register my shock: I would cease immediately and indicate to the client that I was going outside, hoping that he would follow. I suspect that the client is as shocked as I am and assume he did not know he was joining in a group in which I was present. My primary concern is the client's well-being, especially in the light of his feelings around sex. The client may feel unable to continue therapy with me; it is therefore also a dilemma for him.

Professional codes
In addition to sex with a client, have I also broken contracting codes, as I may not have raised at the outset how we'd deal with meeting in this sort of setting?

Identify possible courses of action
- Leave the sauna immediately
- Remain at the sauna but move to other spaces which are better lit, and avoid further sexual contact with the client
- Indicate to the client I am leaving and that he is welcome to come outside and discuss this

Select the most appropriate course of action

As I am aware of the client's conflicts about sex I would seek to reassure him that I didn't know that it was he, that I am somewhat shocked and need time to collect myself. I would probably let him know that I was going home (in order to reflect on this). I would indicate that I would like us to discuss this at our next session. Acknowledging that he may be surprised to see me here and might want to discuss this before our next appointment, I would encourage him to telephone me. I would want my tone to indicate that I saw nothing wrong with being at the sauna, or having casual sex, and that I am leaving because I want some time out.

Evaluate the situation

In my reflections afterwards I would wonder if my behaviour breached the BAC *Code*. Did we, in the spirit of the *Code*, engage in sexual activity? Casual anonymous sex is a feature of gay men's subculture. Many gay men use casual sex as a way of meeting people. This and other cultural differences need to be borne in my mind when considering ethical dilemmas.

I am uncertain whether our encounter in the dark room would be seen as unethical if neither of us knew the other was involved and as soon as we realised this we stopped. The BAC *Code* is particularly concerned with exploitation of clients by counsellors. I think it unlikely that I would be seen as exploiting a client in the circumstances outlined above.

Did the client know I was part of the scene when he joined in? If he did, then we have issues to work out about our boundaries, that's for sure! It would be important to reflect on the positive or erotic transference that might exist between us. If there were a strong transference, I'd be wondering whether he had planned to be there. The place to sort this out would be in the therapy room with the client, after having some supervision.

If he didn't know I was at the sauna, how does he feel about what occurred? If he were open-minded and familiar with the context he may not be worried by it and we'd need to be clear, and take steps to ensure that it would not happen again. This is unlikely to be the case with this client.

What of the therapist's own attitudes to sex in saunas? It is possible that internalised shame will be triggered by this experience. Some therapists may feel they had let the profession down, and in part this reflects society's negative messages about sex, reinforced by some therapeutic modalities. Casual sex may be seen as pathological, avoidant of mature adult intimacy, commitment and fidelity. Others might describe these as heterosexist assumptions not consistent with gay men's subcultural and psychosocial contexts.

Closer attention to my contracting with clients would be essential, as I had clearly breached this code and could perhaps have anticipated this situation better. In this dilemma it would depend on how comfortable the client would be in continuing with me as his therapist. The possibility of working through the experience at the sauna holds great potential for understanding his conflicts about sex. However, it is possible the client would feel the relationship had been irrevocably damaged by this intimacy, and would prefer to continue his therapy with someone else.

Key points when considering dilemmas in dual relationships

Theoretical and conceptual influences

Counselling theory has offered inadequate concepts, theories and frames of reference for affirmative work with clients from sexual minorities and for working through dilemmas in dual relationships in general. The decision making and process models illustrated here transcend theoretical perspectives and offer a generic frame for practitioners to use in such dilemmas.

Affirmative psychology and therapeutic theory and practice need to be developed – and be appropriate to client work within community contexts (see Introduction to this volume).

Practitioners can consider how their own theoretical perspective would encounter and perceive the case studies, and 'rehearse' (particularly within a training or supervision arena) ethical means of resolving each case.

Client-counsellor dialogues

Potential overlap between therapy and community can be discussed in contract building at the outset of the therapy relationship and renegotiated as appropriate.

Acceptable behaviours where overlap occurs need to be negotiated – for example, 'What is appropriate outside the therapy relationship?' Client and therapist can rehearse possible scenarios and consider ways of becoming 'fluent' in a range of dual and overlapping roles. Supervision can facilitate this process. Client and therapist may agree a rota for participating in social or community events. The counsellor, the boundary rider, remains the guardian responsible for the ethical and professional handling of boundary overlap where dilemmas or conflicts arise.

The ending of the therapeutic relationship may be necessary in some situations; this process needs to be negotiated and managed sensitively and humanely. Decisions need to be reached about ethical obligations to former clients; for example, what decisions are taken about opportunities for future counselling work? What preparation is made for possible future dual roles and relationships?

Conclusions

The overlapping situations exemplified raise a number of concerns. Those stated are drawn from the myriad of possible questions and issues. Grounding our anxiety and concern through utilising a process model to work through the dilemma can help us to deal with personal and professional issues that arise. Reasoned, relevant and ethical actions are possible, despite any initial shock or concern we may experience when encountering our clients in situations outside therapy. Witnessing and welcoming one another in a range of roles need not be inappropriate or unmanageable. Where overlapping connections and role conflicts are unavoidable, realistic and respectful ways of developing what Clarkson (1995) terms 'role fluency' need to be developed. Although this is new territory for sexual minority counselling theory, it is possible that we can positively mediate between therapy and community and become fluent in a range of situations yet to be explored and articulated.

Above all, we must remember that the counsellor and client will at times fall short of ideals. Humans make mistakes, regret things spoken or acted upon; even wish they could be the perfect therapist or client. The therapist, being human, will struggle at times in the work. Where conflicts and dilemmas are encountered, we need not set ourselves up to be perfect – instead, we can draw upon personal strengths and skills and permit ourselves to learn from our anxieties and concerns. Our personal and professional skills do not desert us the moment we encounter a dilemma. We may be challenged to remain aware of them, however, as we struggle to engage with conflicts without resorting to acting-out or denial.

Dialogues about dilemmas need to be brought into mainstream literature. Counsellor training needs to address the issues discussed here and ensure that trainee counsellors are equipped to deal with the management of crises and dilemmas. We need to explore how to develop and manage 'role fluency'. Importantly, we need to determine how our clients perceive and experience dual and overlapping roles.

Acknowledgement

The authors wish to thank Toni Wright, whose valued participation in a working group within ALGBP UK informed the ideas contained in this chapter, and Tim Bond, Alan Jamieson and Charles Neal for their feedback on earlier drafts.

References

Anderson, S.K. and Kitchener, K.S. (1996) Non-romantic, nonsexual post therapy relationships between psychologists and former clients: an exploratory study of critical incidents. *Professional Psychology: Research and Practice*, 27(4): 59–66.

BAC (British Association for Counselling) (1998) *Code of Ethics and Practice for Counsellors*. Rugby: BAC.

Berman, J.S. (1985) Ethical feminist perspectives on dual relationships with clients, in L.B. Rosewater and L.E.A. Walker (eds) *Handbook of Feminist Therapy: Women's Issues in Psychotherapy*. New York: Springer Publishing Company.

Betan, E.J. (1997) Towards a hermeneutic model of ethical decision making in clinical practice. *Ethics & Behavior*, 17(4): 347–65.

Bond, T. (1993) *Standards and Ethics for Counsellors in Action*. London: Sage.

Bond, T. (1997) Therapists' dilemmas as stimuli to new understanding and practice, in W. Dryden, (ed.) *Therapists' Dilemmas*. London: Sage.

Borys, D.S. and Pope, K.S. (1989) Dual relationships between therapist and client: a national study of psychologists, psychiatrists, and social workers. *Professional Psychology: Research and Practice*, 20(5): 283–93.

Brown, L.S. (1984) The lesbian therapist in private practice and her community. *Psychotherapy in Private Practice*, 12(4): 9–16.

Brown, L.S. (1985) Power, responsibility, boundaries: ethical concerns for the lesbian feminist therapist. *Lesbian Ethics*, 1(3): 30–45.

Brown, L.S. (1989a) Beyond thou shalt not: thinking about ethics in the lesbian therapy community. *Women and Therapy*, 8(1/2): 13–25.

Brown, L.S. (1989b) NEW VOICES, NEW VISIONS: towards a lesbian/gay paradigm for psychology. *Psychology of Women Quarterly*, 13(4): 445–58.

Brown, L.S. (1994) Boundaries in feminist therapy: a conceptual formulation. *Women and Therapy*, 15(1): 29–38.

Browning, C., Reynolds, A.L. and Dworkin, S.H. (1991) Affirmative psychotherapy for lesbian women. *The Counseling Psychologist*, 19(2): 177–96.

Burgess, N. (1997) All in the mind: the ethics of gay counselling. *Gay Times*, September: 39–42.

Clarkson, P. (1995) *The Therapeutic Relationship*. London: Whurr.

Concise Oxford Dictionary. (1982) (7th edn). Oxford: Oxford University Press.

Coyle, A. (1993) Gay and lesbian mental health: in defence of a radical psycho-therapy. *Directory of Lesbian and Gay Studies in the UK*, 4: 10–12.

Coyle, A. (1995) *What are we affirming in lesbian and gay affirmative psychology and therapy?* Conference paper, Association for Lesbian, Gay and Bisexual Psychologies annual conference, Nottingham, 14 September.

Davies, D. and Neal, C. (eds) (1996) *Pink Therapy: A Guide for Counsellors and Therapists Working with Lesbian, Gay and Bisexual Clients.* Buckingham: Open University Press.

Dworkin, S.H. (1992) Some ethical considerations when counselling gay, lesbian and bisexual clients, in S.H. Dworkin and F.J. Gutierrez (eds) *Counselling Gay Men and Lesbians: Journey to the End of the Rainbow.* Alexandria, VA: American Counselling Association.

Dworkin, S.H., and Gutierrez, F. (1989) Counselors be aware: clients come in every size, shape, color, and sexual orientation. *Journal of Counseling and Development*, 68(1): 6–9.

Epstein, R.S. and Simon, R.I. (1990) The exploitation index: an early warning indicator of boundary violations in psychotherapy. *Bulletin of the Menninger Clinic*, 54(4): 450–65.

Gabriel, L. (1996) 'Boundaries in lesbian client-lesbian counsellor relationships'. Unpublished MEd thesis, University College of Ripon and York St John, York.

Gabriel, L. (1998) Materials presented at ALGBP-UK Annual Training Conference, March 7th.

Gartrell, N.K. (1992) Boundaries in lesbian therapy relationships. *Women and Therapy*, 12(3): 29–50.

Gonsiorek, J.C. (1994) Foreword, in B. Greene and G.M. Herek (eds) *Lesbian and Gay Psychology: Theory, Research, and Clinical Applications.* Thousand Oaks, CA: Sage.

Gutheil, T.G. and Gabbard, G.O. (1993) The concept of boundaries in clinical practice: theoretical and risk-management dimensions. *American Journal of Psychiatry*, 150(2): 188–96.

Henry, C. (1996) Taking an ethical position on standards. *British Journal of Guidance and Counselling*, 24(1): 35–43.

Heyward, C. (1993) *When Boundaries Betray Us.* San Francisco, CA: HarperCollins.

Jamieson, A. (1998) *Personal communication.*

Kitchener, K.S. (1984) Intuition, critical evaluation and ethical principles: the foundations for ethical decisions in counseling psychology. *The Counseling Psychologist*, 12(3): 43–55.

Kitchener, K.S. (1988) Dual role relationships: what makes them so problematic? *Journal of Counseling and Development*, 67(4): 217–21.

Kitzinger, C. (1987) *The Social Construction of Lesbianism.* London: Sage.

Lago, C. and Thompson, J. (1989) Counselling and race, in W. Dryden, C. Edwards and R. Woolfe (eds) *Handbook of Counselling in Britain.* London: Routledge.

Langs, R. (1976) *The Bipersonal Field.* New York: Jason Aronson.

Langs, R. (1978) *The Listening Process.* New York: Jason Aronson.

Langs, R. (1979) *The Therapeutic Environment.* New York: Jason Aronson.

Lyn, L. (1995) Lesbian, gay, and bisexual therapists' social and sexual interactions with clients, in J.C. Gonsiorek (ed.) *Breach of Trust: Sexual Exploitation by Health Care Professionals and Clergy.* Thousand Oaks, CA: Sage.

McGrath, G. (1994) Ethics, boundaries, and contracts: applying moral principles. *Transactional Analysis Journal*, 24(1): 7–14.

McLeod, J. (1993) *An Introduction to Counselling*. Buckingham: Open University Press.

Margolies, L. (1990) Cracks in the frame: feminism and the boundaries of therapy. *Women and Therapy*, 9(4): 19–36.

Meara, N.M. and Schmidt, L.D. (1991) The ethics of researching counseling/therapy processes, in C.E. Watkins, and L.J. Schneider (eds) *Research in Counseling*. Hillsdale, NJ: Lawrence Erlbaum.

Milton, M.J. (1993) The frame in psychotherapy: Langs and Casement compared. *Counselling Psychology Quarterly*, 6(2): 143–53.

Pearson, B. and Piazza, N. (1997) Classification of dual relationships in the helping professions. *Counselor Education and Supervision*, 37(2): 89–99.

Peterson, M.R. (1992) *At Personal Risk: Boundary Violations in Professional-Client Relationships*. New York: Norton.

Pope, K. (1991) Dual relationships in psychotherapy. *Ethics and Behaviour*, 1(1): 21–34.

Roll, S. and Millen, L. (1981) A guide to violating an injunction in psychotherapy: on seeing acquaintances as patients. *Psychotherapy: Theory, Research and Practice*, 18(2): 179–89.

Sim, J. (1997) *Ethical Decision Making in Therapy Practice*. Oxford: Butterworth-Heinemann.

Vasquez, M.J.T. (1988) Counselor-client sexual contact: implications for ethics training. *Journal of Counseling and Development*, 67(4): 238–41.

Webb, S.R. (1997) Training for maintaining appropriate boundaries in counselling. *British Journal of Guidance and Counselling*, 25(2): 175–88.

Young, V. (1995) *The Equality Complex: Lesbians in Therapy – a Guide to Anti-Oppressive Practice*. London: Cassell.

Issues in HIV/AIDS counselling

In its early days, HIV/AIDS was seen as a gay disease, as is reflected in its initial name, 'Gay-Related Immune Deficiency' (GRID). In my perception, the gay and bisexual communities were unable to cope with the burden of the epidemic without external resources and, therefore, a struggle to widen it as an issue for everyone (whether gay or not) followed for several years. However, some of the arguments of gay and bisexual activists were used to serve the diminishing of the statutory resources, aimed at the prevention and treatment of HIV/AIDS, addressing the specific needs of gay and bisexual people.

For the last few years there has been a strong movement to reclaim the 'gayness' of HIV/AIDS: in Britain, as in the rest of Europe and North America, HIV and AIDS are still primarily affecting gay and bisexual people. Men who have sex with men constitute the vast majority of people with AIDS in the UK and North America. According to April 1995 statistics (PHLS 1995) men who have sex with men comprise 74 per cent of people with AIDS in the UK. Despite evidence of a levelling-off in the incidence of HIV in this population (Loveday *et al.* 1989; PHLS Working Group 1989; PHLS 1995) following changes in risk behaviour (Evans *et al.* 1989; Johnson and Gill 1989) they will continue to represent the most infected and affected group in the UK for quite some time (Hart *et al.* 1990).

HIV and AIDS does not affect only gay and bisexual people infected by the virus. It also affects their partners and friends, and the wider sexual minority communities as a whole. Hart *et al.* (1990) conducted a non-clinical British study with 502 men who had sex with men within the previous five years. The vast majority (78 per cent) identified themselves as gay and a further 9 per cent as homosexual. By definition, men who were isolated from other gay men and unable to confide in, or discuss issues of sex and sexuality with others, were not included in the sample. Of the participants, 63 per cent knew or had known at least one person who was HIV antibody positive and between 42 and 46 per cent knew or had known a person or persons who were HIV antibody positive and ill (with HIV symptomatic disease), someone with AIDS or somebody who had died from AIDS. The figures are even higher for the big cities; for example, 68 per cent of the respondents interviewed in London and Manchester knew of someone who was HIV antibody positive. Finally, 85 men in the total sample (17 per cent) had a close friend, lover or former lover who had died of AIDS.

These interconnections relate to the psychological identification of gay and bisexual individuals with the 'collective of gay and bisexual people' – by which I mean the psychosocial representation of all gay and bisexual people regardless of their participation in sexual minority communities which might provide a sense of belonging and psychological safety, in counterbalance to not belonging to the majority heterosexual group.

For lesbians and, to a lesser extent bisexual women and transgender people, the connection does not appear to be so much in having an HIV positive status themselves but being associated with HIV and affected by it at various levels including community and self-identity. This does not mean that there are no bisexual or lesbian women, or transgender people at risk from, even infected by, HIV.

Laura was a symptomatic, bisexual woman who had been infected by her bisexual ex-boyfriend, with whom she had an HIV negative 9-year-old daughter. For the last seven years she had been living with her HIV negative girlfriend. I saw Laura and her daughter for family therapy because her daughter's teachers informed her that other girls at school were physically attacking her. At a later stage I saw Laura and her girlfriend for some couple sessions.

Alison was a 21-year-old, lesbian woman I saw at a crisis intervention service the morning after the night she had unprotected sex with her HIV positive, 19-year-old gay male flatmate, while intoxicated. She looked pretty rough, having thrown up a few minutes prior to our session the several chocolates she had had for comfort since she had woken up. Interestingly, although she often said that they were 'out of their heads', she did not state that she did not know what they were doing nor pretend it had not happened.

The multiplicity of experiences is one of the most striking characteristics of the psychological impact of HIV and AIDS on gay and bisexual people. What stands out for me is the multiplicity of losses.

Biller and Rice (1990) provide data that highlight the inability of survivors of multiple losses to resolve their grief, because preceding losses compound each loss and time for recovery is relatively brief. The stages of grief (avoidance, confrontation and re-establishment) happen simultaneously in response to each loss and the boundaries between the stages become unclear. The subjects were bereft not only of close friends and lovers but also of entire personal support networks. The normal process of grieving was further undermined by the society's lack of acceptance of their sexual identity and the resulting breakdown in familial and community support.

Grothe and McKusick (1992) refer to McKusick and Hilliard's (1991) research on gay men in San Francisco, which reveals on the one hand increasing levels of depression with each year of the epidemic, and on the other a greater likelihood of depression among men experiencing a higher number of deaths, and among men who are HIV infected and symptomatic.

Many men who have sex with men experience the loss of their own health when they become HIV symptomatic, but in several cases even before: when they are HIV positive and in anticipation of the symptoms some time in the future. At the time of writing, there is still no known vaccine against infection nor a cure or disease management for HIV related symptoms and AIDS that does not compromise the person's duration and quality of life. HIV infection is still a shortening of the journey to death, despite recent detours and delays associated with medical developments. The advancements in drug treatments (such as triple combination therapies) have resulted in significant drops in the death rate: therefore, there are more people alive and suffering, to some extent, from AIDS.

Moreover, psychological experiences of loss of health are observed in some men who have sex with men who do not know their HIV status. Several avoid the test, feeling terror when they contemplate, at whatever level of consciousness, that they might be infected. The terror is so strong that it dictates their avoidance behaviour. At that level of consciousness they get in touch with the actual or fantasised infected self and they are faced with the loss of health.

In addition to loss of health, HIV evokes in several people experiences of loss of life itself: loss of existence and of all possibilities of change.

Some people who are HIV negative (especially if they know a lot of people who have been infected with HIV, developed AIDS symptoms and died) start, at some level of consciousness, to believe that HIV infection is only a matter of time. They experience the loss of their own health linked to the loss of health of the collective with whom they have psychologically identified.

At an individual and collective level, people follow a pattern of spirals of excitement followed by disillusionment with medical advancements which do not prove to be the miraculous cures yearned for. Feelings of disappointment, stuckness, bitterness, anger, vast sadness, anguish, despair and terror are often present. Grothe and McKusick (1992) describe how urban gay men, in particular, are subject to multiple loss and mourn not only those who have died but also their own hopes for the future and their fondness of the time before the epidemic. Gay and bisexual people in Western Europe and North America have been losing the lightness of being and optimism that they had arrived at. Moreover, at a community level, there has been a loss of leaders and role models, who were providing concrete contributions by their actions and, at a psychological level, safety and support. All these losses pile up.

Hays and Tobey (1990) indicate that social support is crucial in mitigating symptoms of depression in men with AIDS. However, the deaths that cause the depression also deplete the social support networks necessary to deal with multiple loss. It has been further suggested that, particularly in conditions of chronic or severe stress, social support may prove a disappointment because it is hard to mobilise or simply cannot meet the extreme demands (Hobfoll 1985; Hobfoll and London 1986). Britton *et al.* (1993) point out that support systems for men in gay and bisexual communities may be particularly vulnerable to this phenomenon.

The intensity of such loss is closely interlinked to existential fears of death. For some, these are related to a sudden deeper realisation of futility and meaninglessness in human existence. People who believe that death is the ultimate state, nullifying all possibilities of change, often feel under tremendous pressure to 'get things right' now, and this gives rise to fears of 'getting it wrong' – especially in relation to lifelong struggles that really matter to them. Most people suffer from anxieties about being dead. Religious people might have fears related to their beliefs about post-death unpleasant experiences (e.g. physical and soul pain in 'hell') arising from feelings of guilt. People are generally aware that pain becomes more difficult to bear after a long period of physical suffering linked to demoralisation.

Case example 1

Luca, a 23-year-old bisexual man, who was HIV-positive symptomatic and an intravenous heroin user, had acute fear of pain.

From my brief work with him, the connections between chronic back pains associated with a motorbike accident, his intense emotional distress and his drug use were apparent. These connections included his use of heroin as a painkiller and his difficulty getting painkiller prescriptions. When they discovered Luca's ongoing use of illegal drugs, his medical practitioners felt justified in mistrusting him. Luca was scared that his prescribed dosage of pain killers would not be enough; the more anxious and worried he became, the less the drugs were able to sedate him, fulfilling his fear and reinforcing his mistrust of the medical practitioners. He would resort to heroin to top up his prescribed medication. I was stunned by the frantic escalation of his panic when he believed that he was going to experience physical or emotional pain, and his desperation to do anything to prevent feeling it. He was in such terror of 'free-falling in a pit of panic, dreading eventually crashing at the bottom' that he would often end up overdosed, not prepared to err on the side of lower dosage.

In this vicious circle it seemed that he and the doctors were feeling despair and frustration in gaining control over the panic. These struggles for power were underpinned by a core perception that the panic was not part of Luca's self. At some level, both parties were desperately seeking something concrete. However, pain is not objectively measurable. People have individual experiences of severity and tolerance thresholds of the same pain stimulus.

Although Luca was unable to break free from the vicious circle he realised that his panic was accompanied by muscle tension, which in turn increased his pain due to spasm. The muscle tension that often accompanies pain can be understood as an attempt to numb sensation. It is unfortunate that when people desensitise, neither unpleasant nor pleasant sensations are felt. People end up being afraid of living because opening up to experience through physical sensing results in more awareness of fears, loss and pain.

Luca had told me he was worried that if he were to have fun 'life would soon give him an even harder time'. He feared being punished for having fun. His past fear of punishment by God, linked to his Catholic background, was less, but his dread of pain was dominating his attitude to, and experience of, life. It appeared that struggling with pain, fear and uncontrollable changes for the worse had become integral aspects of Luca's identity. He had generalised his fear of physical deterioration to a fear of change in general, thus eliminating the possibility of changes for the better. Therefore, although he was craving for fun and aliveness, the dominant feeling was of being afraid of it.

Case example 2

Two other fears in relation to HIV and AIDS in connection to belonging to a sexual minority are the fear of ostracism and the fear of isolation, possibly triggering earlier traumatic experiences of abandonment. Gareth was a 37-year-old Welsh manual worker who moved to East London seven years earlier because he 'could not connect with anyone in Wales'. Initially I thought that he was referring to his experiences of being abandoned as a child by his biological parents and, following a period at an orphanage, being adopted at the age of 5. At our fourth meeting he told me that he was gay and had been having sex either in public toilets or in his local sauna. He said that two years earlier he had had some treatment at a sexually transmitted diseases (STD) clinic, developed health problems and was soon after diagnosed as HIV symptomatic. He had not disclosed his gayness or his HIV status to his adoptive parents or workmates for fear of prejudice and aggression. From comments about television characters he was aware of his parents' homophobia supported by religious beliefs. He was aware of his workmates' homophobia through name-calling, scapegoating and intimidation of staff in other teams who were suspected to be gay. The homophobic name-calling that had the most impact on Gareth was that linked to HIV and AIDS.

In the case of gay and bisexual people, HIV related distress interacts with distress experienced through being members of a minority group (Barrows and Halgin 1988). The 1987 British Social Attitudes survey (Jowell *et al.* 1988) indicates that oppression of gay men has dramatically increased with the emergence of the AIDS crisis. The 1986 report (Airey and Brook 1986) reveals an increase in the proportion saying that homosexual relationships were 'always' or 'almost always' wrong, while responses in respect of pre- and extra-marital sex remained largely unchanged between 1983 and 1985. In 1987 the data reveal a sharp increase in the proportion censuring sex outside marriage and a further climb in the proportion critical of homo- sexuality. There has been a steady increase in censoriousness since 1983, when 62 per cent took the view that sexual relationships between two adults of the same sex were 'always' or 'mostly' wrong. By 1987 the percentage had risen to 74. In both reports (Airey and Brook 1986; Jowell *et al.* 1988) the increase in hostility towards homosexuality has been linked to the asso- ciation of AIDS with the gay community in the public's consciousness. Barrows and Halgin (1988) and Herek and Glunt (1988) emphasise that the escalation of homophobia in and of itself has contributed to further distress in these communities.

Gareth's only friends were the homophobic guys at work. He wanted to belong but not to the group that was the target of scapegoating and other forms of aggression. Actually, his social contact with his workmates was limited to drinking at the pub near the warehouse after their shift. The rest of the time he would spend alone watching television and drinking. At the sixth session I learnt that he was cutting his wrists with broken beer bottles when he had more than one day's break from work; he said that it made him feel relief.

Bulmer (1987) emphasises that community care in the UK in relation to other illness relies to a large extent on unpaid, informal carers, often women. However, Hart *et al.* (1990) point out that in the gay population, which is distributed unevenly throughout the country and which cannot assume the presence or availability of partners or relatives at times of serious illness, men not willing or able to disclose their sexual orientation may be even less likely to expect or receive such support. It is not unknown for friends and relatives to reject those found to be living with HIV or AIDS.

Case example 3

All the above fears add up to the fear of being overwhelmed by the accumu- lation and interaction of pain and loss. This does not only apply to people infected by HIV but also to their partners and carers. Due to the stigma attached to HIV related issues, gay and bisexual men report feeling tentative and fearful about disclosing their HIV status or that of a friend to anyone (Lopez and Getzel 1984). That was the case with Jonathan, a bisexual senior teacher and his partner Olu, a black American. When Olu found out his HIV positive status seven months after they had been with each other, he did not tell Jonathan. Instead, he started doing hours of bodybuilding, trying to block it out of his mind, believing that telling Jonathan would make it even more real and harder to forget for a while. Besides, he would then have to deal with Jonathan's reactions and the implications for their new relationship, including the possibility of Jonathan leaving, or not wanting to leave him. Olu did not know what he wanted or what he was most scared of. Jonathan started to notice changes in Olu's mood and behaviour and, when these piled up, realised that it was something significant. Jonathan found it difficult to believe that this was temporary but he was scared to address it. Was it problems at work or with his family of origin, or was it another man in Olu's life? He was dreading what he might find and concerned that bringing the problems up would make them harder to solve. They both became depressed, having explosive arguments and avoiding each other by working longer hours than ever before. At weekends when they were together they would get stoned smoking cannabis and get drunk. Eventually, they came for couple counselling where they got some support and felt able to bring together the different pieces of the picture.

Case example 4

Unlike Jonathan, Jason, a 29-year-old African-Caribbean gay man came for counselling only when his Zimbabwean partner, Kayode, died from an AIDS related illness.

When a partner or friend is the only person who 'knows', there is pressure to provide support in a multitude of roles, often overwhelming. In addition, the significant other may not be free to discuss the problem and, thus, be left handling their own pain in isolation, with the mutual secrecy becoming an obstacle to processing and moving through the emotions (Britton *et al.* 1993). Kayode had asked Jason not to talk about his illness with anyone, as they and their families of origin were part of a closed community with strong Christian evangelical anti-gay beliefs. This secrecy was ever present in the long process of tentative consolidation of trust in the therapeutic relationship. My being white evoked fear in Jason and relief that his black environment would be far removed from me (see also Chapter 1).

If the biological family of a gay man infected with HIV learns about his HIV status significant others, and especially the partner, often get blamed following the hostility and resentfulness biological families often experience over the closeness they perceive between their family member and such others (Britton *et al.* 1993).

Families have belief and value systems which shape patterns of behaviour (Rolland 1988), and may experience value dissonance, shame and fear concerning a family member's disclosure of HIV antibody positive status, because HIV is attached to values about sexuality, religion and lifestyles. Relatives often express concern about the effect it may have on their lives and communities. Britton *et al.* (1993) give the example of a young mother who operates day care in her home and is worried whether her neighbours will allow their children over if they discover her brother's HIV antibody positive status.

It is not uncommon that a family's rule in dealing with a gay member has been not to discuss the situation. Their form of 'accepting' means that 'it' goes unstated. Consequently, if HIV issues surface, the family has no formulated manner of processing the emotions, as the rule has been 'don't talk about anything related to it'. Besides, families may simply lack competency in dealing with HIV issues; they may not know how to cope with the plethora of concerns and emotions, feel inadequate and become awkward. Even if the family desires to be supportive it may become immobilised and inefficient as a source of support (Britton *et al.* 1993).

Establishing new relationships evoked more guilt for Jason and ambivalence about his sexuality itself. As he vacillated between denying and accepting the loss of his lover, he perceived the threat of loss in new relationships and alternately denied or accepted the possibility of his own mortality from HIV disease.

Sowell *et al.* (1991) indicate that normal bereavement is confounded by limited social support, by the social stigma surrounding the diagnosis and the gay lifestyle itself, and by the survivor's own risk status. Survivors felt isolated from family and friends and from themselves; they reported going through the 'motions of life'. Emotional confusion, manifested in feelings of guilt and vulnerability, was common.

Besides comfort-food binging, excessive work, exercising (especially bulky muscle building), escapist sex, reading and television watching (which are deflection activities), alcohol and other psychotropic drugs are used as coping strategies to numb feelings of becoming overwhelmed by pain and fear. I keep noticing the large prevalence of alcohol and other drug use in the gay population and have witnessed the unfolding of this theme especially in my experiences at lesbian and gay alcohol counselling services.

Pivar and Temoshok (1990) in their research with 100 homosexual seropositive men found that 22 per cent evidenced a 'control/denial' response style to HIV related stressors. This group utilised strategies of escape/avoidance, distancing self, rationalisation and distraction. Almost a quarter reported impulsive or self-destructive behaviours, including alcohol and drug abuse. Such clients are characterised by the intensity of emotions that they are struggling to suppress and by their extensive use of desensitisation and deflection as coping strategies.

The McCann and Wadsworth (1992) study provides some British data regarding the informal carers of gay men who have HIV related illness. Respondents were recruited through the genito-urinary medicine and immunology clinics and the designated wards of a London teaching hospital. Of all gay men who attended the hospital between November 1988 and June 1989, 80 per cent completed a form expressing interest in the study, and structured personal interviews took place with 265 men. The whole range of HIV disease was represented, from HIV positive (without symptoms), to AIDS. In the next stage 125 informal carers were interviewed: these were most commonly identified as a close friend (45 per cent) or a partner (42 per cent) and the majority were male (77 per cent). When asked the question 'Do you worry or have you ever worried or thought about being HIV positive yourself?' only a third of carers (34 per cent) said that they did not. Actually, one in ten carers were positive themselves. As the majority (70 per cent) did practical tasks and provided emotional support (26 per cent gave *only* emotional support), this was one of the main areas where they felt unsupported or in need of additional assistance.

Research on the volunteers of British AIDS service organisations is another source of data illuminating aspects of the impact of HIV and AIDS on gay people. Bebbington and Gatter (1994) present data from a South London AIDS organisation regarding its volunteers, which they find typical of most of the researched 14 other non-profit south-east AIDS service organisations that do not operate a health model. The unusually high percentage of male volunteers (compared with most social welfare voluntary organisations) was attributed to the high percentage of gay men. From the 95 volunteers studied, 13 per cent were black and over a third unemployed. Their choice to volunteer for an HIV/AIDS organisation and lack of interest in other areas provides further evidence for the impact of HIV/AIDS on gay people as individuals and as a community. The predominately gay subjects felt that HIV was an issue affecting them personally, either directly through knowing someone living with the virus (or who had died), or from a general sense of the impact of HIV on their communities. In the process of recruiting volunteers, this AIDS service organisation, like others, turned down those who were not realistic about the practicalities of the work, its potentially stressful nature and their own support needs. They provided training which served the additional purpose of bonding volunteers and dealing with sensitive and personal issues, and offered fortnightly to monthly meetings with clearly designated support. They also provided ongoing training on support skills. Despite all this, turnover was high with half the volunteers dropping out in their first year, 40 per cent of them due to personal problems or problems related directly to volunteering. This accords with two Australian studies which report that over a third of

AIDS volunteers showed evidence of psychological morbidity (Guinan *et al.* 1991).

Lesley, a 67-year-old lesbian helpline volunteer saw me after crying on the phone while talking with a 69-year-old caller, who was a fellow wheelchair user. She did not manage to stop until well after a colleague took over the call. She could not understand the intensity of her emotion especially as, from an intellectual perspective, the call did not appear to her exceptionally distressing. It seems that she had underestimated the impact of this work on her. Working with people leads to lowering of interpersonal barriers and weakens the mechanisms utilised to suppress emotional pain.

At one period of my own work experience, when I was mainly providing short-term counselling to people in crisis, I would frequently burst into tears in my clinical supervision and sob for most of the time. I was 'burning out' through death and loss counselling, especially as I work from a model that emphasises the importance of engaging not just intellectually but also through my emotions.

I noticed the petrifying fear and tremendous sadness that we members of sexual minority communities are holding and am aware of the piling up of the effects of homophobia and heterosexism, HIV and AIDS. Unlike heterosexual people, we go through a psychological process of accepting a sexual identity for which we are not psychologically prepared, mainly due to lack of educative and social support. In my experience there is insufficient support to make us safe and thus enable the flow of grief. Moreover, some expressions of the grief response, such as anger, are deemed unacceptable both at societal and individual levels: many people are afraid that the accumulated grief will be overwhelming and that anger will be expressed as aggression. Unacceptable feelings of anger and sadness are therefore continually suppressed and numbed at the expense of psychological, physical and cultural well-being.

Guidelines for good practice

- As appropriate, provide information to clients regarding HIV prevention and be willing to refer on to specialists in fields such as treatments, housing, benefits, etc., taking into account the probability that the client might not follow up the referral to another professional.
- Challenge self-harm with compassion without compromising the clarity of challenge; in this way you will deliver the message undiffused with minimal erosion of the working alliance.
- Assess clients' internal and external resources to cope with the therapeutic exploration of suppressed areas. Teach clients skills such as 'grounding' to deal constructively with avoiding becoming overwhelmed.

- Attend to client's environmental support utilising existing abilities and resources. Consider initially prioritising physical safety and basic comfort and sharing with the clients *simple* maps of understanding what might be going on, what processes they have gone through and where they might go next. Small improvements in physical and cognitive levels might be the only manageable way, while large physical changes might override defence mechanisms.
- Consider primary focus on emotional support at later stages, because such support might act as a catalyst contributing to relaxation of defences resulting in increased physical sensation, awareness and experiencing. This might be followed by more rigidification of defences and the self as a whole (e.g. experiences of feeling overwhelmed leading to not returning for another session).
- Notice interruptions to the grieving process, paying attention to how the client does this, and explore with the client desirable and undesirable aspects of alternative ways of grieving.
- Monitor the support you have yourself in this work. Attend to your own motivation for working in the field of HIV and AIDS. How appropriate is it? If appropriate for you at this time, what areas of your well-being might you need to monitor particularly carefully?
- Take into account your personal life and the emotional demand of your caseload (i.e. working with people with personality disorders, very fragile clients or clients going through bereavement). Monitor your burnout level by attending to your sensitivity to noise, your energy levels, mood, sleep, appetite and eating patterns. Attend to your needs for time to process losses and monitor to what extent you meet them.
- Monitor the degree to which you meet your support needs within work (e.g. from clinical supervisor or consultant, line manager, colleagues, etc.) and outside work (e.g. personal therapy, partner, family of origin, friends, spiritual practice, hobbies or recreational activities, food, exercise, material comfort, etc.). Be aware of the difference between peer and horizontal emotional support and vertical or one-way emotional support.
- Other useful questions to ask yourself might be whether you are receiving empathy or sympathy, how the provider of support meets their own needs and what the motivation is of the person with whom you have an implicit or explicitly contracted arrangement for one-way emotional support.

Acknowledgements

The author wishes to thank his clients, trainers, colleagues, friends and family for teaching him what is included in this chapter, and Charles Neal for his patience and editorial support in writing it.

References

Airey, C. and Brook, L. (1986) Interim report: social and moral issues, in R. Jowell, S. Witherspoon and L. Brook (eds) *British Social Attitudes: The 1986 Report*. Aldershot: Gower.

Barrows, P.A. and Halgin, R.P. (1988) Current issues in psychotherapy with gay men: impact of the AIDS phenomenon. *Professional Psychology: Research and Practice*, 19(4): 395–402.

Bebbington, A.C. and Gatter, P.N. (1994) Volunteers in an HIV social care organization. *AIDS Care*, 6(5): 571–85.

Biller, R. and Rice, S. (1990) Experiencing multiple loss of persons with AIDS: grief and bereavement issues. *Health and Social Work*, 15(4): 283–90.

Britton, P.J., Zarski, J.J. and Hobfoll, S.E. (1993) Psychological distress and the role of significant others in a population of gay/bisexual men in the era of HIV. *AIDS Care*, 5(1): 43–54.

Bulmer, M. (1987) *The Social Basis of Community Care*. London: Allen & Unwin.

Evans, B.A., McLean, D.A., Dawson, S.G. *et al.* (1989) Trends in sexual behaviour and risk factors for HIV infection among homosexual men, 1984–1987. *British Medical Journal*, 298: 215–18.

Grothe, T. and McKusick, L. (1992) Coping with multiple loss. *Focus: A Guide to AIDS Research And Counselling*, 7(7): 5–6.

Guinan, J.J., McCallum, L.W., Painter, L., Dukes, J. and Gold, J. (1991) Stressors and rewards of being an AIDS emotional-support volunteer: a scale for use by care-givers for people with AIDS. *AIDS Care*, 3(2): 137–50.

Hart, G., Fitzpatrick, R., McLean, J., Dawson, J. and Boulton, M. (1990) Gay men, social support and HIV disease: a study of social integration in the gay community. *AIDS Care*, 2(2): 163–70.

Hays, R.B. and Tobey, L.A. (1990) The social support networks of gay men with AIDS. *Journal of Community Psychology*, 18(4): 374–85.

Herek, G.M. and Glunt, E.K. (1988) An epidemic of stigma: public reactions to AIDS. *American Psychologist*, 43(11): 886–91.

Hobfoll, S.E. (1985) Personal and social resources and the ecology of stress resistance, in P. Shaver (ed.) *Review of Personality and Social Psychology*. Thousand Oaks, CA: Sage.

Hobfoll, S.E. and London, P. (1986) The relationship of self-concept and social support to emotional distress among women during war. *Journal of Social and Clinical Psychology*, 4(2): 189–203.

Johnson, A.M. and Gill, O.N. (1989) Evidence for recent changes in sexual behaviour in homosexual men in England and Wales. *Philosophical Transactions of the Royal Society*, B325: 153–61.

Jowell, R., Witherspoon, S. and Brook, L. (eds) (1988) *British Social Attitudes: 5th Report*. Aldershot: Gower.

Lopez, D.J. and Getzel, G.S. (1984) Helping gay AIDS patients in crisis. *Social Casework*, 65(7): 387–94.

Loveday, C., Pomeroy, L., Weller, I.V.D. *et al.* (1989) Human immunodeficiency viruses in patients attending a sexually transmitted diseases clinic in London, 1982–7. *British Medical Journal*, 298: 419–421.

McCann, K. and Wadsworth, E. (1992) The role of informal carers in supporting gay men who have HIV related illness: what do they do and what are their needs? *AIDS Care*, 4(1): 25–34.

McKusick, L. and Hilliard, R. (1991) Multiple loss accounts for worsening distress in a community hard hit by AIDS. Presentation from the VII International Conference on AIDS, Florence, 16–21 June.

PHLS (Public Health Laboratory Service) (1995) *Communicable Disease Report: Data to 31 March 1995.* London: Public Health Laboratory Service.

PHLS (Public Health Laboratory Service) Working Group (1989) Prevalence of HIV antibody in high and low risk groups in England. *British Medical Journal,* 298: 422–23.

Pivar, I. and Temoshok, L. (1990) Coping strategies and response styles in homosexual symptomatic seropositive men. Paper presented to International Conference on AIDS, San Francisco, 20–24 June.

Rolland, J.S. (1988). A conceptual model of chronic life threatening illness and its impact on families, in C.S. Chilman, E.W. Nunnally and F.M. Cox (eds) *Chronic Illness and Disability.* Thousand Oaks, CA: Sage.

Sowell, R.L., Bramlett, M.H. and Gueldner, S.H. (1991) The lived experience of survival and bereavement following the death of a lover from AIDS. *Image: Journal of Nursing Scholarship*, 23(2): 89–94.

Expressive therapy: freeing the creative self

Background

I remember being 10 years old at school and making a painting for a parents' evening. For two weeks I painstakingly worked with poster paints and glue, to produce a textured picture of a wonderful white fluffy dress that my mother had in her wardrobe, which I had worn. I was delighted with what I saw as being a really good piece of work. Quizzed by a teacher, 'Well dear, what exactly is it you've drawn?' I replied, 'It's a nice party dress of my mother's which I've worn.' My work was removed with the response, 'Well, we don't think that is really appropriate, do we Timothy?' I was the only kid in the class not to have a picture on display, and my creativity went through the floor. Crash! It stayed there for almost 20 years.

At that same time in school, during our physical education lessons, we had just started dance as part of the programme. Many gay men have told me in therapy they were terrified of their own enjoyment of this type of physical activity, because their pleasure would be seen as a sign of effeminacy. Therefore they would be seen 'not to enjoy the activity'. Put theoretically, an 'imposed condition of worth' (as the person-centred model would describe such attitudinal conditions) was at odds with the experience of the organismic self. Incongruence occurred and somewhere the trauma associated with the difference between the organismic self and the external self was stored by the body.

As one of a growing number of practising expressive therapists I venture to suggest that such theory can now be substantiated and confirmed.

For 20 years after those primary school experiences I never really allowed my own creativity and physical expression to resurface. For me there was little or no dancing. Drawing, story telling, dressing up, or many of those other things which, as a child, had been useful tools for self-expression, and which had included the expression of my developing sexuality, were now missing.

These two personal anecdotes I include to illustrate how the creative process, alive within everyone, can so easily be arrested and hidden, particularly when one's creativity might in other people's eyes indicate to them certain characteristics associated with the behaviour of sexual minorities. Young boys dancing, dressing up, playing with dolls, dress making; young girls playing with soldiers, wanting to play with wood, cars, and so on.

Many times I have heard clients recount stories about their formative years of playing, being creative and expressive, and being met with at best lack of parental support and validation and at worst disapproval from parents or authority figures, peers and a society in general which subliminally or actively promotes stereotypes of the camp, effeminate gay man, or the masculine, coarse lesbian.

Subtle forms of phobia, deriving from sexism and the 'policing' of gender roles are at work here. It is important that we identify these in order to illustrate and illuminate clients' early life experiences. Here I identify the following dimensions:

- *Fear of association*: if I'm seen to be in their company, others may think I am one of them.
- *Fear of contagion*: if I'm spending time with them, I may become one of them.
- *Fear of attraction*: if I consort with them, they might sexually arouse me.
- *Internalised homophobia*: fear, denial and dislike of my own homosexuality.

At the age of 28 I attended a residential workshop where I was introduced to drawing and crayon work, psychodrama and other expressive mediums. For the first time since childhood I found that through my expressive self a real and meaningful understanding of my deeper self was experienced. From those days in the early 1990s I have developed my own way of working with various media.

Theoretical paradigm

I seek to respect humanistic principles – that we have within ourselves a capacity to grow and achieve our full potential through a process of self-actualisation. As a humanistic expressive therapist I also accept the validity of the *six necessary and sufficient conditions* postulated by Carl Rogers (1990), and believe that these, modelled by the therapist, will bring about changes desired by the client. Readers unfamiliar with the theoretical concepts of client-centred psychotherapy are referred to Rogers (1990) and in relation to using a client-centred approach to working with lesbian, gay and bisexual clients to Davies (1998, 2000). Other texts recommended for a sound, theoretical and practical understanding include Farber *et al.* (1996), Ivey *et al.* (1993) and Fadiman and Frager (1994).

My work also incorporates parts of a model called *the 'creative connection'* devised by Carl Rogers' daughter, Natalie. Those unfamiliar with her work might want to read *The Creative Connection: Expressive Arts as Healing* (1993) and *Emerging Woman: A Decade of Mid Life Transitions* (1995).

I hope that this chapter will encourage those working in the helping professions to trust themselves to allow both their own inert creativity and expression and those of their clients to come to life.

Professional perspectives

A participant on Natalie Rogers' expressive therapy training course describes what Rogers calls a 'creative connection' thus:

> The [creative] connection [is] between movement, art, writing and sound. When I move with awareness, it opens me to profound feelings, which can then be expressed in colour, line or form. When I write immediately after the movement and art there is free flow – sometimes poetry – which emerges. When I discovered this process for myself, I wanted to expand it and create an environment where others could explore themselves in this way.
>
> (Wenner, personal communication)

Carl Rogers (1961: 350) wrote of the motivation for creativity:

> The mainspring of creativity appears to be the same tendency, which we discover so deeply as the curative force in psychotherapy, as man's tendency to actualize himself, to become his potentialities. By this I mean the directional trend, which is evident in all organic and human life – the urge to expand, extend, develop, mature; the tendency to express and activate all the capacities of the organism, or the self. This tendency may become deeply buried under layer after layer of encrusted psychological defences; it may be hidden behind elaborate facades, which deny its existence. It is my belief however, based on my experience, that it exists in every individual, and awaits only the proper conditions to be released and expressed. It is this tendency which is the primary motivation for creativity as the organism forms new relationships to the environment in its endeavour most fully to be itself.

We have here a working hypothesis which says that all human beings have within them a capacity for, and drive towards, creativity and expression.

They may for several reasons, once they experience them, come to repress these feelings. With these feelings suppressed, individuals may then receive the approval of those around them. However, the cost of stifling this expression and creativity will be a damaging incongruence between the inner, organismic self and the self-concept. If a model of working can be found to allow the client to access their inner self through experiencing their own creativity and expression, their organismic and self-concepts have the potential to merge and thus to heal resulting psychological disturbances.

Methodology

Rogers (1993) illustrates, through her understanding of an 'individual creative force', a process whereby a client can move from medium to medium. There is a releasing of layers of inhibitions and the client is brought nearer to a deep and significant relationship with their organismic self. With lesbian, bisexual and gay clients, expressive therapy has the potential to liberate expression that has been hidden and suppressed for fear of disclosing sexual identity.

In Figure 5.1 we see how Rogers (1993) demonstrates that the integration of movement, colour, art, writing and sound can provide insight for the client so that they may benefit from greater understanding of themselves and their experiences. Rogers says of the creative connections her clients make that they help them become aware of their past (childhood and early years), their present (What am I feeling now?), their inner reality of unconscious and also their spirit, or higher consciousness. I find that the greater the awareness of these four states with clients, the greater their opportunities to improve their concept of self and their self-esteem.

In my work I have available space for movement, paper for writing, and fabric for dressing up in for any client who wishes to work with these things. When working within the arena of art, I also have available clay, pastels, oils, crayons, fabrics and a whole host of other materials that would make any art and craft practitioner excited!

Movement

Something that is often given little consideration with people from sexual minorities is the way the body moves and the way in which the person interacts with, and feels about, their own body. For example, clients report to me experiences, particularly as children, of being told to sit properly: 'not like a woman' to young boys and 'more like a lady' to young girls. At perhaps 6 or 7, the young child would not be expected to relate a developing sexual orientation with their own patterns of movement, although of

Figure 5.1 The creative connection process

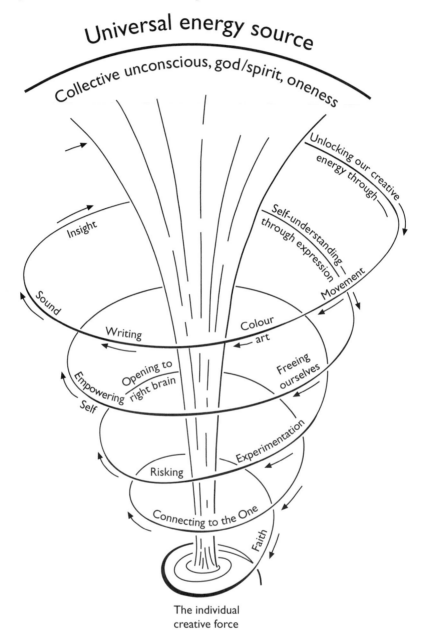

The individual
creative force

By moving from art form to art form, we release layers of inhibitions, bringing us to our centre – our individual creative force. This centre opens us to the universal energy source, bringing us vitality and a sense of oneness.

Source: Rogers (1993).

course the parent may well do so. A person whose general way of being and moving differs in any significant way from the ways of the majority may well suppress their individuality in order to satisfy the demands of the majority and to continue to 'belong'.

Children and adolescents will experience incongruence between their own desire to be the person they want to be in their bodies and the desire to conform in order to maintain approval. Very frequently their own will gets lost. Boys learn to walk like men and sit with open legs, and girls to take small steps and sit with legs tightly crossed. These early messages, learnt in order to receive parental love and peer acceptance, can come at a heavy cost to our true organismic self. The way somebody sits can inhibit the flow of their natural energy. If a client wishes to dance, I say let them dance!

Therapeutically, I believe it is essential to follow the lead of a client. Consider your responses to a request from a client to dance with them during their session with you. How would you react if they wanted to dance to a 1960s girl band like *The Ronettes*? Would you feel comfortable trusting yourself to do the twist with a queen or dance the locomotion with a dyke? If yes, why? And if no, why not?

Would you be prepared to sculpt yourself around your image of your client, and then allow them to look at your 'body sculpt' of them? I ask you to consider the implications, positive and otherwise, of shadowing your client as they move about the room for two minutes. How would you feel, acting as a witness to somebody being a horse, running as if in a pasture, giving them feedback on how you experienced them and then facilitating their own experience of the exercise?

How would you facilitate a client beginning contact with their bodies, allowing them to touch base with each part of their anatomy? 'Hello hair, hello scalp, hello eyebrows, hello breast, hello penis, hello thigh, hello kneecap, hello toes' and so on. Encouraging the client to feel connected to the physical aspects of themselves, to reconnect their being is, I believe, an essential yet often ignored area of therapeutic work, especially with clients from sexual minorities who have so often been taught to be guarded and suspicious about their body's sensations, desires and feelings.

Rogers (1993: 62) writes of a female client, Dean, who reported real fear in her movement. Dean recalls her experiences of that work:

> And I stood there, not moving, for what seemed like an eternity. And then I started to shiver-shudder in some sort of defiance and resistance to the exercise. And something in my body said yes to the feeling of resistance. To go ahead and really experience resisting. To really experience resisting to melting, to letting go. Because that was the way it had been for me. Strong, strong resistance.

Rogers went on to report the big risk her client took 'to give in just a tad'. She described the subsequent transformation as her client felt the forces of life, movement and ground enter her body. The client acknowledging her resistance rather than fighting it meant she could use it as an ally – an energy force – and integrate it into her own healing. Rogers postulated that cognitive change took place as the connection was made into other media.

In his discussion of gay affirmative therapy and Clark's (1987) guidelines for retraining and ground rules for helping, Davies (1996: 32–3) reminds us (point six) of the very 'anti touch' society within which we live, and speaks of the therapeutic value of touch with a client, while remaining mindful of ethical conduct.

Back to dancing! Here is one type of movement I find useful with clients. First I position myself opposite my client and then allow hand on hand contact, allowing the first to lead, the other following, secondly allowing the first to resist, the other trying to lead, and finally both dancing mutually. Then we swap around so that the client has the opportunity of experiencing the movement from both perspectives. From a therapist's point of view, I find this a particularly attractive tool to use. With this exercise one doesn't need to stand. It is therefore suitable for people with mobility impairments. It is completely non-verbal so it can be very effective when faced with communication problems through language difficulty, speech impairment or psychological barriers. It's really like a kind of 'hand dancing'. Puppetry can also be a powerful medium here. After partaking in any exercise like this, on a stand-alone basis, I encourage the client to express their experience in their own words. My empathic and congruent response to the exercise as I experienced it can further broaden this experience for the client.

Much of the work suggested here requires body contact with the client, and readers considering undertaking this type of therapy would be well advised to look at their own reactions to, and experiences of, touch. Other writers – Keleman (1971), Lowen (1975) and Bodella (1973) for example – have written more extensively on touch and body therapy and the reader is recommended to read about this exciting and much underutilised field of work. For many clients, touch from the hands of an encouraging yet ethical therapist may be one of the first times they have experienced safe touch in a way that doesn't threaten them or exploit their sexuality.

Colour

Working with clients through the use of colour is particularly fruitful, be it materials for dressing up, poster paints to splash onto paper, oil pastels to delicately shade a drawing or even the choice of colour of clay with which to sculpt. The client's choices and subsequent use of colours, and their understanding about this process usually surprises them. Sometimes these new understandings come to them not at the time but maybe a session or so later.

I dislike the notion in analytic art therapy where, as a client, I would be told what my choice of colour signified. I would not want to know that my choice of pink or yellow relates to an ethereal aspect of my personality. I would feel threatened and unwilling to risk exposing other aspects of myself to *my* therapist, no matter how well intentioned he or she might be. I find my clients want to tell *me* what the significance for them is. I also find that clients derive value from my relating *my* experience of *their* exercise.

Art

I referred earlier to many aspects of art (painting, drawing, clay work and so on), so will briefly look at how these media can be used.

Painting

Whether clients simply want to amass colours on paper, without any recognisable form, or to paint their own story in more detail, they will do what is right for them at the time. I have available a selection of about ten colours, always making sure the primary colours of red, yellow and blue are there, as well as black and white. Poster paints, finger paints or other watercolours are all suitable for use, and can be easily mixed at the time. Sheets of paper and card of various sizes, and maybe a solid surface or drawing board are all one needs to allow clients to create whatever images they need to.

I often find it useful to work alongside my client, relating empathically to them in the painted form, painting my response to their work as a kind of mirror, always following on from them, never making a verbal interpretation. Frequently this process takes place without dialogue. For clients new to this medium, or for those who lost that creative connection as a child, work often follows a pattern. From the abstract through to landscape, portrait or still life then back to abstract as clients make their journey from here and now experiences to then and there experiences and back again.

In my personal journey I found art to be the most healing medium when dealing with the processing of my experiences of the *Marchioness* pleasure boat disaster (the loss of one friend and the survival of another). A year and a half of my personal therapy had been instrumental in my development, but it was the painting of individual coffins of all those who died which finally healed me, seven years after the sinking.

Drawing

Art pastel crayons are the medium most used by clients when drawing. Pencils, or better still charcoal, have often allowed clients to express pain and hurt initially too difficult to speak about. Again, the presence of the therapist alongside the client, quietly sketching their empathic response is frequently very cathartic for the client.

I want to re-emphasise the value of working with the 'hidden creativity' of our clients. Allowing them the space to freely access their creativity, without labels of 'queer', 'bent' or 'dyke', will bring out a whole range of emotional issues which were internalised with their creativity.

Blue Peter *creations*

I use this title after the British children's television programme, with a degree of humour, referring to the enormous collection I have of old bottles, boxes, sticky-back plastic, felt, sticky stars, glue and so on. All part of the presenter's box of tricks, and an essential kit for expressive therapy. It is interesting that *Blue Peter* is widely acknowledged to have been a big favourite with gay men in particular when they were small children.

A few years ago I was surprised when two separate clients asked if they could make their own 'Tracey Island', based on a commercial toy from the cult TV series *Thunderbirds*, which had apparently taken children all over the country by storm. The first client, a lesbian in her forties, was distressed when her own child wanted to make his 'Tracey Island', and the mother realised how she had been denied any practical creative fun as a child. She recalled with anger how both her brothers had been given encouragement to build with balsa wood and had frequently received much praise from their parents. Her parents' denial of her need to build toys with wood resulted in her one day smashing up most of her younger brother's constructions. The memories of an ongoing programme of savage beatings from that point on were only healed, finally, when this client built her own wooden and papier mâché 'Tracey Island'.

The other client, a gay man in his thirties, once having completed his 'Tracey Island' disclosed for the first time his feelings that now there was somewhere safe to which he could escape: this led to his disclosing the story of the 'prison of his childhood'. These two examples served to teach me the real impact of working with whatever medium the client chooses to bring to the relationship.

A particular favourite of clients and trainees with whom I work is the 'self box'. It warrants mention here, since it is applicable for use within the confines of a therapeutic session. A 'self-box' requires a little planning in order to invite the client to bring with them to a session an unwanted shoe box, complete with lid. Therapists who find this a useful technique, however, may want to stock themselves with a number of lidded boxes for this purpose.

The reader familiar with the 'Johari window' (Sanders 1996: 40) may see some similarities with this exercise. In essence, I invite my client to create the outside of the box as the world sees them and the inside as they see themselves, but which is hidden from the view of the outside world. It is quite likely the outside would portray the client's adapted or passing self, and the inside their true transgender, lesbian, bisexual or gay spirit.

I like to work with clients over two hours for this exercise, rather than starting and stopping over two sessions. Most clients use the first hour for decorating the box, as they want, accessing many of the *Blue Peter* materials already described. Other materials such as newspapers and magazines are invaluable, since they contain words and images clients can paste on, but may not yet speak about. Wool, yarn, string, fabrics, buttons, seashells, dried pasta and rice are all useful additions to an art tool box.

The sharing of a 'self box', which follows its creation, is invariably moving, frequently distressing and generally cathartic. In my experience, having created a self box, a client would want to use it as part of a therapy relationship for several weeks and, from feedback I have received, clients tend to keep their self boxes for many years.

Clay work

Not nearly as messy as it may seem, clay work is an extremely grounding way of working for a client. Most children's play centres and shops sell sculpting clay, usually available in a variety of colours. Again clients may choose to trust their gut feelings, to make a form, and then explore the significance of what they have created; others may have a very specific form in mind.

I never cease to be amazed at the creativity, talent and strength of my clients and trainees when expressing themselves with this medium. I will forever remember working with a trainee over three years when towards the end of her training she sculpted a trumpet. In the presence of her peers and tutors she announced with great glee and satisfaction, as she put her trumpet to her lips, that for the first time in her life she was able to 'blow her own trumpet', something until then she had been unable to articulate. Sometimes clients choose to take their sculpts with them, other times I look after them.

Pipe cleaners

This innovative medium is fairly new to me. Queueing in my local supermarket for my lottery ticket, I noticed packets of pipe cleaners on the cigarette stand. Since I don't smoke a pipe I'm not sure why I bought a pack, but I found the following week I was using several to respond to a client empathically. They are now a firm favourite with clients, supervisees and trainees alike. In periods of silence the sculpted and twisted pipe cleaners speak in their eloquence of shape and form. This medium is sometimes used for checking in, checking out, or communicating something altogether different. For example, a client arriving to a session late after being stuck in traffic jams may choose to represent their stressed state of mind with several pipe cleaners all bunched together in knots. Whereas another client having reflected on issues to work on, may mould pipe cleaners gently together to give form to some past experience.

Dressing up and make-up

This takes considerable planning and is most appropriate to working in groups, where there are normally resources for collecting the clothes, fabrics and other paraphernalia needed. However, the reader would do well to consider their responses to, for example, a male client who wishes to attend therapy in the attire of a woman or to a client who attends in a costume or uniform which has some psychological meaning for them.

While acknowledging the stable from where expressive therapy comes, I do find Jungian concepts of archetypes fascinating. At risk of raised eyebrows from some of my person-centred colleagues, I believe archetypes do exist within clients' own frames of reference and can be useful tools that they can explore when adopting the attire or costume which symbolises a particular archetype. One example might be the female client who dresses in some militaristic uniform to represent an authority figure from her childhood.

One area of work which I do find practical within an hour is the use of face paints. There are four options. A client may choose to paint their own face, using a mirror, as they see or feel about themselves. Second, the therapist paints the face of the client on the client, as the therapist sees or feels it. Third, the client paints their own face on the therapist's face, as they feel or see it. Or finally, the client paints the face of the therapist on the therapist as the client sees or feels about the therapist. The client usually answers the question of who does what to whom. Following the face painting, clients talk about what they see and feel, followed by the therapist giving feedback. It is essential to have a good supply of cleansing lotion and cotton wool for afterwards! These activities take considerable trust on the part of both client and therapist. My experiences of all four have been exceptional. In terms of allowing touch and intimacy, the healing can be profound and I have often found this to be a useful way of deepening the relationship. Once the client has experienced this intimacy with their therapist they are more likely to feel safer to explore unaddressed issues, which may include elements of touch and identity.

Writing and storytelling

Storytelling, poems, prose, letters and song libretti may all fall under this category. Many therapists work with clients writing letters, whether posted or not, and may even have experienced the joy of listening to clients read poems they have written. The luxury of an hour with an individual makes therapy almost unique – a captive audience! I wonder, however, how many therapists have spent an hour with their clients beginning with the phrase 'Once upon a time'?

The art of storytelling goes back many centuries but seems to have been lost in the late 1990s: at least that is what clients and trainees report. In every situation – individual, couple or group – I have found storytelling to be often humorous and more likely deeply moving and cathartic. A fictional narrative can allow the client to tell their story with a degree of security, safety and even confidentiality. In groups, or individually with their therapist, they can listen to the way others respond to their characters' dilemmas. The client is given scope and licence to play, celebrate, mourn, understand and finally integrate their learned experiences from feedback received.

To illustrate the relevance of narrative, I refer to a story written by a dear friend and colleague, an accomplished expressive therapist from whom I have learnt much. Her story was about a rhinoceros that was befriended by a little bird which settled on his horns, and about a seal that on the surface was mean and fierce. Through a journey involving seals in supermarkets, animal deaths and binoculars the writer traversed many areas of her experience. The little bird was in fact her small and beautiful self, often disallowed. The 'supermarket' seal mirrored the religious doctrine she had encountered as a child. My friend's increasing awareness of her relationship with seals in her story mirrored her increasing capacity to be aware of, and act on, her internal locus of evaluation:

> Now Jongo seemed weak and vulnerable, but he was very, very wise, because his tummy told him not to go to the supermarket seal and ask for help, but to hop three times in a circle, and then fly straight to a baobab tree on the edge of the desert where he would find a seal basking in the sunshine. Nothing doubting, little Jongo kissed Ping Pong goodbye, and flew off to beg the seal to come and heal Ping Pong . . .
> And Seal gently opened his flippers and gave Ping Pong the jewel, the token of his caring. And Ping Pong knew, and Jongo knew, and Seal knew that now was the time for the handing over of precious loves.
> (Davidson 1997, personal communication)

My colleague subsequently described in her final chapter the 'God within', guarding and nurturing the 'self' – not dependent on external clarification.

Sound

Whether it is primal screaming, humming, singing or something completely different, sound plays an important role in healing. Too many times I hear clients talk about their quiet childhood, with 'never a raised voice, either in anger or joy'. Frequently, I also hear clients talk of the opposite end of the spectrum: rage, swearing and shouting and voices being spoken over each other. I don't see these experiences as uniquely belonging to clients from sexual minorities, but I know these clients may have been especially denied the freedom to express themselves in ways that were organismically right.

A healthy environment for a developing individual should include a whole repertoire of vocal experiences to illustrate the ranges of their emotions and accompanying physical experiences. Natalie Rogers (1993: 81) speaks of the voice being where the body and mind connect: 'Our vocal chords, located between our head and body, are the channels through which we link these two aspects of self'. A participant in one of Rogers' workshops speaks in detail of her experience with using sound:

> My experience with sound. Sound is a release for me. If I do something that is not quite right, the judge in me condemns me and I let out a barely audible squeal, more like a whimper. Over the weeks and months these add up. There is so much hurt, guilt, not-able-to-please-ness, and frustration. Friday I let out a scream that came from my gut – I know it did because right before it was released I felt such a turmoil going on down there. I didn't want to let out any feelings. I was trying so hard to sit on them, to contain them, telling myself don't let it out, don't let it out . . . Let it out! . . . Hold on, contain, and put your feelings away . . . LET IT OUT! Aaaaaaaaaeeeeehhhh. I collapsed into myself, exhausted, crying, spent.
>
> (Rogers 1993: 84)

Experiences of clients are similar: most expect little or nothing to come out of their bodies and are amazed, but shocked too, at the strength that their voice has when safe conditions are present in the therapy room.

Bringing it all together

The techniques I refer to in this chapter are each strong enough alone to use with clients. However, the reader will, I am sure, also see the exciting possibilities of incorporating and linking a number of them.

I sometimes feel that there is a temptation to become too dogmatic when working with a therapeutic model which espouses stages of change. I prefer to see how and where clients choose to go in their choice of media, and if that means that they start off with writing and later sculpt or draw an image that has come from the writing, all well and good. Movement and sound may then come to the client's here and now experience. The client chooses to make these connections. They are *their* connections.

The importance of the expressive approach in therapy with our lesbian, transgender, gay and bisexual clients is that it offers the potential to bring them fully to life once more. The power of their creativity and expression can flow again through their veins and arteries and back into their hearts where previously they may have been too scared and too traumatised to feel the power of their own fullest expression.

As an expressive therapist I would expect my clients' internalised homophobia, particularly *their* fears of association, experienced by themselves and witnessed by others, to diminish, if not disappear in the long term. Clients should eventually be able to take their own creativity into many other areas of life, for example art, drama, physical exercise and writing.

One final thought: Hancock (1986) warns of the dangerous underlying beliefs some therapists (even those who are themselves from sexual minorities) may have relating to the physical, sexual aspects of clients' lives. He says:

> Some therapists who have rejected the grosser forms of prejudice nevertheless have a lingering belief that interpersonal love, sensual pleasure, and erotic experiences of intimacy that are unrelated to a biological procreative process are in some way inferior, and that couples of the same sex cannot experience the qualities of personal intimacy and physical pleasure that are possible for couples of different sexes.
>
> (Harrison 1987: p. 222)

As therapists working in an affirmative way with creative media, which have the potential to expose our own creativity, we cannot be sure our internalised oppression will not surface as we, for example, watch clients dancing with coloured fabric around themselves. My experience is that expressive therapy offers more opportunities than usual for therapists to confront their own internalised homophobic feelings.

Guidelines for good practice

- Ensure you have the correct support before engaging in expressive work with clients. Look *professionally* at your supervision relationship. How will your supervisor react to your working in different media? *Personally* experience the power of expressive therapy.
- Do not allow your own process to get caught up with your client's process! Work through your own inhibitions and internalised oppressions via supervision and your own personal therapy.
- Think about ways of grounding yourself and your client, before and after a session. Sometimes the creative arts are slow to work – like a sustained release vitamin supplement. Drinking water, eating nutritious food and good firm shoes are all important!

- Regularly practise expressive therapy for yourself by yourself or with peers. Draw, paint, write and move.
- Read widely and keep a journal of your own and your clients' experiences of the power of expressive therapy.
- Above all, *have fun* and enjoy being witness to the rebirthing of your clients' and your own creativity!

References

Bodella, D. (1973) *Wilhelm Reich: The Evolution of his Work*. London: Vision Press.

Clark, D. (1987) *The New Loving Someone Gay*. Berkeley, CA: Celestial Arts.

Davies, D. (1996) Towards a model of gay affirmative therapy, in D. Davies and C. Neal (eds) *Pink Therapy: A Guide for Counsellors and Therapists Working with Lesbian, Gay and Bisexual Clients*. Buckingham: Open University Press.

Davies, D. (1998) The six necessary and sufficient conditions applied to working with lesbian, gay and bisexual clients. *The Person-Centered Journal*, 5(2): 111–24.

Davies, D. (2000) Person-centred therapy, in D. Davies and C. Neal (eds) *Therapeutic Perspectives on Working with Lesbian, Gay and Bisexual Clients*. Buckingham: Open University Press.

Fadiman, J. and Frager, R. (1994) *Personality and Personal Growth*. London: HarperCollins.

Farber, B., Brink, D. and Raskin, P. (1996) *The Psychotherapy of Carl Rogers*. London: Guildford Press.

Harrison, J. (1987) Counselling gay men, in M. Scher, M. Stevens, G. Good and G. Eichenfield (eds) *Handbook of Counselling and Psychotherapy with Men*. Newbury Park, CA: Sage.

Ivey, A., Ivey, M. and Simek-Morgan, L. (1993) *Counselling and Psychotherapy: A Multi-cultural Perspective*. London: Allyn & Bacon.

Keleman, S. (1971) *Sexuality, Self and Survival*. London: Lodestar.

Lowen, A. (1975) *Bioenergetics*. Harmondsworth: Penguin Books.

Rogers, C. (1961) *On Becoming a Person*. London: Constable.

Rogers, C. (1990) The necessary and sufficient conditions of therapeutic personality change, in H. Kirschenbaum and V.L. Henderson (eds) *The Carl Rogers Reader*. London: Constable.

Rogers, N. (1993) *The Creative Connection: Expressive Arts as Healing*. Los Angeles: Science and Behavior Books.

Rogers, N. (1995) *Emerging Woman: A Decade of Mid Life Transitions*. Manchester: PCCS Books.

Sanders, P. (1996) *First Steps in Counselling*. Manchester: PCCS Books.

Psychosexual issues

Introduction

The concept of 'psychosexual problems', as applied to gay men, lesbians and bisexuals has traditionally been used to focus on the supposed pathology, distress and difficulties of same-sex attraction. Psychological theories have abounded regarding the causation of homosexual feelings and identities, and clinical approaches have aspired to promote the development of hetero-sexuality regardless of the means. Even when not aiming for orientation change, clinicians were at best interested in the 'problems' associated with developing a non-heterosexual identity: confusion, conflicts and the diffi-culties of coming out, or 'ego-dystonic homosexuality'. It is only in the past 15 years or so that clinicians have paid attention to psychosexual factors with the aim of helping individuals and couples to achieve positive and satisfying same-sex relationships and lifestyles, overcoming problems of sexual func-tioning which may be preventing or interfering with this.

Even now, while the provision of sex therapy and medical approaches to sexual dysfunction are fairly widely available within the British National Health Service and in private practice, it appears that services directed at the needs of people from sexual minorities experiencing sexual problems are limited to a few metropolitan clinics and agencies. Ussher (1990) has argued that a lack of referrals of gay couples and individuals, combined with an absence of appropriate training or supervision for counsellors and therapists has led to reluctance among professionals to take on this client group. Neglect of sexual minority issues in psychosexual literature and assessment tools perpetuates this phenomenon. Gay clients themselves may be equally likely to avoid contact with therapists due to the traditional therapeutic stance outlined above, and to their perception that services are not oriented towards their needs (Davies 1996). Bisexual issues and needs are almost completely absent in psychosexual literature and services.

The aim of this chapter is to present an overview of the literature on sexual dysfunction in lesbians and gay men, with a focus on factors specific to sexual orientation which need to be considered in therapeutic approaches and service delivery. We will also consider the adequacy of the standard diagnostic and classification systems for sexual dysfunction in addressing the sexual norms and problems of non-heterosexual groups. We are aware that at present there is little to report on the needs of bisexual people, although we have noted when the issues raised are likely to be applicable to bisexuals. We are not attempting to give an authoritative account of the nature and treatment of psychosexual dysfunctions (see Bancroft 1989) or of the principles and practice of psychosexual or couples therapy (see Crowe and Ridley 1990). For a discussion of more general issues in working with couples in same-sex relationships see Carl (1990) and Simon (1996).

Standard definitions and approaches to treatment

Current approaches to the classification and treatment of sexual dysfunction owe much to the pioneering work of Masters and Johnson (1970). In their clinical descriptions, mainly of heterosexual couples, they were concerned with problems of function: loss of erection, premature or delayed ejaculation, vaginismus (muscle spasm preventing penetration), dyspareunia (pain during intercourse) and anorgasmia (absence of orgasm). Later Kaplan (1979) introduced a classification based on a description of a 'sexual response cycle', which included problems associated with lack of sexual desire, as well as problems of arousal and orgasm. The diagnostic classification system, which is currently most widely used in the assessment of sexual dysfunction, is described in *DSM-IV Diagnostic and Statistical Manual of Mental Disorders* (4th edition) (American Psychiatric Association 1994) and is illustrated in Table 6.1.

The main features of the majority of therapeutic approaches (following Masters and Johnson 1970) usually include a combination of work on sexual communication and permission giving, education, anxiety reduction, exercises encouraging physical contact without demand, exploration of new ways of pleasuring and specific training techniques for specific problems – for example, vaginismus and premature ejaculation. These are combined with a focus on background individual and relationship issues which may include traumatic sexual experiences, dysfunctional sexual beliefs and attitudes, interpersonal dynamics and communication styles (Crowe and Ridley 1990).

In recent years awareness has increased about the range of organic factors which can contribute to sexual issues, particularly for men. These include

Table 6.1 *DSM-IV* classification of sexual dysfunction

Aspect of sexuality affected	Women	Men
Interest/desire	Hypoactive sexual desire disorder; sexual aversion	Hypoactive sexual desire disorder; sexual aversion
Arousal	Female sexual arousal disorder	Male erectile disorder
Orgasm	Female orgasmic disorder	Male orgasmic disorder ('retarded ejaculation'); premature ejaculation
Genital pain/spasm during intercourse	Dyspareunia; vaginismus	Dyspareunia

hormonal, neural and vascular causes, illness, ageing and the use of medications, alcohol and recreational drugs. It now seems likely that the traditional view of mainly psychogenic causation will be replaced with an assumption that the majority of problems involve a combination of organic and psychological aetiology (King 1998).

Any classification system reflects the moral values of the majority culture and the classification of sexual problems is no exception (Daines 1988). What is regarded as normal and problematic will be relative to the predominant culture (Ussher 1993). Boyle (1993) makes the point that current *DSM-IV* criteria reflect two key assumptions. First, that sexual disorders are seen as the problem of the individual, rather than existing within the relationship and second, that they reflect a 'dysfunction' of presumed normal sexual functioning. Current classification systems reflect the common expectations of heterosexual intercourse: that it is penetrative, vaginal and follows a prescribed 'sexual response cycle', beginning with desire, followed by arousal and resulting in orgasm.

Loulan (1984) argues that the concept of a sexual response cycle may not be relevant for many sexual minority couples (or even some heterosexual couples), as the primary goal of sex may not be penetration or orgasm when there are many routes to, and varieties of, sexual satisfaction. In an attempt to circumvent the problems associated with current thinking, Loulan developed what she terms the 'willingness model'. This involves the additional stage of willingness in the sexual response cycle, which can be a starting point for women (or men) who are not necessarily experiencing desire but wish to be actively sexual. Her model also includes the stages of desire, arousal and orgasm but the sense of necessary progression from one to another is removed, allowing the individual to move fluidly between stages and stop at any time.

Examples of bias in the *DSM-IV* classifications include the absence of a female equivalent for 'premature ejaculation'. There are some women who reach orgasm before they or their partner wish but this is not recognised in the literature as a potential problem. For gay men or lesbians who include anal penetration in their sexual activity, a category defining pain on anal intercourse, 'anodyspareunia', (Rosser *et al.* 1998), would be relevant.

Psychosexual issues for lesbians

Prevalence

There is very little empirical data on the type or prevalence of sexual problems in lesbians. This section reviews the main difficulties reported by researchers and clinicians but it should be noted that this generally reflects clinical observation rather than formal studies.

In the first reference to the area, Masters and Johnson (1979) report no difference in sexual dysfunction between gay, lesbian and heterosexual couples. However, clinicians, writing in the 1970s and 1980s, began to report high levels of inhibited sexual desire and desire discrepancies in lesbian couples (Todor 1978; Nichols 1983; Loulan 1984). Nichols (1983) reported that problems of desire discrepancy or inhibited sexual desire accounted for 75 per cent of her requests for sex counselling from lesbians. Todor (1978) also reports a high incidence of desire discrepancy in lesbians, as compared with heterosexual couples, with other difficulties reflecting observed differences in lovemaking techniques. For example, greater discrepancies in attitudes towards oral sex were reported suggesting that this practice is more common. Similarly, the reported low incidence of vaginismus suggests that lesbians have a greater sexual repertoire which can avoid penetration if preferred.

The most consistently reported sexual difficulties in lesbians appear to be those relating to sexual desire. The popular lesbian press has referred to this phenomenon as 'lesbian bed death'. This has been investigated indirectly through studies of the frequency of sexual activity among lesbians. Sociologists Blumstein and Schwartz (1983) found that in the first two years of relationships 76 per cent of lesbians and 83 per cent of heterosexual couples had sex once a week or more. However, after two years, this gap widened with only 37 per cent of lesbians still having sex this frequently compared with 73 per cent of heterosexual couples. So, while frequency of sexual activity may be high in the initial stages of a relationship, it seems that it becomes much less so after the first two years (see also Loulan 1988; Rothblum and Brehony 1993).

What is not clear from the frequency data is the extent to which the women themselves consider this a problem. Blumstein and Schwartz (1983) reported that a greater number of the lesbian couples they surveyed would prefer to have sex more often, compared with heterosexual women, heterosexual men and gay men. However, in spite of this, it does seem to be the case that sexual satisfaction in lesbians is generally high. Coleman *et al.* (1983) report that despite the fact that lesbians have sex less often than heterosexual women, they have more frequent orgasms (both through masturbation and partner sex), greater sexual satisfaction and a greater number of partners. Schreurs (1993) reviews 20 studies and reports that, overall, 75 per cent of lesbians have either a satisfying or extremely satisfying sex life, a figure which appears to be equivalent to, or greater than, that for heterosexual women.

It seems that while in general lesbians may have rewarding sex lives, there are still a significant number who are experiencing difficulties, particularly with sexual desire, and who are requesting professional intervention. The following discussion therefore examines the literature on lack of sexual desire in lesbians and some of the relevant therapeutic issues.

Aetiology and specific therapeutic issues

In spite of the limited research into the prevalence of sexual problems in lesbians, some attention has been paid to the possible causes of these. While this may reflect the tendency to pathologise lesbian sexuality, the literature may provide a framework for understanding psychological processes in low sexual desire. What follows are brief descriptions of the ideas and issues which have been explored.

Lesbian sexuality as women's sexuality

Schreurs (1993) argues that the most important variable in lesbian sexuality is gender. Schreurs reviews several studies noting similarities between lesbians and heterosexual women on issues such as motivations for sex, importance of emotional involvement and attitudes to monogamy. Leigh (1989) found that heterosexual and lesbian women rated expressing emotional closeness as more important than physical pleasure during sex, in comparison with heterosexual and gay men.

In general, women appear to be either biologically or socially conditioned to expect and desire different elements of sex from men. If women are believed to have a lower sexual drive, two women in a relationship may be expected to place less emphasis on frequency of sexual activity. Studies show that lesbians have sex less often than heterosexual couples (Coleman *et al.* 1983), but heterosexual women may have sex more often as a result of their partner initiating, rather than because they desire it before a sexual encounter begins (Leigh 1989). The same woman in a lesbian relationship may have sex less often as neither she nor her partner would be as likely to initiate sex. With this perspective, low sexual desire in lesbians is not a 'dysfunction' but a natural consequence of two women having a relationship.

Homophobia

Homophobia has an impact on sexual relationships in a variety of ways. Lack of information, lack of role models and even lack of acknowledgement of sexual difficulties can make establishing a satisfying sexual relationship difficult. Negative messages about lesbian and gay relationships can become internalised, creating guilt or anxiety about sexual feelings. Sexual desire may be present but cause such distress that it is not acted upon. In some cases, women may feel that if they choose not to be sexually active within their relationships they can avoid having to identify with a stigmatised group – i.e. they are 'not really a lesbian'.

The two forces of homophobia and sexism can create a double bind for lesbians – if you have a high sexual drive you are not a 'nice' woman but if you are not sexual you are not really being a lesbian, as identity is usually defined by sexual activity. This may be particularly true for older lesbians who have very few positive sexual role models.

Sexual politics

The pressures exerted by a heterosexual and homophobic community can also lead to a rejection of sexual behaviours which are perceived to be associated with heterosexuals, especially men. This may lead to beliefs that sex should always be egalitarian, that each partner should experience equal pleasure, that sex should always be gentle and tender and that both partners should have orgasms, thus placing a great deal of pressure on women to have 'perfect' sex. Some sexual behaviours have attracted strong political debate – for example, 'butch-femme' roles, penetrative sex, the use of vibrators, dildos and pornography, SM and 'kink' sex. Problems may arise when couples do not share the same values or feel guilty for having particular sexual fantasies. This can result in anxiety, guilt and poor sexual communication. Akkerman *et al.* (1990) report that one third of lesbians had sexual wishes their partners did not know about, suggesting that it is not always easy to be explicit with a partner about sexual interests.

Expression of anger

In her study of lesbian couples seeking therapy, Loulan (1984) found that on initial presentation many couples appeared to be very loving and considerate, physically affectionate and reported no difficulties other than their lack of sexual desire or desire discrepancy. However, on closer questioning, long-standing resentments were apparent. Loulan suggests that women are socialised not to express anger and lesbians in particular are reluctant to complain about sex, feeling this is behaving 'like a man' and being 'selfish'. However, this taboo on the expression of anger manifests itself in the avoidance or withholding of sexual activity.

Previous experiences with men
A lesbian with a history of unsatisfactory relationships with men may approach sex with different expectations compared to a lesbian with no heterosexual experience. This may manifest itself in a desire to be different from the male partner, a pressure for sex to be perfect or resentment and disappointment if the sexual relationship is not sexually satisfying.

Sexual abuse
Loulan (1988) reports that 30 per cent of her sample of lesbians had experienced sexual abuse as children. This figure may be significantly different to an equivalent heterosexual population. In addition, the likelihood of any lesbian couple having at least one partner with a history of sexual abuse is greater than that for a heterosexual couple. Experience of childhood sexual abuse can have a significant impact on self-esteem, sexual confidence and intimacy and is associated with sexual difficulties in adults (Becker 1989; see also Chapter 9).

Substance abuse/alcohol problems
Loulan (1988) also reports a 30 per cent rate of alcohol and substance misuse in her lesbian sample. Other research has also suggested a higher rate of alcohol use in lesbians in comparison with heterosexual women (see Kowszun and Malley 1996). Both alcohol and substance use affect sexual performance directly physiologically and indirectly if their misuse leads to relationship difficulties.

Fusion/merger
Fusion or merger in relationships refers to a process of connection through loss of individuation. Without the gender differences inherent in heterosexual relationships, some therapists believe that lesbians form much closer emotional ties which, taken to the extreme, may mean that the expression of any difference of thought, feelings or beliefs becomes threatening to the existence of the couple. This process has been suggested by some therapists as a root cause of lack of sexual desire.

Hall (1987) describes several alternative explanations for the relationship between merger and low sexual desire:

- *Avoiding intimacy.* Psychodynamically, relationships between women are seen to replicate the mother-daughter bond. Both women are seen to crave the closeness of this relationship yet simultaneously fear the powerlessness of the infant's position. In this context, sexual desire of the partner is believed to increase the fear component and is thus repressed.
- *Lack of difference.* Social gender conditioning theories suggest that women identify with others through affiliation (connection) and that their ego boundaries are less discrete. Thus women in lesbian relationships might lose their individuality as the relationship develops, enhancing empathy.

If erotic desire is believed to stem from difference, the effect of greater affiliation is to lower the erotic potential.

- *Lack of adversity*. Hatfield and Walster (1978) go further and suggest that erotic feelings can only flourish under conditions of adversity, not just difference. The safe, nurturing fused lesbian relationship eliminates adversity and therefore removes the potential for sexual desire.

- *Sex as bridging process*. Krestan and Bebko (1980) argue that lesbian merger or fusion is an essential form of defence against a hostile and homophobic environment. This 'us against the world' stance protects the couple from negative external messages but also reinforces the union of the couple. Sex therefore becomes redundant as a bridging mechanism.

As we have noted, lesbian sexual problems have received very little attention from researchers and much of the preceding text reflects only those aspects which have attracted discussion. The focus on lack of sexual desire ('lesbian bed death') may be seen as a reflection of unhelpful stereotypes about female, or lesbian, sexuality. Equally, the greater focus on fusion/ merger theories could also be seen to reflect a simplistic pathologising of relationships between women, with the assumption that gender creates the only difference and other differences such as race, age or social class are ignored. While it may be the case that issues such as lack of sexual desire and difficulties arising from fusion prove to be particularly relevant for lesbians, it may be that other sexual difficulties are as yet unrecognised or unnamed. The empirical research to date is not conclusive and a broader perspective is needed to reflect the diversity of individual experience.

Psychosexual issues for gay men

Prevalence

As with lesbian sexual difficulties, there is no established body of empirical data on the types and prevalence of problems experienced by gay men. Early studies (McWhirter and Mattison 1978; Masters and Johnson 1979) suggested that gay and heterosexual men present with similar problems, with erectile dysfunction experienced most frequently by both, although there is some evidence that premature (rapid) ejaculation may be less common in gay men while retarded (delayed or absent ejaculation) seems to occur more frequently (Reece 1982; Green and Miller 1985; Paff 1985). There is also evidence that situational rather than global erectile problems may be more common in gay men, tending to occur more frequently among intimates rather than in casual sexual encounters (Paff 1985). George and Berhrendt (1988) reported seeing inhibited sexual desire as the most frequent presentation in their practice with gay couples, followed by retarded ejaculation, arousal problems and premature ejaculation.

Reece (1988) notes that the definition of disorders needs to be expanded to include problems with sexual acts more common among gay men, including desire, arousal, and penetration difficulties specific to anal sex. This would include painful intercourse and 'anodyspareunia' (Rosser *et al.* 1998). Lack of interest in fellating a partner due to aversions and difficulty overcoming the gag response have also been reported (Paff 1985). In a recent community study of nearly 200 gay men, Rosser *et al.* (1997) found that gay men report a higher lifetime prevalence of all sexual problems than heterosexuals (apart from premature ejaculation), although this could be an artefact of having more sex as a whole.

Aetiology and specific therapeutic issues

Many of the psychological, organic and interpersonal factors which lead to and maintain sexual problems are similar for gay, bisexual and heterosexual men. The following factors, however, are likely to be specific to or have a greater effect on non-heterosexual men, and should be considered in the formulation and treatment of their presenting problems.

The effect of male gender roles
Zilbergeld (1992) has argued that beliefs relating to masculinity play a key role in male sexual problems generally. Sexual potency is highly valued as a representation of manhood and when a man fails to 'perform', a cycle of anxiety, perceived weakness and low self-esteem can result which maintains sexual problems. Many gay men may feel that they happily sidestep such stereotypes. However, Bhugra and Wright (1995) note that these pressures may have a greater effect on some gay men, particularly when coming to terms with sexual identity. A desire to escape from suggestions of 'femininity' or weakness, especially where these have been the focus of childhood and adolescent attention or mockery, may lead many gay men to strongly equate a stereotyped 'masculinity' with attractiveness and acceptability.

Internalised homophobia
This issue is covered widely throughout *Pink Therapy* (Davies and Neal 1996) and contributes to many psychological problems. In the context of sexual functioning, cognitive dissonance between the sexual behaviour in which an individual engages and their belief that the behaviour (or the sexual identity that it may signify) is 'bad' often contributes to problems with desire, arousal, penetration or orgasm. This is particularly the case around anal sex, where there may be specific beliefs (sometimes at a pre-conscious level) about unnaturalness and immorality. In an extreme form internalised homophobia can lead to complete absence of sexual desire, sexual aversion or phobias (see also Chapter 11).

At a more subtle level, unrecognised homophobia may lead a gay or bisexual individual to devalue their relationships, making it less likely that they will be motivated to work on overcoming sexual problems that may arise. Conversely they may be more likely to maintain self-esteem and sexual functioning by engaging only in sex where personal contact is minimal. In the context where casual sex is an accepted part of gay culture it becomes difficult to make a distinction between lifestyle choice and avoidance of intimacy or relationships.

Compensation

As a consequence of internalised homophobia or beliefs about personal failure linked to homosexuality, some men may compensate by adopting idealised standards in many areas, including the need to be an 'ideal' gay man (or couple). This pressure to succeed contributes to sexual problems both directly through performance anxiety or difficulty in recognising or accepting problems, and indirectly through increased stress in life generally. Similar pressures may apply to bisexual men.

Identity and intimacy problems

Coleman *et al.* (1992) and Coleman and Reece (1988) provide an extremely useful discussion of the specific effects of intimacy and identity difficulties on sexual functioning, including problems with compulsive sexual behaviour, hyperactive and hypoactive sexual desire. Coleman *et al.* propose that:

> Failure to develop a positive and integrated identity – including a posit-ive appreciation of and congruence between one's sexual orientation, sex role and behaviour – may result in ambivalence about intimacy and development of identity disorders. The imbalance seen in intimacy dysfunction is characterised by interpersonal communication problems, unresolved intrapsychic and interpersonal stress, and behaviour patterns designed to cope with unresolved stress [e.g. compulsive sex].
>
> (Coleman *et al.* 1992: 262)

They suggest that gay males seem more at risk of this type of presentation due to growing up with a 'hidden' aspect of their identity as well as to the lack of positive reinforcement and role models for this aspect. Neal (1998, personal communication) has also drawn attention to the role of unexpressed anger (a consequence of the trauma and oppression resulting from homophobia) which additionally may be an inhibiting factor in gay men and their intimate relationships. The interpersonal and psychosexual issues for gay relationships, often discussed in the literature in terms of the dynamics of maintaining a separate identity in the context of same-sex attachment and identification, are similar to those raised in our discussion of lesbian sexual problems (under 'Fusion/merger').

Abuse or traumatic early experiences
It is well documented that a history of abuse is associated with the development of difficulties in sexual functioning and may require prolonged therapy when present (Becker 1989). While this issue affects heterosexual men too, many gay and bisexual male clients have histories of childhood abuse and trauma as well as physical and emotional neglect. This is particularly true among men who work in prostitution, which in itself may increase the likelihood of current sexual trauma (Coleman and Reece 1988). On the basis of clinical population and gay community studies it seems that abuse and trauma issues are relatively more likely to affect gay and bisexual men (see Chapter 9 for further discussion of this issue).

Reactions to HIV and AIDS
Again this issue frequently affects heterosexual clients also, but is more likely to present as a contributing factor in gay or bisexual men. For some this may be due to adopting celibacy because of their fears of HIV infection, which would result in a lack of sexual experience. It may be a factor contributing to internalised homophobia, or sex may become associated with having acquired HIV, raising issues of guilt, self-blame and depression. It may contribute directly to sexual anxiety and problems (particularly of desire and arousal) due to associations of sexual acts with risk of transmitting HIV. Condoms are frequently an issue in presentations of erectile difficulties. Not only does putting them on interrupt sensuality, reduce sensitivity and place a focus on the 'active' partner to continue the 'performance'; they also carry symbolic importance regarding disease and the need to be 'safe'. For some men this, and the need to 'play safe' generally, interferes with excitement and sexual activity.

There are also interpersonal aspects of HIV. Where one partner in a relationship is positive, the increased pressure on the other to stay 'healthy' can contribute to stress on the relationship (Bhugra and Wright 1995). If HIV illness is present, the sexual and relationship dynamics can also be affected by the development of 'carer/cared for' roles or pressures (see also Chapter 4).

Organic factors
Those organic causes of sexual problems which arise more frequently in the assessment of gay men usually relate to the effects of HIV illness and medications, although the underlying mechanisms are not well understood. Care has to be taken however to identify psychological and interpersonal aspects of illness and treatment which are often found to be equally important in the maintenance of problems. Gay men also have a higher risk of contracting certain other sexually transmitted infections (e.g. anal warts) and discomfort or anxiety relating to these may contribute to sexual problems, particularly if the individual has current or past experience of symptoms.

Interpersonal factors

We have already considered some of the interpersonal issues arising from individual psychological factors. In addition sexual problems may arise in the context of a discrepancy between partners in beliefs about homosexual lifestyles and attitudes to 'coming out'. Conflicts, doubts or misunderstandings arising from this may increase anxiety or stress and lead to sexual problems, particularly of loss of desire and arousal in one partner. Discrepancies between partners in terms of level of sexual desire have already been described for lesbians and may apply also to gay and bisexual men, although these are less prevalent in the literature.

Socio-cultural factors

We have already considered how lesbian sexual politics may influence sexual beliefs and behaviours, and similar issues apply to gay and bisexual men. A wider range of sexual lifestyles and relationships are available in comparison with heterosexual norms, and there are fewer institutionalised pressures towards lifelong monogamy (Bell and Weinberg 1978); indeed there are social pressures to reject 'heterosexual' values of exclusivity and permanence. As a result of this, apart from the possibility of clear 'discrepancies' in sexual attitudes and values between partners as described above, there is a general lack of established 'rules' for relationships with which to identify (or reject). George (1993: 237) suggests that these rules instead have to be individually negotiated and created in gay and bisexual relationships, and are then more frequently questioned as the relationship progresses: 'What frequently appears to happen is that gay and bisexual men feel torn between what they perceive as the norm for gay lifestyles and the ideal of heterosexual society'.

Where not resolved, the uncertainty and anxiety that result from this are likely to increase pressure on individuals to be sexually 'successful' within the relationship as a way of feeling reassured. However, the anxiety and uncertainty also create emotional blocks which make it more difficult for sexual success to be achieved. Additionally, an individual may be more able to find sexual or emotional reassurance outside the relationship as an alternative way of dealing with the anxiety raised. All of these factors can then contribute to the development and maintenance of sexual problems, and to a couple seeking solutions through external sexual contact rather than working within the relationship.

Pressures to be sexually successful are not limited to gay men who are in relationships. Shires and Miller (1998) studied psychological factors associated with erectile dysfunction in gay and straight men, regardless of relationship status. They found that gay men generally were more likely to describe themselves as sexual failures as a result of erectile loss (internalising the problem in terms of failure to be a 'proper' gay man), while straight men described bad luck, frustration or simple performance anxiety more often. Shires and Miller conclude that:

the crucial factor in the experience of erectile dysfunction seems to be a successful sexual performance in the context of a specifically characterised sexual identity (including beliefs about mode and frequency of sexual relationships), rather than being a simple question of sexual functioning *per se*.

(Shires and Miller 1998: 47)

It seems therefore that gay men are under even more pressure than straight men to perform sexually, 'a situation in which an erection becomes a necessary but problematic rite of passage to further relationships' (Shires and Miller 1998: 46).

This linking of potency with gay identity may become even more problematic for older gay men, for whom the experience of normal erectile function decline with age will be exacerbated by the increasing discrepancy from the youth-oriented imagery and values of the gay scene. The prevalent use of alcohol and recreational drugs (Kowszun and Malley 1996) also contributes to sexual problems (both directly through their physiological affect on the sexual response cycle, and indirectly through relationship problems which may result from their use). Additionally, problem drinking or drug use is likely to prevent successful participation in sexual therapy or treatment.

Medical treatments
A specific issue for HIV positive men, as well as gay and bisexual men as a whole, arises regarding medical treatments for erectile problems. There is debate in the medical literature regarding the ethics of offering treatment to HIV positive individuals. Schover (1992) states that treatments such as the vacuum pump device, intracavernosal injections or penile prosthesis should not be offered without involving a partner and making sure that safer sex counselling has been provided. At a 1995 conference at the Royal Society of Medicine on the interdisciplinary management of erectile dysfunction (regarded as sufficiently ground-breaking that a supplement of the *International Journal of STD and AIDS* was published on the proceedings) the question was asked 'Does anyone on the panel treat HIV positive individuals with intrapenile injections?' The only published reply (it is not known if there were others) came from a leading clinician and researcher in the field of impotence, from whom general practitioners and others may be expected to take a lead. It merits full quotation:

We do see a number of patients who are gay and we treat patients who are HIV positive but there are differences in different parts of the country. It is very difficult for a hospital such as St. Mary's, which receives £14 million a year for AIDS treatment to avoid treating patients who are homosexuals and who have erectile problems. I understand completely that other units do not wish to do it.

(Brindley 1996: 15)

With the advent of new medical treatments and the possibility that services for male sexual problems will increasingly be influenced by such views, the knowledge and attitudes of professionals about homosexuality is likely to remain a significant barrier to treatment unless training improves. At the time of writing, the Department of Health is in the process of developing guidelines on the possible use of Sildenafil (Viagra) for erectile dysfunction and early indications are that they will advise against its use for 'recreational' sex. Again, stereotyped views and prejudice about gay sexuality and lifestyles may lead to denial of medical treatment, which might otherwise improve quality of life for both individuals and couples.

Case example 1

Lauren, a 35-year-old lesbian woman presented with lack of sexual interest over the previous five years, with no sexual activity at all for the past two years. She had been in her present relationship for seven years. Two years into the relationship she had an abnormal cervical smear, which necessitated laser treatment. After the surgery she was advised to abstain from penetrative sex for six weeks. Lauren and her partner did resume sex after this time but Lauren described finding sex physically uncomfortable and rarely feeling sexually aroused. She described her relationship with her partner as extremely close, neither herself nor her partner expressing any other concerns about the relationship aside from the lack of sexual contact.

Initially, after two sessions of assessment, it seemed appropriate to formulate Lauren's difficulties in terms of a learned aversion to sexual contact as a result of pain experienced during sex. However, Lauren experienced strong negative emotional reactions to the homework exercises. Through discussion with both partners, it became apparent that there were long-standing difficulties within the relationship which had never been openly acknowledged. Lauren felt that her partner was too involved in her work and thought this reflected a lack of commitment to the relationship. Her partner experienced Lauren's lack of sexual interest as rejecting but felt as if she was 'complaining' if she expressed this and therefore avoided spending time with her partner. Both women felt uncomfortable about discussing differences in opinion and felt that this heralded the end of the relationship.

The second formulation focused on low sexual desire as secondary to communication difficulties, specifically difficulty expressing dissatisfaction, even anger, at behaviour perceived as rejecting. In this scenario, withholding sex becomes a powerful, if subconscious, means of maintaining emotional distance. The focus of the therapy shifted to working with the couple to communicate anger and dissatisfaction assertively, increasing toleration of difference and discussing their fear of abandonment. After 15 sessions Lauren's sexual desire began to return and they resumed a sexual relationship.

Case example 2

Adam, a 26-year-old man attended with his 33-year-old partner of two years' duration, complaining of a loss of interest in sex and frequent episodes of loss of erection or inability to ejaculate. This was his first relationship, following several years of short affairs in which he was always 'let down'. Having found the 'perfect' partner he had always assumed and hoped that they would be together and monogamous for life, but was now distressed and confused that they had not sustained what was a passionate beginning. His partner had had a previous five-year relationship, which had ended when they 'drifted apart'. Adam and his partner were living together and reported being content although Adam was now worried that the relationship would not last.

This example illustrates how a client may attempt to compensate for low self-esteem resulting from internalised homophobia, but nevertheless become anxious as a result of uncertainty over how sexual relationships 'should' be. Here the therapist needs to consider the following possibilities:

- What is the likely aetiology of the sexual difficulties and which could be regarded as the most useful focus for sex therapy? Are there any related problems that have not been mentioned? In this case, assessment revealed that Adam experienced difficulties with both insertive and receptive anal intercourse, which had led to them not including this in their sexual activity. Although they had not talked about this aspect of the problem, it was central to Adam feeling that he was not able to fulfil either sexual 'role'.
- What is the client's own definition of a good relationship, including sex, when it is not determined by the need to be 'ideal' or to match gay cultural expectations of sexual fulfilment? (For a further discussion of this point see Simon and Whitfield 2000.)
- Is the client strong enough to accept that as a result of his dependence on his partner he undermines himself and is inevitably 'let down'? Are his projections of being let down based on homophobic beliefs (e.g. 'gay people are disloyal', 'gay relationships don't last')?
- Adam may need to recognise not only his own tendency to idealise but also that he is now internally supported enough to sustain a more stable relationship and to accept help to reflect critically on his own values. The therapist needs to acknowledge the client's strength and self-determination in coming to therapy.

Therapeutic implications and recommendations

The clinical case examples illustrate how the issues we have identified can be applied to clinical work. It is clear that therapists who work with clients from sexual minority groups need to be aware that the range of presenting psychosexual problems is different from that of heterosexual clients, and that the standard classification and treatment approaches which characterise formal psychosexual therapy training may therefore be limited or inappropriately used. Problems which are not currently classified may be overlooked, while the aetiology of recognised problems may be incorrectly formulated and treated (e.g. erectile dysfunction which has developed secondary to painful receptive intercourse in the male partner). In addition, the definition of what constitutes 'satisfactory' sexual relationships and practices may differ from heterosexual norms, which may lead to an inappropriate focus in therapy on heterosexually-defined goals and patterns of behaviour. Therapists also need to be aware that aetiologies of sexual problems are less likely to be 'simple' manifestations of sexual anxiety compared with heterosexuals, and greater attention needs to be paid to issues of sexual identity as a whole and the role of sexual behaviour in defining and supporting this.

The need for therapists to recognise their own sexual feelings, values, prejudices, and limitations in knowledge around gay or lesbian sexuality has been discussed throughout *Pink Therapy* (Davies and Neal 1996), as has the need to provide affirmation for the client's sexuality and relationships. What has received less attention are the issues raised for lesbian and gay therapists working with lesbian and gay clients. One issue which is particularly relevant in psychosexual therapy concerns the therapist's own beliefs about gay and lesbian sexuality – for example their attitudes to monogamy, SM or anonymous sex. For many therapists it can become difficult to separate personal agendas from professional views. We have discussed in this chapter how there are no established 'rules' for same-sex relationships and lifestyles, and instead these have to be created and negotiated, either in isolation or drawing on perceived gay community norms (Simon and Whitfield 2000). Therapists as well as clients engage in this process, which in addition to enabling their creativity and insights, may also result in shared 'blind spots'. Thus there may be a parallel process in which a therapist with the same cultural values colludes with the defensive part of the client that doesn't want to change. Growth in therapy usually occurs when a client's anxiety is supported enough to experiment with alternatives. If the therapist colludes on the basis of shared values, progress may be inhibited. Good practice guidelines should ensure that therapists have the opportunity to acknowledge and explore these issues in supervision and training.

As we have noted sexual problems among minority groups have received limited attention and further work is essential if we are to be confident that individual needs are being fully and appropriately addressed. In order to improve clinical practice we need information on the prevalence of sexual problems, the form difficulties take and how these may differ from those in the heterosexual population. We need new models of sexual behaviour which incorporate the wide variety of sexual expression across all sexualities, and an understanding of the individual, interpersonal and wider socio-political issues which impact on sexual functioning. Training courses need to acknowledge the importance of raising awareness of sexual minority issues when teaching about sexual dysfunction, rather than working with an assumption of heterosexuality. Finally, clinicians themselves need to be aware of the limitations of the traditional theoretical approaches and to be inventive in their application of traditional therapeutic techniques.

References

Akkerman, A., Betzelt, S. and Daniel, G. (1990) *Nackte tatsachen. Ergebnisse eines lesbisches forschungsprojekts, Teil I, (Bare Facts: results of a lesbian research project) Zeitschrift fur Sexualforschung*, 3: 1–24.

American Psychiatric Association (1994) *Diagnostic and Statistical Manual of Mental Disorders*, 4th edn. Washington, DC: American Psychiatric Association.

Bancroft, J. (1989) *Human Sexuality and Its Problems*. Edinburgh: Churchill Livingstone.

Becker, J. (1989) Impact of sexual abuse on sexual functioning, in S.R. Leiblum and R.C. Rosen (eds) *Principles and Practice of Sex Therapy*. New York: Guilford Press.

Bell, A.P. and Weinberg, M.S. (1978) *Homosexualities: A Study of Diversity Among Men and Women*. New York: Simon & Schuster.

Bhugra, D. and Wright, B. (1995) Sexual dysfunction in gay men: diagnosis and management. *International Review of Psychiatry*, 7: 247–52.

Blumstein, P. and Schwartz, P. (1983) *American Couples*. New York: William Morrow.

Boyle, M. (1993) Sexual dysfunction or heterosexual dysfunction? *Feminism and Psychology*, 3(1): 73–88.

Brindley, G.S. (1996) Intrapenile drug delivery systems. *International Journal of STD and AIDS*, 7 (suppl. 3): 13–15.

Carl, D. (1990) *Counseling Same-Sex Couples*. New York: Norton.

Coleman, E. and Reece, R. (1988) Treating low sexual desire among gay men, in S.R. Leiblum and R.C. Rosen (eds) *Sexual Desire Disorders*. New York: Guilford Press.

Coleman, E., Hoon, P. and Hoon, H. (1983) Arousability and sexual satisfaction in lesbian and heterosexual women. *The Journal of Sex Research*, 19: 58–73.

Coleman, E., Rosser, B.R.S. and Strapko, N. (1992) Sexual and intimacy dysfunction among homosexual men and women. *Psychiatric Medicine*, 10(2): 257–71.

Crowe, M. and Ridley, J. (1990) *Therapy With Couples*. Oxford: Blackwell.

Daines, B. (1988) Assumptions and values in sexual and marital therapy. *Sexual and Marital Therapy*, 3(2): 149–64.

Davies, D. (1996) Homophobia and heterosexism, in D. Davies and C. Neal (eds) *Pink Therapy: A Guide for Counsellors and Therapists Working with Lesbian, Gay and Bisexual Clients*. Buckingham: Open University Press.

Davies, D. and Neal, C. (eds) (1996) *Pink Therapy: A Guide for Counsellors and Therapists Working with Lesbian, Gay and Bisexual Clients*. Buckingham: Open University Press.

George, H. (1993) Sex, Love and relationships: issues and problems for gay men in the AIDS era, in J. Ussher and C. Baker (eds) *Psychological Perspectives on Sexual Problems*. London: Routledge.

George, K. and Berhrendt, A. (1988) Therapy for male couples experiencing relationship problems and sexual problems, in E. Coleman (ed.) *Psychotherapy with Homosexual Men and Women*. New York: Haworth.

Green, J. and Miller, D. (1985) Male homosexuality and sexual problems. *British Journal of Hospital Medicine*, 33: 353–5.

Hall, M. (1987) Sex therapy with lesbian couples: a four stage approach. *Journal of Homosexuality*, 14(1/2): 137–56.

Hatfield, E. and Walster, G. (1978) *A New Look at Love*. Reading, MA: Addison-Wesley.

Kaplan, H.S. (1979) *Disorders of Sexual Desire and Other New Concepts and Techniques of Sex Therapy*. New York: Bruner/Mazel.

King, M. (1998) Sexual dysfunction needs an integrated approach. *Trends in Urology, Gynaecology and Sexual Health*, March: 27–8.

Kowszun, G. and Malley, M. (1996) Alcohol and substance misuse, in D. Davies and C. Neal (eds) *Pink Therapy: A Guide for Counsellors and Therapists Working with Lesbian, Gay and Bisexual Clients*. Buckingham: Open University Press.

Krestan, J. and Bebko, C. (1980) Problems of fusion in the lesbian relationship. *Family Process*, 19: 279–86.

Leigh, B. (1989) Reasons for having and avoiding sex: gender, sexual orientation and relationship to sexual behaviour. *The Journal of Sex Research*, 26: 199–209.

Loulan, J. (1984) *Lesbian Sex*. San Francisco: Spinsters/Aunt Lute.

Loulan, J. (1988) Research on the sex practices of 1566 lesbians and the clinical applications. *Women and Therapy*, 7(2/3): 221–34.

McWhirter, D. and Mattison, A. (1978) The treatment of sexual dysfunction in gay male couples. *Journal of Sex and Marital Therapy*, 4: 213–18.

Masters, W. and Johnson, V. (1970) *Human Sexual Inadequacy*. Boston, MA: Little, Brown.

Masters, W. and Johnson, V. (1979) *Homosexuality in Perspective*. Boston, MA: Little, Brown.

Nichols, M. (1983) The treatment of inhibited sexual desire (ISD) in lesbian couples. *Women and Therapy*, 1(4): 49–66.

Paff, B.A. (1985) Sexual dysfunction in gay men requesting treatment. *Journal of Sex and Marital Therapy*, 11: 3–18.

Reece, R. (1982) Group treatment of sexual dysfunction in gay men. *Journal of Homosexuality*, 7 (2/3): 113–29.

Reece, R. (1988) Causes and treatments of sexual desire discrepancies in male couples, in E. Coleman (ed.) *Integrated Identity for Gay Men and Lesbians*. New York: Harrington Park.

Rosser, B., Metz, M., Bockting, W. and Buroker, T. (1997) Sexual difficulties, concerns, and satisfaction in homosexual men: an empirical study with implications for HIV prevention. *Journal of Sex and Marital Therapy*, 23(1): 61–73.

Rosser, B., Short, B., Thurmes, P. and Coleman, E. (1998) Anodyspareunia, the unacknowledged sexual dysfunction: a validation study of painful receptive anal intercourse and its psychosexual concomitants in homosexual men. *Journal of Sex and Marital Therapy*, 24: 281–92.

Rothblum, E. and Brehony, K. (1993) *Boston Marriages: Romantic but Asexual Relationships among Contemporary Lesbians*. Amhurst, MA: University of Massachusetts Press.

Schover, L. (1992) Erectile failure and chronic illness, in R.C. Rosen and S.R. Leiblum (eds) *Erectile Disorders: Assessment and Treatment*. New York: Guilford Press.

Schreurs, K. (1993) Sexuality in lesbian couples: the importance of gender. *Annual Review of Sex Research*, 4: 49–66.

Shires, A. and Miller, D. (1998) A preliminary study comparing psychological factors associated with erectile dysfunction in heterosexual and homosexual men. *Sexual and Marital Therapy*, 13(1): 37–50.

Simon, G. (1996) Working with people in relationships, in D. Davies and C. Neal (eds) *Pink Therapy: A Guide for Counsellors and Therapists Working with Lesbian, Gay and Bisexual Clients*. Buckingham: Open University Press.

Simon, G. and Whitfield, G. (2000) Social constructionist and systemic therapy, in D. Davies and C. Neal (eds) *Therapeutic Perspectives on Working with Lesbian, Gay and Bisexual Clients*. Buckingham: Open University Press.

Todor, N. (1978) Sexual problems of lesbians, in G. Vida (ed.) *Our Right to Love. A Lesbian Resource Book*. NJ: Prentice Hall.

Ussher, J. (1990) Couple therapy with gay clients: issues facing counsellors. *Counselling Psychology Quarterly*, 3(1): 109–16.

Ussher, J. (1993) The construction of female sexual problems, in J. Ussher and C. Baker (eds) *Psychological Perspectives on Sexual Problems*. London: Routledge.

Zilbergeld, B. (1992) The man behind the broken penis, in R. Rosen and S. Leiblum (eds) *Erectile Disorders: Assessment and Treatment*. New York: Guilford Press.

| CHARLES NEAL

We are family: working with gay men in groups

There is so much healing to be done, so much mending and so much tending; and time may be shorter than we know. Out of history we emerge. A separate people whose time is at hand. Out of the mists of our long oppression we bring love for ourselves and for each other, and love for the gifts we bear ... 'tis a gift to be gay! Share the magic of it!

(Hay 1987: 290–1)

The scene

Since I began practising as a psychotherapist with individuals I have been keen to offer 'affirmative' therapy (for discussion of this term see Davies and Neal 1996, 2000) for clients from sexual minorities. It became obvious that many gay male clients especially would benefit from sharing their experiences and issues within a group. Many were wary of groups altogether and of male (and gay male) groups particularly. Being in intimate groups touches unconscious issues and memories about our families of origin and the wider communities in which we have lived, from which we have felt excluded, or by whom we have been oppressed. I knew from personal experience how healing and beneficial a safe, challenging group could be for a gay man, as well as how threatening and frightening joining a group could be.

I would like to share here some of the issues, concerns and structures which have occupied gay men and myself working in ongoing therapy groups in London over past years. I believe such work to have great significance in healing and empowering men for whom prejudice has denied representation, equality and status in our society. All quotations from members of the groups are here with their consent, for which I am deeply grateful.

My original 'Coming Out and Coming In' groups ran over eight weeks with one three-hour evening meeting each week. Men who came had either worked with me as individual clients, been referred by colleagues or responded to flyers distributed within the gay and personal growth communities. Their commitment was to attend every meeting and membership was closed for the whole period. This format proved perfect for men ready for short-term work, wanting a discreet, satisfying connection with other gay men in a new way, and for others with some experience of group work or 'men's work' who wanted more. Following an experience of a group in which I felt frustrated by time limits when several participants were fearful and withholding, I decided to go with my own preference for depth and breadth and started ongoing groups for men wanting to work longer-term together.

The first of these new-style groups, also called 'Coming Out and Coming In', attracted several men from the shorter groups and lasted over three years until I went abroad and closed the group. The second, 'Coming Home', with more than half its members returning from the first group, is entering its fifth year. Ten men work with me for one whole day and six or seven evenings for three 'terms' a year. Originally we met every week but, because of my schedule, this changed two years ago to fortnightly meetings.

The groups have all been held at Spectrum in London, one of the oldest established humanistic therapy centres. I have been a client, trainee, supervisee and practitioner there over many years. Two areas of specialism, led by founders of Spectrum and both programmes in which I have fully participated, provided significant contexts for my work there. In 1973, Jenner Roth began a sexuality programme as a place for 'men and women to explore their sexuality as an integral part of themselves, rather than as an isolated or dismembered part with little or no relationship to the rest of their lives'. This, their first programme of personal development, develops every year as an 'essential part of our work and beliefs' (Spectrum 1999: 36). Few other therapy training institutions give sexuality prominence.

Another large area of work, 'Men for Men', under the direction of Terry Cooper includes ongoing men's groups, an annual conference, retreats and workshops designed to be 'for men and not against women . . . and to . . . increase men's awareness and vocabulary of feeling so that emotional bonding is possible' (Spectrum 1999: 53). Again, 'men's work' in the UK has generally been developed outside formal therapy establishments.

The issues

Multiple issues become figural individually and collectively within the general fields 'group', 'men' and 'gay'. I will look at these clusters in turn.

Being a group

For hundreds of years men who are sexually attracted to men in our culture have been vilified and rejected and their contributions to wider communities diminished or denied (Duberman *et al.* 1990; Grahn 1990). Every 'gay' man – as most have latterly come to be known – in Britain has grown up taught that he is worth less than others and that what he has to offer is, in some regard, unwanted. Having ingested this homophobia, it is common for members of gay subcultures to reproduce notions of themselves as shallow, narcissistic, sexually uncontrolled and predatory people. This further weakens their significant connections with their wider communities. For these reasons alone it is profoundly important that gay men organise groups which seek to heal these experiences. This includes the importance of meeting with people of all sexual orientations involved in personal, group, women's and men's work in environments where individual sexuality is respected and celebrated. Group work includes many facets: family, belonging, having value, being known and cherished, position and status, conflict, love, anger, intimacy and trust are some.

'There's a slight touch of Falstaff's army about most of us when we first turn up at an interpersonal group. For many of us, being direct with people, letting ourselves be straight [*sic*], knowing what we are feeling, even listening, are much harder than we suppose' (Houston 1984: 2). Joining, belonging to and leaving a group all touch upon relationships to inclusion and exclusion with all groups in our life. How we have been and felt included or excluded, how we exclude and include ourselves. Is individuality acceptable? What do we share with these people and what marks us out from them? How do we, and they, tolerate differences between us? What does it take, and mean, to be a 'real' member? What is our history and current relationship to being wanted, rejected, sought after or marginalised? What does 'family' mean to us now?

> A history of exclusion made self-exclusion second nature, as if by definition I would never find a group in which I was openly and happily gay . . . I used to behave extremely competitively with other gay men ('Don't look at him, look at me'). I now have enough confidence in who I am to feel I can occupy any public gay space I choose without projecting negative fantasies onto whoever might be there.
>
> (Group member)

In a trustworthy group we can learn to tolerate movement and pulsation (the varying levels of energetic engagement with a position or identity, attitude or belief) in others and develop for ourselves an expectation of pulsation in life and people rather than one of fixedness or static identities. Understanding and empathising with others helps us to reduce harsh judgements of ourselves as well. We have a great deal in common in respect of feelings. The ongoing, gradual process of 'coming out' to the group – as to ourselves – has many dimensions and a different pace and depth for each of us. Witnessing the lives and processes of one another, especially when our wider culture has shown disdain or lack of interest in these, is an immeasurably valuable function:

> Challenges for me being in a group: being accepted on every level, developing trust, being seen and visible, being there to meet my needs, to ask for help, to be vulnerable and emotional, to connect with my heart and my stomach and not just my head, to sort out issues I may have with individuals.
>
> (Group member)

A group is important as a container for experiencing the self in relationships. We are helping each other build a sense of safety, trust, cohesiveness and continuity of experience. Setting and keeping boundaries, negotiating and contracting are all important skills for development here. We agree rules about confidentiality, timekeeping and ways of interacting. We commit for specific purposes, contract to attend all group meetings and are willing to meet between times to do 'homework' exercises one to one. When members have broken agreements and suddenly left the group, the grief, anger and loss has been processed and we have asked anyone leaving to give at least one term's notice so that we can close with them satisfactorily.

Group members do form friendships at various levels outside meetings and these are openly talked about in the group. The only sexual relationship which developed while both members were in the group, which had an unhappy course, was negative for both men because of secret-keeping. It made their time in the group less productive and contributed to one leaving.

We occasionally invite another facilitator in to lead a specialised theme for the day – for example, massage training, voice and movement work – in which case I participate as a group member and then facilitate part of the day.

Gay men's gatherings are often stereotyped in one of two ways. The first genuinely celebrates diversity – the annual 'Pride' celebrations, for example, display a vast range of human expression and tolerance. The second is ultra-critical and competitive. Our men's group is diverse in terms of age, class, ethnic origin, religion, politics and occupation. Dealing with stereotypes is most effectively managed within groups (see Clark 1997). It is more productive in groups than in individual therapy to challenge talk of 'us' and 'them', speaking for *all* gay men or about *all* straight people: 'Participation has resulted in me becoming less judgemental of others and myself, through increased awareness of the differences between feelings, thoughts and judgements' (Group member).

Internalised oppression is easier to spot in others. Participants strive not to be assumptive or judgemental, to treat one another with respect and goodwill, to speak their own truth for themselves, not to speak for others. Modelling these principles and creating a shared 'culture', we increase our expectation that we will be treated in these ways elsewhere. It can, of course, be a shock or continuing disappointment when this does not happen!

A group setting affords rich opportunities for practising new ways to be with others and develop our communications, social and relational skills. We can see how we are behaving as usual, how we are willing to try something different. It becomes a place to develop trust, explore and work through feelings, assert needs, negotiate conflict or intimacy. No one was originally socialised as gay: each of us has been primarily socialised as if we would become heterosexual. In the group we can learn to be authentic rather than 'passing' (as heterosexual) or merely decorative, to be real rather than only nice, whole rather than just sexual: to experience and express the whole of our innate emotional range.

We work on how we each make and maintain contact and connection, how we reach for others and withdraw, how we are different alone, with another or with many. We investigate how each of us has different energetic needs and how and when group energy depletes or enhances us. This small, trustworthy group acts as a reality check in participants' lives. Members are encouraged to experiment in working with a range of partners within group meetings and in tackling homework exercises which enhance the work. Our own reactions to experiences often make sense when contextualised with those of others. We cannot easily disregard multiple feedback on how others experience us.

The group becomes an excellent place to facilitate increased awareness, and constructively channelled expression, of both anger and openly-given affection. The former is made safer through teaching and using anger rituals in the group and the latter through structured contact exercises. (John Stevens' 1988 book, *Awareness*, has some excellent material.) Lots of men find it difficult to receive or give appreciation so we employ regular structures to practise this. Similarly we spend time learning the differences between thoughts, fantasies, sensations, emotions and behaviours. These are of huge significance. The wounds inflicted on gay men have created powerful fantasies of being boundless and overwhelming and fears of being invaded or overwhelmed. The considerable shame and deceit around these issues has led to myriad forms of 'acting out'. Isensee (1991), for example, lists alcohol and substance abuse, sexual and other compulsions, unsafe sex, overwork and overachieving, food abuse, debt, self-deprivation, co-dependency, revictimisation and domestic violence as self-destructive outcomes of homophobic abuse.

One of the greatest tragedies of our history in this culture is the way in which gay men have been sexualised: the term 'homosexual' indicates this and much of the male gay 'scene' enacts it (Neal 1998). Significant healing of these wounds and misappropriations means emphasising appreciation of our bodies as the site of our 'self' and our emotions; increasing our sensitivity to our own bodily sensations and needs and those of others; the importance of touch and breathing, of caring gestures and clear boundaries; and the widest range of possibilities of non-sexual contact.

Group members work on these elements through Gestalt 'zones of aware-ness' exercises, (Stevens 1988), massage, movement, voice work and games (see Brandes and Phillips 1977). The group provides adequate social controls for safety – gradually members can lessen fears surrounding their own responses and those of others and see that there are no automatic next steps to sexual activity. Participants learn to offer and receive mutual respect, acceptance, value and support: most of us grew up feeling different, bad and alone. 'For the first time I have close relationships with other gay men where I feel completely comfortable about the boundaries between intimacy and sex . . . I feel much less confused about these boundaries' (Group member).

A group can also serve to provide a more equal power relationship between therapist and client. After all, there's only one facilitator and ten other members: strength in numbers! I generally do the homeworks and often partner participants for exercises within the group. This democratisa-tion is not unimportant when gay men have been criminalised and persecuted by 'authorities' in psychology as much as elsewhere.

Being men

People of all sexualities can assume that gay men do not share issues with other men about intimacy, touch, support, and softness. They may have been recruited into stereotypical ideas of gay men as not men at all but false women or an altogether different kind of being. (Women, of course, are often seen by some men and some women as *entirely* different from men.) On closer examination, these notions are not borne out by our experience of others or ourselves. A world of only two genders denies each of us the internal experience we have of both and neither.

Many gay men have distanced themselves from masculinity as a defence mechanism. Coming home to, acknowledging and valuing our masculinity can be profound. Much valuable work has been done in recent years on the anxieties of modern masculinities and the emergence of a masculine con-sciousness: the work of The Achilles Heel Collective, Wild Dance events and so on.

> Participation has . . . transformed my relationships with straight men. In my twenties I spent an immense amount of effort with my erotic focus on straight men as if I could persuade them, by loving them enough, to change from straight to gay. If anyone had suggested this was tyrannical delusion, I would have been horrified.
>
> (Group member)

Being gay raises issues of gender identity and loyalty, and gives rise to further patterns of inclusion and exclusion. How gay men may be the same as, and different from, other men is one consideration. We begin to learn more about how we were first socialised as men, then rejected as inadequate men. Many men came, unsurprisingly, to prioritise their gayness over their maleness. Other key issues evoked include power and its uses, size, status, intimacy, pornography, trust, competition, aggression, fear, anger and violence. Many men fear further failure, assault, invasion or tyranny. They fear being found wanting as 'proper' men (see Stoltenberg 1990): 'Many of my relationships with women were imprisoned in the dysfunction of fag/hag . . . we got together to complain about men – a negative contract on a huge scale which yielded some intimacy but only at the cost of structuring men out of my life and confirming my own disappointments' (Group member).

Being in an all male group raises anxieties about being without women, so often the mainstay of support in straight and gay men's lives, frequently representing not-male, split-off characteristics for them. Questions arise about how we relate to men (straight and gay) and how we relate differently to women. Absent or unavailable fathers remain sadly figural. Old injuries concerning brothers, lovers, friends and enemies come out, as do the terrors of school experiences (Rivers, in Chapter 10, discusses the lifelong effects of bullying): 'Men who have been abused as children often anticipate feeling uncomfortable in a group of men. The majority were abused by men and many felt alienated by typical role expectations while growing up' (Isensee 1991: 176).

Being gay

This raises complex issues of sexual identity and orientation. There are lots of fears and anxieties about gayness as well as about being with other gay men for purposes other than sex and the commercial gay 'scene'. Being intimate and open is frequently experienced as threatening and there are fears about being found wanting as 'real' gay men, not being gay enough or gay in acceptable ways – having been taught originally that 'real' men are not gay. These fears arise from introjected oppression (absorbed into the self), through the homophobia which surrounds us all in Britain, and the manifestations of this within 'gay communities'. Sexism, ageism, racism, objectification, body fascism, addiction, unsafe sex and self-abuse have grown in response. 'Positive evidence that gay men can be, and are, very different to the limiting and oppressive rules and behaviours of "the scene" . . . it's so important that gay men become aware that their sexuality and difference is an integral and positive aspect of their lives and extends beyond the merely physical' (Group member).

It is shocking how widespread is the learnt dislike of other gay men (ourselves?) and mistrust or disapproval of them (us? me?). A lot of our work involves working through negative stereotypes within and between ourselves and dealing with the resulting 'dispiritation' (spiritual malaise), lack of value or purpose. This frequently takes the form of decreased awareness of the self and one's own feelings. Many men find it easier to feel sorrow or anger in response to someone else's story while being able to report terrible things in their own biography without emotion. Depression is never far away. Identification can be a stimulus for realising the wide range of one's own feelings.

Key for gay men will be recovering from the damage experienced around desiring and being desired by other men: for example, erotophobia, compulsions, body hatred, shame, denial, panic, guilt. There are specific issues in approaching and being in a group of men for gay men. Who will I desire? Will anyone desire me? Who is most desirable? We discuss cottaging, cruising, phone lines, masturbation, pornography and safer sex. We work on healthy models of relating to our own desire, appropriate containment and expression of it and learning that we are, despite contrary narratives, able to control acting out our desires and to express them in satisfying ways. Level, intimate, authentic relationships are rehearsed within the group. For some this means tackling 'passing' as heterosexual, secrecy or game playing and celebrating their sexuality and individuality. Can we succeed in building satisfying and committed relationships (stay the course, trust and give of ourselves) when negative 'scripts' in our culture tell us we cannot?

> The group was never dramatic or artificially intense – and I think this is vital. I think the way the closet works is that it makes our straightforward desires and loves into dramas. They have to be hidden or announced – rather than just lived. Your style . . . calm, using skills in a simplified, very compassionate way, is perfect for reversing the drama of 'coming out' and welcoming the process of 'coming in'.
>
> (Group member)

An existential question permeating much of our work concerns what gay men are other than sexual beings; what our gayness consists of, other than certain sexual preferences. The sexual acts we perform do not differ much from those enjoyed by people of other sexualities, after all! What is our gay spirit or nature? Is there a special gay sensibility or soul? (See Thompson 1987, 1994; Walker 1994; Ramer 1995; Roscoe 1995.) It is refreshing, especially for those who learned to sexualise all feelings, to begin to see themselves more completely.

One term each member had an hour or more to present their 'gay identity', or spirit, to us all. The range, individualism, creativity and depth of these presentations was fascinating and deeply moving. It is an immense privilege to be invited to tell our story at our own pace and to hear the stories of others.

Individual queer clients, having assured themselves of a non-pathologising therapist, often need to talk little about sexual orientation or sex itself. Similarly, in an effective gay group, members are relieved to freely illuminate their wider lives. Issues raised one year have included childcare, ageing parents, identity, ethnic differences, work problems, spiritual hunger, fear, money, sexual abuse, finding partners, bullying, self-employment, friend-ships, illness, depression, holidays, moving house, anger and self-esteem. 'I've learnt from the group that I don't have to be lonely or depressed, I'm still learning how to take control of my life . . . thinking about the group assures me I can do this' (Group member).

How?

Often a circle of chairs delineates a workspace contained by us all. I like to challenge complacency by configuring the space differently whenever I feel that more contact or movement may be productive. So, at times, we begin with everyone on the floor, maybe for meditation, breathing or contact exercises, massage or relaxation; or with everyone standing and using the whole space, perhaps to indicate their feelings about their position in relation to the group that evening, or to begin to work on someone's issue through a 'sculpt' using the other members in some way. I sit in a different place each time. We have a break in the communal dining room about two-thirds of the way through the evening sessions and make a very enjoy-able shared lunch together there on our whole day.

Most evenings several individuals raise something they wish to tackle and they suggest a way of working or receive suggestions. I also introduce structured exercises, often arising from 'themes' and sub-themes emerging in individual work or in clusters of issues in a series of meetings. If work has been deep or distressing we sometimes end with physical contact, or a visualisation or brief meditation, bringing people back to themselves.

At the start of a term or year each person identifies a personal goal for their work. Recently some members appointed others as observers to feed back to them on specified issues or behaviours of concern. We usu-ally identify a general theme for a term, like making relationships, sub-personalities, anger or self-assertion. Sometimes pressing current issues, such as the Gay Pride carnival, the age of consent debate in the House of Lords or the bombing of a pub in Soho's gay village in London in 1999, demand our attention. Most sessions lead to a 'homework' in which mem-bers meet in pairs to follow up something that came up that evening. Par-ticipants are encouraged to keep personal journals on their process in and out of the group.

I continue to work in individual therapy with about half of the group; some see other practitioners and some are not in therapy. One or two have been members of other kinds of personal development group, a few belong to other gay interest groups or attend Edward Carpenter Community Gay Men's Weeks. Members sometimes join other groups at Spectrum, such as the anger management workshops or the sexuality programme, and particip-ate in the annual men's conference there.

I work with an eclectic toolkit, mostly humanistic. Gestalt (Perls *et al.* 1951) predominates, and I draw upon transactional analysis (Perlman 2000), existentialism (Milton 2000), expressive and art therapies (see Chapter 5 and Cameron 1994), my previous training in libertarian education, Zen Buddhism (Center for Practice of Zen Buddhist Meditation 1988) and psychodrama (Moreno 1948). I am strongly influenced by somatic psychology, especially the work of Stanley Keleman (1971, 1975, 1979, 1985, 1994) at the Center for Energetic Studies in California, and am informed by very many years' personal experience of psychoanalysis.

One important procedure used regularly is the '*daily temperature reading*' (Gordon 1975), used either for ourselves or as a 'go around' in the group. The following are worked through in sequence: *appreciations* for ourselves or one another, or for someone outside the group; *new information* about our internal or external lives; genuine *puzzles* we have for each other or about ourselves; *complaints* about one another's behaviours with *clear recommendations for change*; and, finally, sharing our *wishes, hopes and dreams* about our own lives, one another's lives and for the world in general. This order is very important to the success of the exercise. This is an extremely effective way to keep in touch with our own, and one another's, process and to monitor dynamics between us. Keleman (1994) says the most loving thing one person can do for another is to keep them as fully informed as they are able about themselves.

Over a representative 18 months or so, the group engaged in: visualisations and drawings, breathing and touch exercises, contact and self-awareness games, Gestalt two or more chair dialogues, intimate relationship skills exercises (Gordon 1975), the Karpman (1968) persecutor-victim-rescuer drama triangle from transactional analysis, somagrams (making templates of the whole body to work on history or trauma located there), 'life maps' of the development of sexual identity, dream work, enacting conflicted parts of someone to clarify an issue, anger rituals, Neuro-Linguistic Psychology reframing, a day trip to the sea and, most of all, talking, talking, talking. We are presently in the process of planning the first of what I hope will become an annual residential weekend together in the countryside.

Conclusions

The first gay men's therapy group, to my knowledge, was that led by Daniel Rosenblatt, the Gestaltist, in Manhattan from the mid-1960s to 1992, and it is grounding to feel part of a tradition now spanning 40 years. Many themes and concerns are similar in the groups then and now (Rosenblatt 1998). It is poignant to note our group's great good fortune in having lost none of the 30 or so men involved to AIDS, when Rosenblatt's group was eventually tragically reduced to one living member.

This style of work has a powerful significance for gay men in Britain in the late 1990s. We face a new wave of uniformity inside the gay community ... less support for making the most of ourselves by accepting who we are (at a physical as much as at an emotional level) ... This is rooted in self-hatred and it's profoundly threatening to the survival of the current generation.

(Group member)

I agree. I believe our healthy survival depends on working to heal the wounds to ourselves inflicted by growing up gay in a sexist and homophobic environment; on our empowering ourselves individually and as communities with the intrapersonal and interpersonal skills and resources needed to flourish. On an individual level, all of the men have made many transformations in their lives, work and relationships with themselves and others with support, challenge and feedback from the rest of the group. Frequent references are made to '*the* gay community' and many gay men have been massively disappointed and disenfranchised in trying to find this entity, or trying to connect with its forms. A group such as the one with which I have the privilege to work builds a genuine community, which serves many of the functions of a healthy family and tribe. We are doing what many women have done in the development of their own liberation movements: 'the love, wit and support of those men ... what makes me so proud and excited as I write is the feeling that this isn't a set of separate appreciations – it's gratitude for a whole single precious journey which we all contributed to with love' (Group member).

I have personally derived enormous richness, pleasure and satisfaction from working with the men in my group and I hope this chapter will encourage other affirmative therapists to venture to establish gay groups elsewhere.

With the love of comrades,
With the life-long love of comrades ...
We are nature, long have we been absent, but now we return ...
We have circled and circled till we have arrived home again.

Walt Whitman, 'Leaves of Grass', 1855

Guidelines for good practice

- Interview participants beforehand to ensure that their hopes and expectations are commensurate with what the group offers.
- Agree 'rules' at the first meeting, including confidentiality (e.g. no one 'outs' anyone as a group member if they meet outside). Refresh agreements clearly each term or whenever a new member joins. Preferably run a closed group, whether time limited or open-ended. These two factors enhance a sense of safety.

- Teach members to speak for themselves, to express a range of feelings honestly, to be clear and assertive, non-assumptive, non-threatening and non-blaming towards others.
- Set homework exercises that help make a bridge to socialise learning from group work into 'real' life, and offer members further opportunities for personal connection and growth.
- Facilitate the development of skills for the safe expression of anger and frustration, grief, tenderness and love.
- Encourage trusting physical and emotional connections between men.
- Gradually teach a range of skills and 'techniques' for working through emotional, physical and psychological material as alternatives to 'acting in' or 'acting out'.
- Model compassion, authenticity and goodwill as much as possible.
- Disallow collusion in 'them' and 'us' stereotyping about men, women, gays, straights, bisexuals, the scene, queens, the church, anything. Such stereotyping avoids truth.
- Encourage the identification of the enduring, sometimes subtle, effects of oppression in gay men's lives. Discourage pathologising of the self and others. The real sicknesses are homophobia, hatred and lack of love.

Dedication and acknowledgements

To the group I love working with; to my sons, Sam and Jago and my life partner, Jeremy – their manly beauty shines so brightly in my life. To the men I live, love, play and work with, for inspired masculinity. With great big thanks to Martin, Jef, Steve, John, Jenner and Liz for invaluable feedback.

References

Brandes, D. and Phillips, H. (1977) *Gamester's Handbook*. London: Hutchinson.
Cameron, J. (1994) *The Artist's Way*. London: Pan Books.
Center for the Practice of Zen Buddhist Meditation (1988) *The How You Do Anything is How You Do Everything Workbook*. Mountain View, CA: Center Press.
Clark, D. (1997) *The New Loving Someone Gay*. Berkeley, CA: Celestial Arts.
Davies, D. and Neal, C. (eds) (1996) *Pink Therapy: A Guide for Counsellors and Therapists Working with Lesbian, Gay and Bisexual Clients*. Buckingham: Open University Press.
Davies, D. and Neal, C. (eds) (2000) *Therapeutic Perspectives on Working with Lesbian, Gay and Bisexual Clients*. Buckingham: Open University Press.
Duberman, M., Vicinus, M. and Chauncey, G. (1990) *Hidden from History: Reclaiming the Gay and Lesbian Past*. New York: Meridian Books.
Gordon, L.H. (1975) *The PAIRS Handbook: Practical Application of Intimate Relationship Skills*. Falls Church, VA: PAIRS Foundation Ltd.

Grahn, J. (1990) *Another Mother Tongue: Gay Words, Gay Worlds*. Boston, MA: Beacon Press.

Hay, H. (1987) A separate people whose time has come, in M. Thompson (ed.) *Gay Spirit: Myth and Meaning*. New York: St Martin's Press.

Houston, G. (1984) *The Red Book of Groups*. London: Rochester Foundation.

Isensee, R. (1991) *Growing Up Gay in a Dysfunctional Family*. New York: Fireside Books.

Karpman, S. (1968) Fairy tales and script drama analysis. *Transactional Analysis Bulletin*, 7: 51–6.

Keleman, S. (1971) *Human Ground: Sexuality, Self and Survival*. Berkeley, CA: Center Press.

Keleman, S. (1975) *Your Body Speaks Its Mind*. Berkeley, CA: Center Press.

Keleman, S. (1979) *Somatic Reality*. Berkeley, CA: Center Press.

Keleman, S. (1985) *Emotional Anatomy*. Berkeley, CA: Center Press.

Keleman, S. (1994) *Love: A Somatic View*. Berkeley, CA: Center Press.

Milton, M. (2000) Existential-phenomenological therapy, in D. Davies and C. Neal (eds) *Therapeutic Perspectives on Working with Lesbian, Gay and Bisexual Clients*. Buckingham: Open University Press.

Moreno, J. (1948) *Psychodrama*. New York: Beacon House.

Neal, C. (1998) Queer therapy, past and future. *Counselling News*, 4: 20–3.

Perlman, G. (2000) Transactional analysis, in D. Davies and C. Neal (eds) *Therapeutic Perspectives on Working with Lesbian, Gay and Bisexual Clients*. Buckingham: Open University Press.

Perls, F., Hefferline, R. and Goodman, P. (1951) *Gestalt Therapy: Excitement and Growth in the Human Personality*. London: Souvenir Press.

Ramer, A. (1995) *Two Flutes Playing: A Spiritual Journeybook for Gay Men*. San Francisco: Alamo Square Press.

Roscoe, W. (1995) *Queer Spirits: A Gay Men's Myth Book*. Boston, MA: Beacon Press.

Rosenblatt, D. (1998) Gestalt and homosexuality. *British Gestalt Journal*, 7(1): 8–17.

Spectrum (1999) *Spectrum 1999–2000*, programme brochure. London: Spectrum.

Stevens, J. (1988) *Awareness*. London: Eden Grove Editions.

Stoltenberg, J. (1990) *Refusing to be a Man*. London: Fontana Paperbacks.

Thompson, M. (1987) *Gay Spirit, Myth and Meaning*. New York: St Martin's Press.

Thompson, M. (1994) *Gay Soul: Finding the Heart of Gay Spirit and Nature*. San Francisco: Harper Collins.

Walker, M. (1994) *Men Loving Men: a Gay Sex Guide and Consciousness Book*. San Francisco: Gay Sunshine Press.

Further information

Achilles Heel Collective. The *Achilles Heel* bi-annual anti-sexist men's magazine, 48 Grove Avenue, London N10 2AN.

Edward Carpenter Community. Contact ECC, 1 Cambridge St., Hebden Bridge, West Yorkshire HX7 6LN.

'Wild Dance' events. An annual programme of non-sexist men's work, and men and women's work. Details from BCM, Box 8059, London WC1N 3XX. Tel./fax: +44(0)20 78134260. Email: wild_dance.events@virgin.net

| ELIZABETH OXLEY AND
CLAIRE A. LUCIUS

Looking both ways: bisexuality and therapy

Introduction

We are two women therapists who identify as bisexual, who got to know each other as a result of talking about our shared experiences within a professional psychology association. The prevailing attitudes and poor levels of awareness we find generally in society, and within such professional associations in particular, make us wish to discuss the universal nature of good therapeutic practice across this and other issues, as well as particular issues about bisexuality.

We have used the terms gay, lesbian and bisexual to refer to people who use these words to describe themselves. We recognise that such terms are inadequate and over-defining.

In this chapter we hope to:

- distinguish issues that are specific to bisexual psychology;
- explore definitions of bisexuality, how a person may come to identify as bisexual, and how this differs from identifying as lesbian or gay;
- look at some of the psychological consequences of embracing such an identity (or of showing what may be construed as 'bisexual behaviour');
- outline some issues for therapists and counsellors to consider;
- give examples of issues clients may bring to therapy;
- give examples of helpful and unhelpful practice;
- suggest guidelines for good practice.

Definitions

There are many ways of conceptualising bisexuality. An initial temptation
was to come up with a narrow definition in order to aid clearer discussion
and avoid some of the confusion that often seems to surround this term.
Instead we have chosen to give an idea of the range and some of the difficulties inherent in trying to pin down meaning when the subject is amorphous and shifting. We recognise that the discussion can only be limited in
the space available and that many other ways of thinking about bisexuality
would be possible.

Sue George, in *Women and Bisexuality*, states: 'For me ... women who
change their sexuality from completely heterosexual to completely lesbian
(or vice versa, or back and forth) are not necessarily bisexual, as according
to my definition, to be bisexual means always consciously feeling some desire
for one sex when loving the other' (George 1993: 58).

In 1979 Gore Vidal wrote in *Playboy*:

> There is no such thing as a homosexual person, any more than there
> is such a thing as a heterosexual person. The words are adjectives,
> describing sexual acts, not people ... Many human beings enjoy sexual
> relations with people of their own sex, many don't; many respond to
> both. The plurality is the fact of our nature and not worth worrying
> about.
>
> (Vidal 1993: 550)

Marjorie Garber, author of *Vice Versa*, comments:

> Gore Vidal's distinction between essence and practice points up yet
> another paradox in the definition and discussion of bisexuality. Is it
> the potential to have sexual feelings for members of both sexes? Or the
> acting, or the sex itself? This explains why statistics about bisexuals
> vary so spectacularly, from the 10 per cent of an *Essence* magazine poll
> (based on people who called themselves bisexual) to the original Kinsey
> report's figure of 15 per cent (for both men and women) to bisexual
> activist Maggi Rubinstein's whopping 80 per cent, a figure she deduces
> from the number of people who've had, or say they've had, same-sex
> fantasies, feelings, or dreams.
>
> (Garber 1995: 249)

Lucius and Allen (1993: 2), exploring theory, write that recent research
poses 'a serious challenge to traditional and limited views of bisexuality'.
One finding of particular interest is that for some bisexuals at least, gender
may not be a defining factor in determining sexual attraction or the choice
of sexual partner. For some people it seems that personality and social and
physical characteristics unrelated to gender might govern the choice of sexual

partner (Ross and Paul 1992). This strengthens the argument that bisexuality is a distinct form of sexual orientation that cannot be understood within the framework of purely biological or gender-specific conceptions of sexuality. Ross and Paul propose an alternative to the Kinsey model (Kinsey *et al.* 1947). They place 'homosexuality and heterosexuality at one end of a continuum as gender-linked choices of sexual partner, and bisexuality at the other as non-gender specific' (Ross and Paul 1992: 1).

It has been interesting in writing this to realise that, as two women who identify as bisexual, we have very different views on how we come to define ourselves in this way, what it means to us, and our experience of bisexuality. For one of the authors, Sue George's definition (i.e. feeling a 'pull' towards both sexes) most closely approaches the reality; for the other, it is not about the choice of a partner of a particular sex, or about feeling a pull towards both sexes, but purely based on attraction to a particular individual who could be of either sex.

There are a number of ideas and theories about bisexuality put across by Freud throughout his career, some of which appear to conflict. He made a massive contribution, in the case of Little Hans, (Freud 1909) to the establishment of bisexuality as the norm in infancy and seeing the child as gradually conscripted into the rigid norms of heterogenital sex. He made a distinction between 'genital', (i.e. biological) sex characteristics and 'sexual', in which he noted the influence of social constructions of gender. In relation to sexual development, Freud observed that every individual shows both masculine and feminine character traits and that masculinity and femininity do not exist in a pure or biological sense.

In *An Autobiographical Study* (1986: 222) Freud refers to homosexuality being 'traced back to the constitutional bisexuality of all human beings'. He referred to bisexuality to describe the two-sided nature of both sexes. He also wrote that bisexuality is an 'immature' or transitional developmental stage through which adults should pass in order to move on to a full and adult (i.e. heterosexual) expression of sexuality.

For Kinsey, bisexuality is acknowledged as a stable and enduring orientation. However, he viewed it as the midpoint of a continuum with exclusive homosexuality at one end and exclusive heterosexuality at the other (see Kinsey *et al.* 1947).

The consequence of these ideas has been that bisexuality has, in a sense, been marginalised. It has rarely been studied as a potentially different and informative form of human sexuality. Instead it has been largely regarded as a state of indecision occupying a position between heterosexuality and homosexuality. When bisexuality is seen as existing only within the framework of the latter categories it becomes invisible. In other words, a person who identifies as bisexual is reduced to a person who must have a 'heterosexual side' and a 'homosexual side'. There is no recognition of the potentially unique quality of the bisexual experience.

In *Pink Therapy* there is a helpful discussion with reference to 'biphobia' and the ways in which sexuality is perceived (Davies 1996: 42, 53). This, however, also suggests that biphobia involves people objecting to 'one side' of the bisexual person's sexuality – heterosexuals to the homosexual part and homosexuals to the heterosexual part.

Bisexuality is also rendered invisible when the label 'bisexual' is tacked onto the end of any gay and lesbian issue; it then becomes just another aspect of homosexuality. We need to recognise that while there are points of contact with homosexuality, there may also be important differences. Supporting each other as people of different sexualities fighting common oppressions does not mean that we have to make ourselves into a falsely homogeneous group. If we do this we give up the possibility of learning from our differences and enriching our experience. Similar issues around integration, assimilation and integrity characterised the anti-sexist, anti-racist developments in this century.

Another approach people sometimes take is to say 'we're all bisexual really', making what they intend as a well-meaning comment. However, as Sketchley (1989: 244) points out:

> this over-simplification dismisses the problems as simple and unimport-ant. To state 'you have the best of both worlds' fails to understand the two separate worlds: bisexuals cannot easily reveal their heterosexual interests in the gay world, even less can they reveal their homosexual interests in the heterosexual world. Thus they may feel trapped in two separate closets.

Klein (1993: 43) makes a similar point: 'both the heterosexual and homo-sexual view him or her [the bisexual] as suspect, not a fully paid up member but as someone whose allegiance is with the other group'.

Our personal experience and discussion with others leads us to suggest that there is often an additional type of prejudice in operation against a bisexual person's potential to have relationships with a man or a woman. It seems that here it is the person's bisexuality *per se* that is objected to, not just particular aspects of it. Examples of such experiences follow.

Psychological consequences and possible difficulties of living as a bisexual

The assumptions and stereotypes of others will influence many of the experiences of people who see themselves as bisexual. Negative stereotypes are many and wide-ranging and are discussed more fully elsewhere (e.g. Sumpter Forman 1991; Blasingame 1992; Udis-Kessler 1996). Bisexuals will have to regularly confront and deal with these ideas in their inner and outer worlds. One belief held by some is that to be bisexual means being unsettled. As one client put it, 'I'm destined to be unhappy as a result'. Another example is the view that bisexuality is linked with the transmission of the HIV virus from the 'gay community' to the 'heterosexual community': 'I don't find any difficulty accepting homosexuality or heterosexuality, but I have great problems with bisexuality, and the transmission of AIDS to women worries me greatly' (Blunkett 1994: 15).

One of the authors recently saw two new individual male clients who had been happy to see themselves as 'bi' in the 1980s but were now finding it much more problematic because of their experiences of increased stigma in the wider society. We will refer back to this, and explore possible ways of dealing with similar client issues, in the section on helpful and unhelpful practice (see pp. 125–6).

For some, bisexuality may be a transitional state on the way to identification as gay or straight. For others though, it may be a position reached after a period of identifying differently, based on a belief that this represents a 'better fit' with their sexuality and selfhood. As stated elsewhere, this is not necessarily based on significant differences in behaviour from those identifying differently. For some, 'coming out' as bisexual may represent their second coming out, after a previous identification as lesbian or gay. Describing yourself as bisexual may be important in terms of personal identity, but confusing, alienating or even threatening to those around, involving subtle shifts of alliance.

Acceptance or approval of you as a bisexual person may depend more specifically on the sex of your partner. One of the authors has experienced her mother talking animatedly, openly and at length with neighbours and friends about her daughter's male partner, having been totally silent about her female partner, even though this was a very significant live-in relationship that lasted many years: 'This put me in a very difficult position – I want my partner to be accepted, so I am pleased that my mother accepts him, but I don't want her to implicitly or subtly deny the importance of my previous long-standing relationship with a woman. This is denying a part of me'. Conversely, certain lesbian friends quickly or more gradually drifted away following the author's move to a male partner: this included people who had been very good, close and supportive friends and who had known about, and apparently accepted, the author's bisexuality – in theory at least.

As a result of prejudice towards bisexuality, bisexuals who are still exploring and making sense of their sexuality may find that they have to present themselves to the world as more self-assured and certain than they really are: this may increase feelings of alienation. Bisexuals may feel that they have to defend their corner fiercely against attack from *monosexuals* (by monosexuals we mean people who are exclusively heterosexual or homosexual). Similarly, a bisexual person may have to be more insistent about their identity as, even if the individual's self-image is relatively robust and stable, other people's 'placing' of them may depend largely on the gender of their current partner(s). For example, monosexual friends may choose to see you as gay if you are in a relationship with someone of the same sex, but heterosexual if you have a partner of the opposite sex. Others (e.g. parents) may more readily accept a bisexual label as it is seen as a 'softer' option and keeps you with one foot apparently in the 'normal' camp. It then becomes another way of denying the reality of the individual's experience and the significance of a same-sex relationship, so that this apparent acceptance feels tainted: 'My mother talked about my female partner in a denigrating way – "you're bisexual but she's a real lesbian" – as if being bisexual was obviously better. I found this very offensive and immediately felt driven to downgrade the significance of my feelings towards men' (quotes in this section come from bisexual women of our acquaintance in informal interviews).

Many people choose to restrict their friendships and socialising to homogeneous groups, based on factors such as race, class, religion and sexuality. Many lesbians choose to severely restrict their contact with men:

> As a bisexual woman with a lesbian partner who did not want to mix with men at all, I found socialising exclusively with women ultimately unsatisfying and uncomfortable. I missed having men around and it felt like a part of my reality was missing. However, it was really difficult to acknowledge this as I felt lucky to be accepted by lesbians at all and did not want to rock the boat.

Similarly, for some bisexuals, being in an all-gay or all-straight environment may be uncomfortable and there may be a psychological need to bridge the two worlds.

One of the accusations often made against bisexuals with opposite-sex partners is that of 'heterosexual privilege' – that they can 'pass' in straight society. Yet having incorrect assumptions made about you is as uncomfortable for bisexuals as anyone else. We often do not want to 'pass' but may feel pressure to conform to whichever group predominates. The difficulties of this were well expressed by Naomi Tucker (1996: 33), a Jewish woman writing in *Bisexual Horizons*:

> These experiences of passing – allowing my lesbian friends to assume I'd given up men, allowing my political friends to forget I was Jewish or assume it didn't matter – always involved the painful suppression of some aspect of my identity . . . When I 'pass' as the norm for whatever group I might be in, I give up personal integrity, honesty with myself and the world.

Some bisexuals may feel perfectly comfortable 'placing' themselves according to their current relationship and living within a gay or straight world. However, for others this can be at a considerable psychological price, involving denying a part of oneself for fear of being unacceptable, an outsider and not a 'real' member of the group. Biphobia can lead to there being relatively few places where an individual can feel totally at home and able to bring all parts. It may also lead to a feeling of living a lie. Daring to be out and different may jeopardise the only available source of support (i.e. gay and lesbian groups) in many parts of the country. One of us was asked to leave such a group following a change to an opposite-sex partner, despite having been out as bisexual within the group for some considerable time and an active member for seven years.

One person attending a lesbian and gay group reported that when the subject of bisexuality was broached a decision was made to exclude bisexuals from the group. One of the members proclaimed, 'Why should we include bisexuals? They never attend meetings anyway'. This was a sure way of shutting up all the bisexuals at the meeting – it would have taken a very brave soul to speak up in this context! It seems likely that any bisexual person attending would make the decision that the group was not for them, or continue to attend meetings but not raise the issue unless there appeared to be support. Although there are bisexual groups these are relatively few and bisexuals may still feel very isolated. We hope the reasons for this are apparent from the discussion so far.

Visibility is increasing but there is still relatively little information or discussion about bisexuality. When articles do appear in the popular press it is still often with a frivolous or 'fashionable' tag, and a voyeuristic feel. This presentation may add to the impression that there are 'really' only two legitimate choices – gay or straight. There has recently been a move in the media towards a more positive view of 'gay' lifestyles and sexualities – this does not seem to have permeated through to bisexuality yet, but we live in hope!

As this book is about therapeutic issues we have tended to focus on difficulties or possible negative aspects of being bisexual, as these are most likely to be brought to therapy. As a result, there is a danger that the discussion gives an overly gloomy picture of most people's experience. As with other sexualities and identities, there are many joys and positive aspects to a bisexual identity. The amorphous and fluid nature of the term for some may enhance a feeling of freedom and self-definition. There may be a real feeling of richness in having the potential to bridge what are often seen as very separate gay and straight worlds, and in having the possibility of intimate relationships with either sex: 'Although being bisexual has sometimes been confusing or painful for me, it is not something that I would want to change. It is an integral part of my experience and has enriched my life enormously and given me the opportunity to feel connected to others in many different ways'.

In our own lives we have had many examples of being well supported and accepted by both gay and straight people and of them working to overcome prejudice against bisexuals:

My lesbian partner always accepted me for who I was and respected the ways in which I was different from her. She encouraged me to be myself and knew that my bisexual identity was important to me. She was always supportive of my need to explore my sexuality even when this was painful for her, and she helped me confront and reject my own internalised prejudices about what it meant to be bisexual.

Issues that clients are most likely to bring to therapy

People who are likely to come to therapy may include:

- Those who are 'confused' about their sexuality and not sure what they want, or where to 'place' themselves.
- People who are clear about the bisexual nature of their feelings or experience and are uncomfortable about this and not sure whether they can accept it. They may be wrestling with internalised and unhelpful stereotypes about what it means to be bisexual.
- People who are clear about their bisexuality and comfortable with their identity who are working through what it means to their family and others.
- Those who are feeling rejected or isolated because of their sexuality.
- Individuals in a stable relationship that was previously satisfying but who now feel a pull towards relationships elsewhere. In our clinical experience this has most often been seen in men in long-term relationships with women, who have become increasingly attracted to men. They may be confused and concerned to maintain their existing relationships, but needing to explore boundaries, feelings and options. There is also another group comprising women whose children are grown up and who develop an attraction for a woman when they have previously been in heterosexual relationships.
- Those trying to fit themselves into the most convenient 'box' who have been denying their feelings or not found satisfactory ways of dealing with them. They are likely to attend with a different presenting problem.
- Individuals who may have already had therapy elsewhere but who have not found what they wanted – they have felt that options were closed down for them or that the practitioners' views were too rigid.

Case example 1

An experienced clinical psychologist was referring-on a client for further 'expert' help. He described the client (who was exploring his sexuality and trying to make sense of his experiences and feelings to a point of resolution) as 'wanting to have his cake and eat it'. This comment was made to a colleague he knew to be bisexual – indeed, who had been chosen as appropriate to see the client for this very reason.

Case example 2

Another client attended in the middle of a crisis concerning his personal identity and marriage. He had been happily married for some years and had recently started having occasional sexual relationships with men. He had assumed his wife knew about his sexuality and casually referred to the situation and his bisexuality. His wife had in fact not known and her shocked reaction brought things to a head. He had previously seen another therapist who had talked about his attraction to men being like a room in his house that he must not go into. He reported feeling depressed and unsure about whether he could achieve this and what the future held. The second therapist saw things quite differently, feeling that this 'room' was an important part of the client that needed to be incorporated into the rest of his identity in order for him to feel whole. His feelings needed to be acknowledged at least, not split off as unacceptable or dangerous. Allowing himself to think about things did not mean that he would automatically choose to act upon his sexual feelings by pursuing relationships with men. If he did feel the need to do this, many other issues would need to be taken into account in therapy.

Case example 3

A further example we came across concerned a bisexual woman who started therapy with a counsellor who had undergone two years of training in human sexuality. The client's experience was that any issue she brought to the counsellor was seen through the filter of her sexuality as if nothing else in her life or personality was of any importance, so that in the end she felt as if she was in a psychological strait-jacket.

Case example 4

One of our clients was affected by increased stigma in recent years. As a consequence he was working through the question: 'Is it still OK for me to have these feelings?' Perhaps part of this was to test out with the therapist the question 'Will you see me differently if I reveal this part of myself?' (Incidentally, the therapist's sexual orientation was unknown to this client.) The journey of the therapy involved many different aspects of the client's life, and sexual orientation was only a part. However, for the therapy to progress it was important that there was a space where the subject of sexuality could be explored in as open a way as possible, without the imposition of any fixed thoughts or beliefs.

Case example 5

We know a woman who specifically chose to visit a gay therapist. She told him she was bisexual as part of giving him background information about herself – she was happy with her sexuality and did not see it as a problem. The therapist told her that he believed that there was really no such thing as bisexuality and that it represented a transition point only; it was a sign of confusion and showed that someone did not yet know where his or her true sexuality lay.

Case example 6

Another client described her experience and feelings and her resulting confusion to a therapist who said, 'It sounds as if you're bisexual'. The woman in this case found this helpful and liberating, so it was obviously an appropriate intervention for this client. It gave her another possible way of thinking about herself and the therapist was 'giving permission' for the client to consider bisexuality as an option. However, it occurred to us that in other circumstances this suggestion could feel very confining or frightening, as it might have closed down options too soon and not left room for the client to explore her thoughts, feelings and ideas about *her experiences* within the safety of the therapeutic relationship. It would have been more appropriate for the therapist to encourage the client to examine her confusion and open up the discussion by giving information about different perspectives on sexuality. Bisexuality might have then been explored as one of a range of possible ways of making sense of the client's experience.

Issues for therapists and counsellors

Research on homosexuality has shown that up to '50% of gay clients have reported discontent with their professional counselling experiences, with an average rate of dissatisfaction of approximately 40%, a rate exceeding that usually reported by heterosexual clients' (Rudolph 1988: 166). Research conducted by PACE (Project for Advice, Counselling and Education) (McFarlane 1998) seems to suggest a similar level of dissatisfaction. It seems likely that these figures would also hold true for bisexual clients.

The authors attended three meetings of a professional organisation which focused on issues of sexual orientation and espoused a philosophy of encouraging gay affirmative therapy. The organisation had also made a clear stand on wanting to include discussion and study of bisexuality within its remit, and on encouraging bisexuals among its membership. During the course of these meetings a number of events that were oppressive to bisexuals occurred, as follows:

- A group facilitator said that he had assumed all the men at his workshop would be gay, and was shocked when a bisexual man attended.
- Someone tried to silence particular people or views in a debate by asking about their gay credentials ('Are you gay enough to be listened to?').
- A woman commented, 'I used to identify as bisexual, but it's easier to identify as lesbian'.
- Bisexuality was dismissed in a discussion about homophobia on training courses.
- A trainer in equality issues and anti-oppressive practice continually missed out 'bisexual' from the title of the organisation and, when challenged on this, said, 'I'm used to the old days'.

Although there may be an assumption that lesbian- and gay-identified therapists are better equipped than heterosexual ones to work with clients expressing confusion or exploring ideas around bisexuality, our experience suggests that this may not be the case. Sexual orientation alone does not ensure an open, questioning attitude or professional competence to work on these issues. (See Neal and Davies' Introduction to this volume.)

In order for counsellors and psychotherapists to adequately address the needs and concerns of the growing number of people 'for whom the middle range of the sexual continuum is a reality', it will be important to look beyond the 'two dichotomised monolithic extremes' of sexual orientation (Lourea 1985: 51).

Guidelines for good practice

We feel strongly that good therapeutic practice in the area of bisexuality should be the same as good practice with other client issues. Principles of good practice are universal!

Although a person may come to us with issues around their sexual orientation, this is not all that they come with. Each person is unique, with their own unique experience of their sexuality. We are much more than a collection of adjectives – woman, bisexual, Buddhist, middle class, African-Caribbean, etc. As Charles Neal (1997) suggests, echoing Gore Vidal:

> We're not things. Like every other natural organism, we're in a constant process of change and growth, so are our social groups and the meanings we generate. We use adjectives as if they were nouns, to name

things and fix them and then sort them into different classes because we feel we've got them under better control.

Our own guidelines for good practice include:

- Consider your own sexuality and the potential for fluidity within this.
- Examine your own attitudes towards sexuality.
- Be well informed and familiarise yourself with the likely issues, discussions and prejudices clients may encounter.
- Respect the client's experience and individuality.
- Respect the client's views even if they are different from yours. Seek information, help the client explore meanings and encourage an exploratory, open attitude.
- Be open to a wide range of views and possibilities.
- Do not become over-focused on one issue or 'label'.
- Accept that bisexuality exists as a valid identity rather than merely a transition point.
- Encourage the person to celebrate the unique aspects of their experience and identity.

References

Blasingame, B.M. (1992) The roots of biphobia: racism and internalized heterosexism, in E.R. Weise (ed.) *Closer to Home: Bisexuality and Feminism*. Seattle, WA: Seal Press.

Blunkett, D. (1994) I made the right decision, *The Pink Paper*, 18 March: 15.

Davies, D. (1996) Homophobia and heterosexism, in D. Davies and C. Neal (eds) *Pink Therapy: A Guide for Counsellors and Therapists Working with Lesbian, Gay and Bisexual Clients*. Buckingham: Open University Press.

Freud, S. (1925) Analysis of a phobia in a five-year-old boy, in L. Woolf and V. Woolf (eds) *Collected Papers, Vol. 3. Case Histories*. London: Hogarth Press.

Freud, S. (1986) *Historical and Expository Works on Psychoanalysis*. Harmondsworth: Penguin.

Garber, M. (1995) *Vice Versa*. London: Hamish Hamilton.

George, S. (1993) *Women and Bisexuality*. London: Scarlet Press.

Kinsey, A.C., Pomeroy, W.B. and Martin, C.E. (1947) *Sexual Behaviour in the Human Male*. Philadelphia, PA: W.B. Saunders.

Klein, F. (1993) *The Bisexual Option*. New York: Harrington Park Press.

Lourea, D.N. (1985) Psychosocial issues related to counselling bisexuals. *Journal of Homosexuality*, Special Issue, *Bisexualities: Theory and Research*, 11(1–2): 51–62.

Lucius, C. and Allen, J. (1993) 'Bisexuality and counsellor training; a study of attitudes and beliefs', unpublished paper.

McFarlane, L. (1998) *Diagnosis: Homophobic. The Experiences of Lesbians, Gay Men and Bisexuals in Mental Health Services*. London: PACE.

Neal, C. (1997) *Queer therapy, past and future*. Keynote speech presented to the Annual Training Conference of the Association of Lesbian Gay and Bisexual Psychologies UK, Nottingham, 1 November.

Ross, M.W. and Paul, J.P. (1992) Beyond gender: the basis of sexual attraction in bisexual men and women. *Psychological Reports*, 3(2): 71.

Rudolph, J. (1988) Counsellors' attitudes towards homosexuality: a selective review of the literature. *Journal of Counseling Development*, 67(3): 165–8.

Sketchley, J. (1989) Counselling and sexual orientation, in W. Dryden, D. Charles-Edwards and R. Woolfe (eds) *Handbook of Counselling in Britain*. London: Routledge.

Sumpter Forman, S. (1991) Myths/realities of bisexuality, in L. Hutchins and L. Kaahumanu (eds) *Bi Any Other Name*. Boston, MA: Alyson Publications.

Tucker, N. (1996) Passing: pain or privilege? What the bisexual community can learn from the Jewish experience, in S. Rose, C. Stevens, Z. Parr *et al.* (eds) *Bisexual Horizons*. London: Lawrence & Wishart.

Udis-Kessler, A. (1996) Challenging the stereotypes, in S. Rose, C. Stevens, Z. Parr *et al.* (eds) *Bisexual Horizons*. London: Lawrence & Wishart.

Vidal, G. (1993) Sex is politics, in *United States: Essays 1952–1992*. New York: Random House.

Working with people who have been sexually abused in childhood

Introduction

In this chapter I want to do two things: first, set the context in which people from sexual minorities who have been sexually abused live, and second look at how we, as counsellors and therapists, work with them. People do not exist in a vacuum, but sometimes learning about the complexity of their context, particularly that which is out of our own experience, seems so full of effort that we may push it aside and say 'Well, I can't know about everything'. In order to be able to work with someone with full, honest empathy we have to know at least some of their external world as well as their internal truth. What we *imagine* we know is also important because it influences our thinking and belief systems and thus has a direct bearing on how we relate to our clients.

There is a plethora of books on sexual abuse, mainly about hetero-sexual women abused by heterosexual men (Spring 1987; Bass and Davis 1988; Gil 1988; Blume 1991; Sanford 1991; Walker 1992; Herman 1994). For books on men being abused (Lew 1990; McMullen 1990; Gonsiorek *et al.* 1994), the experience of being abused as a black person (Angelou 1971; Wilson 1993; Fontes 1995) or a disabled person (Kennedy 1996; Westcott and Cross 1996), on women abusing (Elliot 1993) or on ritualised or satanic abuse (Sinason 1994; Gomez 1995), resources are limited. It is even more difficult to find something on the experience of dealing with the aftermath of abuse as someone from a sexual minority group. Isensee (1997), Fontes (1995), and Queer Press Collective (1991) are three worth pursuing but generally the issue tends to be treated as an 'also ran' if mentioned at all.

History

There is reference to the sexual abuse of children by older men in Greece and Rome in ancient times when it was often seen as a part of growing up (Corby 1993: 13). Some have seen this as proof of the sexual freedom of the age. It seems to have less to do with eroticism than the power that abuse offers the perpetrator; men exercised their power over women, children, servants, slaves and other men of lower status. Pederasty on a boy of 'citizen status' was ostensibly a criminal offence in ancient Rome. In other words, it was not the abuse that was important but the status of the victim. Corby tells us that there is little information about sexual abuse in the Middle Ages. Incest was punishable by death in 1757 in Scotland, and Europe had strong social and religious taboos which may account for the lack of legislation.

In the UK in the 1880s the London Society for the Protection of Children, during its first year of operation, dealt with 95 cases described as involving domestic victims. Twelve of these concerned 'an evil which is altogether too unmentionable' (Corby 1993: 20). In a nation of animal lovers where the Prevention of Cruelty to Animals Act came into being in 1822, the Prevention of Cruelty to Children Act had to wait another 67 years. The statistics regarding people who have been sexually abused in childhood vary widely depending on whom you read, from one in three (Herman 1994: 30) to more conservative estimates.

Definitions

Statistics depend on what particular authors regard as abuse: some rely on contact abuse only; others take into account non-contact abuse such as indecent exposure, obscene phone calls and inappropriate sexual language. There are a variety of definitions and many authors describe their own working model. Sue Blume (1991: 1) tells us of the traditional, dictionary and clearly unhelpful definition of incest as 'Sexual intercourse between two persons too closely related to marry legally'. Kempe and Kempe's classic *Child Abuse* (1978: 60) has the following definition: 'Sexual abuse is defined as the involvement of dependent, developmentally immature children and adolescents in sexual activities that they do not fully comprehend, to which they are unable to give informed consent, or that violate the social taboos of family roles'. Although it has been criticised for focusing on the child and not mentioning the abuser's power (Kennedy 1996), I find this definition useful as it takes into account the child's development as opposed to what an adult may see as acceptable. This is important for people from sexual minorities, particularly those young gay men who can be pathologised for what some may believe is having sex 'too early'.

All counsellors or therapists need to work on where they stand on what they define as 'child sexual abuse', where the line is between what they see as 'normal' sexual practices and what not, and what they find difficult about sexual behaviours they may not enjoy or engage in.

'Normal' sex is between consenting 'adults'. 'Adults' need to be defined, depending on your assessment of a young person's maturity (Bond 1993; Jenkins 1997) and your country's laws. Is an adult a person who is 18 or over – i.e. someone who can vote? Or does a person normally defined as a minor become an adult at 16 (UK) in order to be able to consent to sex? Gay men in the UK at the time of writing are deemed incapable of making such a decision until the age of 18 (reduced from 21 in 1994). This links to the given wisdom that homosexuality is an immature sexuality: once they mature they will 'become' heterosexual! Curiously, young women between the ages of 16 and 18 are not deemed to need the same protection.

Yet young people mature at different rates, so we must beware of using any particular age as a yardstick to measure abuse, and remain open to hearing clients' experience, especially when it differs radically from our own cultural knowledge and tolerance.

Political context

There is a political framework for working with survivors of child sexual assault. Until recently the main protagonists have been feminists who taught us important lessons about power and powerlessness and how the favoured portrayal of victims assaulted by monsters does not take into account that most assaults happen within the home. An unfortunate fallout of this approach is that it deals mainly with men abusing female children and we are only just beginning to take on board the seriousness and extent of the abuse of male children (Lew 1990; Gonsiorek 1994a) and of women abusing (Elliott 1993). Many organisations in the UK that work with people who have been sexually abused only work with women. Rape crisis groups that want to work with male survivors have found opposition to this idea is such that they have had to separate from the Rape Crisis Federation. The Federation's remit is women working with women 'from a women's per- spective and not from a gender neutral perspective' (Rape Crisis Federation 1997). They direct male callers to male survivors groups, which are few and far between (although growing in number), and they acknowledge the need for more services. These groups have helped many men: however, some male survivors have found the treatment they received from women working in abuse or rape organisations patronising and hostile. We need to say more than simply 'men are abusers and women are their victims', without losing sight of the fact that this is often true. Children of whichever gender need to be protected from perpetrators of abuse of whatever gender. Maybe it is time for us to integrate, to look at the issue of abuse as a whole rather than separating men who have been abused from women who have been abused, men who abuse from women who abuse. There are differences that need acknowledgement but there are also many similarities. It is up to clients to decide what their requirements are: some may want women-only or men-only counselling environments in order to feel safe enough to start the work.

Myths

In the late 1970s in the UK I was working with children in care, some of whom had been sexually abused. The professionals dealing with them were only timidly airing the subject. In 1986 the *Child Watch* programme burst onto TV screens bringing child sexual assault into the public arena. The backlash came some years later with an ongoing tirade of recovered memories, and paedophiles being perceived as being mentally ill monsters outside the family. It is still difficult to accept the pervasiveness of sexual abuse and even more difficult to believe that the aftermath is long-lasting, painful and difficult to heal. For the general public to think of someone being sexually abused and lesbian, gay, transgender or bisexual as well seems too much. We try not to think about sexual abuse at all. It is understandable: we need to protect ourselves from pain. In order to deal with things that do not make sense to us we create myths that become 'facts'. The myth that is relevant here is of those from sexual minorities being 'that way' because they were sexually abused as children.

Another issue horribly muddled in the minds of many is that paedophilia and (homo)sexual orientation are linked. Given the myth of homosexuality being an immature sexuality one can see how they might become so. In fact, 95 per cent of sexual abuse of children is by heterosexuals (Davies 1996a), whether the child is male or female.

The increased profile of sexual abuse has had a number of effects. People are perplexed and ask, 'Is there more of it than there was?' Parents, particularly fathers, worry about how they are with children. Might the rough and tumble enjoyed be seen as abusive, sexual in nature? If a parent delights in their baby's penis does it mean they are perverted? Teachers are told not to put sunscreen on children because of possible allegations of abuse. People ask whether victims are imagining it. They hear persuasive arguments that recovered memories are in the minds of therapists and not their clients. When the facts can no longer be denied people minimise the harm caused. Judges in rape trials have made public statements declaring that the victim suffered no distress. People still believe that children forget, and that they'll get over it given nothing more than time.

A variety of ideas influence our thinking – ideas that have become part of folklore – and we may not even be aware that we know them. I would like to look at three that are relevant when we are working with lesbian, gay or bisexual people who have been sexually abused in childhood:

- Ideas about how people become lesbian, gay, bisexual or transgender.
- The theory around the sexual abuse of children.
- Ideas that link sexual abuse to sexual orientation.

Ideas about how people become lesbian, gay, transgender or bisexual

Davies and Neal (1996) summarised the history of debates on 'causes' of sexual minority orientations. The dominant narrative seems to be overprotective mothers and emotionally distant fathers, particularly for gay men. The idea that emotionally unstable mothers and cold, rejecting fathers 'make' their children develop a minority sexual orientation has been described as being 'deeply embedded in therapists' thinking in all schools and needs to be challenged' (Samuels 1997). Samuels argues that the response to finding out that their child is not heterosexual could be that the mother, understanding what difficulties may lie ahead for her child, becomes protective and, to show that her love has not diminished, may 'over love'. The father may well deal with it, as many men have learned to deal with emotions they find difficult, by withdrawing and becoming distant. The description could thus be a reaction to the news, rather than a cause of it.

With more people being 'out and proud', the heterosexual community wonders if there is more homosexuality about. Heterosexual parents of children of minority sexuality wonder if they 'caused' it by bad parenting, or think that it is due to mixing with the wrong sort. They may hope that it is a phase and that the safety of the heterosexual life will resume before long.

Sexual orientation is often defined exclusively by sexual coupling. Defining oneself is about more than just sex, and each person's identity is different. The question needs to be: 'What does it mean for you to be lesbian, gay or bisexual?' rather than the therapist trying to give the impression 'I'm cool with this' and misunderstanding the issues or believing that sexual difficulty may be due to being in the 'wrong' sexual orientation.

Case example 1

Karen, who had been sexually abused as a child, had been living with her male partner for five years and was experiencing flashbacks and fear while attempting to make love. After two years' work with a heterosexual counsellor there was little improvement and the counsellor wondered aloud whether Karen was a lesbian. Despite Karen's stated discomfort this became the counsellor's focus and Karen eventually moved to another therapist who worked with her to find her own insights rather than prescribe them.

One of the reasons that the false memory debate still rages is that too many counsellors follow their own agenda, determined to find both a reason and a solution to a problem presented that they find intolerable. In this case the counsellor felt that Karen must be a lesbian as her difficulties had been so pronounced for so long. Crudely, the counsellor was defining a lesbian purely as someone who does not enjoy having sex with a man. Whether Karen is a lesbian or not is irrelevant here: she was trying to deal with her sexual difficulties, not her sexual identity. Such a response was a violation of Karen's boundaries. She did not feel the issue was about being a lesbian but was coerced to spend money listening to the counsellor discussing it. This time, as an adult, she found the strength to leave.

The theory around the sexual abuse of children

Gonsiorek (1994b) critiques current models of thinking about sexual abuse, separating them into four: feminist, psychoanalytic, pro-family and pro-paedophile. He includes a thought-provoking discussion on feminist theory where he honours feminists for the work they did to bring sexual abuse of children into the mainstream. However, he sees the focus on male power over female victims as insufficient for dealing with the realities of male victims and female perpetrators. Gonsiorek views *psychoanalytic models* as minimising sexual abuse as part of Freud's legacy of retraction of understanding that patients were being abused by their fathers, and says that the strength of such models lies in dealing with early history, usually prior to abuse.

Analytic models could be misunderstood by looking at infantile sexuality: an approach uncomfortably close to the pro-paedophile model in that it encourages an understanding of a child's sexual being. However, most post-Freudian analytic therapists would be horrified to be thought of as less than serious about child sexual abuse and an understanding of sexuality is very different to acting on it and using it, and the child, for one's own purpose.

In the *pro-family model* the rights of the family are seen as sacrosanct and therefore intra-familial sexual abuse is denied or minimised. (For a discussion on this in the Cleveland Case where, in 1987, 121 children were taken into care suspected of having been sexually abused, see Campbell 1988.) Sexual abuse, which occurs outside the family and is perpetrated by men, who are presumed to be homosexual, is conceived as a threat by running contrary to the correct order – that of heterosexual family life and the unquestionable masculinity of the head of the family (Gonsiorek 1994b).

The *pro-paedophile model* defends the rights of children to be sexual with adults rather than with each other and denies the trauma caused to the child by sexual abuse (Gonsiorek 1994b). The Paedophile Information

Exchange (PIE) had a saying 'Sex before eight, else it's too late' (origin unknown). The organisation disappeared: nevertheless there is information that organised paedophilia is currently very strong. One might argue that re-releasing films such as *Lolita* brings paedophilia into the mainstream by the acceptable 'art' route. While working on a telephone helpline I overheard a woman talking to a 13-year-old girl who was confused because she was in love, and having a sexual relationship, with her teacher. This child was told that if she told people about their 'affair' she would wreck her teacher's career. We can throw our hands up in horror and wonder what this woman was thinking of: we also need to consider where the idea develops that the adult male is more important than the child.

These theories have certainly affected me. As a social worker I was immersed in ideas of the inevitability of the cycle of abuse and I felt relief when feminist writing spoke some of the truth that I saw in my work. As the image of strong women embracing gravity and burning their bras came into being, feminism also brought the fact of sexual abuse of children to light. Women's resulting assertiveness lasted much longer than the mythical demise of the bra. The movement was necessarily more vehement than some wanted in order to upset the patriarchal boat. Balance is what we need now in looking at abuse as more than male power and domination over females.

Ideas that link sexual abuse to sexual orientation

If, as therapists we have introjected the idea that sexual abuse and sexual orientation are linked then our sexual minority clients have a fight on their hands to be seen as themselves and not people who have made 'neurotic' or 'damaged' decisions about whom they love. There is research into the question of whether lesbian, gay and bisexual people are more likely to have been abused than heterosexual people (Finkelhor 1984; Loulan 1987; Johnson 1993; Gonsiorek 1994c), but I think the question itself is interesting. Why is it posed? People are making the link between being of a minority sexuality and sexual abuse. My theory about this is that, having gone through a coming out process a person has had to reveal things normally kept from public scrutiny. Some people feel uninhibited about asking us personal questions they would not ask anyone else. Being 'out' in a heterosexual gathering often causes curious eyebrows to be raised and the inevitable question. The male driver asked a friend catching a taxi one evening: 'Doesn't your boyfriend mind you being out on your own?' She replied, 'I'm a lesbian'. Silence from the wheel of the cab, long glances in the mirror and finally: 'What do you do in bed?' 'If you don't know,' came the reply, 'your wife must have a very boring sex life!' At which point the taxi swerved across the road and not another word was spoken (Caldon 1989).

With the experience of having to be so open to 'come out', members of these groups who have been sexually abused may find it less difficult than heterosexual people to be public about the fact. It reminds me of Anne Robinson, who said 'If you have ever stood on a chair in front of 200 girls with your green knickers showing, reading out loud from a holy book – nothing truly daunts you after that' (Bennett and Forgan 1991: 157).

Society constructs the traumatic sexualisation of children and minority sexual orientation as intrinsically linked. Magazine stories, TV and film reinforce the idea that one causes the other and can add to what is already a confusing issue to deal with. As a survivor it can be very difficult to throw these myths off. A sexually abused 12-year-old boy I met as a social worker stated, 'I'm going to become homosexual and an abuser aren't I?' The idea of the cycle of abuse was so ingrained in social workers that I often wondered why they bothered to work with sexually abused children if they had no feeling of hope for them. If we pull out the simplicity of how we have constructed this, then we can get the following kind of logic:

- Women go with women because men have sexually abused them.
- Men go with men because they have been sexually abused by women and they hated it or by men and they loved it.
- All lesbians and gay men went to same-sex schools, probably boarding (where, it is believed, all young children are subjected to sexual initiation by the older ones).
- People who are bisexual or transgender are confused because they don't know whether they liked their abuse or hated it.

If we believe this, does it then follow that heterosexuals are 'made that way' because of same-gender abuse?

Practice issues

Models of abuse are seen from the point of view of the 'expert', whether activist, therapist or parent, and this focus mirrors the experience of many abused children who dare to disclose. A knee-jerk reaction by authorities leads to an unheard child. Those who remain silent may do so because they know chaos may erupt should they speak their truth. Add a child's growing awareness that their sexual orientation is different to what they see around them and you have the makings of someone in serious emotional turmoil. In working therapeutically with anyone who has been abused it is import-ant to allow them to tell their own story, from their own perspective, without changing their meaning. This may not be as simple as it sounds. Often people whose truth is one others do not want to hear, like coming out, like having been sexually abused, do not expect to be heard. Their way of telling their story can be muddled and incomplete. As they struggle to let you know what life has been like for them they may believe that you will not want to hear and, even if you say you do, that you are highly likely not to believe them. Remember that they have been conned by apparent empathy before. Abusers are adept at enticing their victims.

People come to therapy to work on their difficulties. This immediately puts them in a vulnerable and scary position where you could be yet another authority figure who abuses power. Therapists are taught to hear with more than just their ears. We do, however, need to listen to the client telling their story even when internal voices and alarm bells beckon. Working with people whose boundaries have been badly violated your insistence on working with your 'internal knowledge' can be received as another form of abuse. If you tell them your theories you could confuse sexually abused clients who are desperately trying to work out what their *own* truth really is. These are people who have had to be expert at hiding their feelings for years. You won't see when you've missed their feelings and may well be led to believe that all is well. There can be tiny clues: a heightening of colour or change in skin tone in neck and face; eyes becoming slightly out of focus; slight shifting of position or fidgeting; a sudden stillness; a sense of the client having 'switched off'. These are signs to note and to make you *think* about what you did before they happened – not necessarily to follow through with your client until your relationship is well established. It is their place of safety and exploration, not yours.

For some survivors it is very difficult to deal with their enjoyment of abuse, either because they received a form of attention that they were otherwise missing or because they were excited by the experience. Often they then believe that they caused or should have been able to stop it, as if the fact of their enjoyment made them culpable. The client's truth, as always, is important to be heard: the truth of the contact received, the truth of the titillation. Many counsellors fall into the trap of 'compassionately' declaring that it was not the client's fault, that they were only a child, a victim, that the powerful one was the abuser. All this is true and denies the curiosity, the experience of moving towards something that was exciting and dangerous:

> Being empathic is a process, an interaction between two persons whereby the empathising person continuously has the willingness to tune into the other person. This implies that the empathising person is willing to let go of his own feelings and views.
>
> (Vanaerschot 1993: 68)

Some people have not thought their experiences were abusive and later begin to realise that they were. Denial is a useful mechanism for keeping away pain. Once a good, solid and safe therapeutic relationship has been established your client will feel more able to explore areas kept well under wraps. Abuse is not a topic to be challenging about. If you think your client has been sexually abused keep it to yourself and discuss it in supervision, with someone who has a sound knowledge of working in this area. Our clients have a right to protect themselves from an area that is painful, exhausting and takes a long time to work through. Stay as a good therapist, not the/rapist, one of the reasons the false memory syndrome debate has not gone away is because there are counsellors and therapists who tell, or suggest to, their clients that they have been sexually abused.

Case example 2

Dan went to a hypnotherapist because he was not sleeping. The therapist told him his older cousin who had lived with them when Dan was a child had sexually abused him on 15 occasions. The therapist then told him to go away and forget about it, not to let it disturb his life. By the time Dan came to me he had confronted his cousin, telling him he had made him gay. The family had supported the cousin and told Dan he was no longer welcome. Dan was thoroughly confused. He had good memories of times with his cousin and had no memory of abuse or any feeling of fear or trepidation when thinking of him. It took a long time for Dan to be able to trust me enough to be able to come to grips with some of the conflicting messages he had received.

   Working with someone who identifies as lesbian, gay, transgender or bisexual has its own political context, which has much to do with power and powerlessness, being stigmatised, shunned and isolated. Coming out to family members and friends can be a traumatic time, where a person's truth can be disbelieved, ridiculed or treated as something disgusting. If a person has lived in a mainly heterosexual environment then there is no minority group 'family' to offer support. No one who can say: 'It's OK, you are not going mad, this is a confusing time when the people you love and thought loved you turn away from you'. No wonder 20 per cent of young people from these groups attempt suicide (see Davies 1996b and Chapter 10 for more detailed figures).

   There may be an assumption that once a person has chosen sexual partners of a different gender to the abuser they will enjoy sex. Not necessarily so. Many survivors manage to have an active, enjoyable sex life but many do not. In Johnson's (1993) research 77 per cent of the lesbians who had been abused in childhood avoided sex with their partner, 72 per cent in McGettingan's study quoted in Johnson (1993: 88).

Case example 3

Nina and Jo were having difficulties relating sexually. A male family friend had sexually abused Nina as a child and, working on this in individual therapy, she was finding her intimate relationship with Jo increasingly difficult. She had identified as lesbian for most of her adult life. Jo was angry that, while Nina had enjoyed sex at the beginning of their relationship she was now likely to cringe when Jo made a loving approach. Jo identified as bisexual, which Nina found threatening, believing Jo might leave her. Nina felt criticised and pathologised; Jo felt deeply wounded by Nina's rejection of her. Fortunately, while there was a great deal of pain there was also enough love and goodwill on both sides to agree to work towards managing the situation. Gradually Jo understood that, for Nina, loving closeness was so intertwined with abuse that she could not see further than that terror. Nina started to understand that Jo felt hurt more than angry, and when she felt criticised learnt to check what Jo had actually meant. They also discussed the nature of their relationship. They concluded that they wanted to stay together for a long time and were committed to each other, which helped dissipate Nina's anxiety about the possibility of Jo leaving. This was a long, careful and slow process and both continued to work individually and together to get through.

For some survivors the concept of sexual choice does not exist in the way one would expect in a person who has had a healthy sexual development. While pressures can be great on young people to have sex before they feel ready, a survivor of the same age will not have learned the assurance necessary for refusal. As they become adults the continuum from no to yes becomes no clearer. In a study of 42 women survivors of sexual abuse, one third felt confusion around their sexual choice, which related to the difference between sex and affection (McGettigan quoted in Johnson 1993). An active change of sexuality may be their first step to feeling in some kind of control. Even though it can be a confusing time, it can also be an exhilarating one.

Loulan (1987) suggests that all lesbians will be affected by abuse at some point. Counsellors working with people from sexual minorities are likely to work with clients who were abused or whose partners have been abused. Most books about working with sexual abuse focus on the survivor, and the needs of the partner can become secondary. Without negating the pain of the survivor, the partner deserves good support to cope with the person they love with compassion, patience and understanding and to keep themselves psychologically healthy. Where there are sexual difficulties, a counsellor needs to hear the client's feelings about the rejection of their love and of their bodies. Working with this dynamic in a couple it can be difficult not to be pulled into whose hurt is greater and wondering 'Will this ever end?'

The media represents child sexual abuse as out of the ordinary, and people from sexual minorities as out of the ordinary. There are parallels here that are important. As a society we tend to individualise both sexual abuse and sexual orientation. This makes it easy for the community to ignore and is exacerbated by our insistence on furthering individualism in psychology and counselling.

In an alien, heterosexual world a child will internalise the sexism and homophobia of society and keep silent, hiding the expression of their sexuality. Without support they become vulnerable to the paedophile looking for just such an unprotected child. Others who carry the brunt of society's prejudices, such as children from ethnic communities and children with disabilities, are also vulnerable. When a client from a sexual minority has other areas of oppression to cope with as well, therapists have a great deal to learn and understand (see Wilson 1993; Keith 1994; Lago with Thompson 1996; Shakespeare *et al.* 1996; Altschuler 1997). Gonsiorek (1994d) quotes Wyatt on the effects of sexual abuse on black children, whom racism in research often stereotyped as being 'more sexual', presuming that the after-effects were less serious than for white children. For disenfranchised children, finding role models becomes a difficult task. Children with disabilities are often seen as unable to think, emote or make judgements and are therefore silenced, sometimes because they literally cannot speak in a way that most people can hear. Counsellors may need particular knowledge and specialist supervision in order to work with people with disabilities. Sinason (1989), Kennedy (1990, 1996), Purdie (1991, 1994), Westcott and Cross (1996) and Zinschitz (1998) all offer advice here.

Somatic presentation

As children, and as adults, many people who have been abused will have been to their doctors with all manner of physical complaints where the underlying message has not been picked up. The classic for children is stomach-ache. Santi Ireson (1995), a counsellor working in a GP practice, looked at the medical histories of 32 clients who had been abused. Their GPs referred three as a direct result of disclosing but 24 women and five men had not disclosed to their doctor. She took the GPs' patients and asked how many the GPs knew had been abused. She then compared these figures with the NSPCC's (National Society for the Prevention of Cruelty to Children) 1990 nationally projected figures (i.e. 12 per cent of women and 6 per cent of men) (see Table 9.1).

Table 9.1   Table showing the discrepancy between patients' history of sexual abuse reported in a GP's surgery and nationally projected figures

	Female patients	Male patients	Known abused females	Possible 12% abused females	Known abused males	Possible 6% abused males
Total	4896	6164	22	630	4	376

Source: Santi Ireson (1995)

Symptoms doctors noticed in patients they knew to have been abused were mainly depression, followed by urinary tract infections, anxiety and interpersonal difficulties. Santi Ireson cites a number of studies looking at the somatic presentation of childhood abuse, increased suicide risk and self-injury such as cutting or burning.

Some attitudes Santi Ireson found among the GPs were alarming. 'Not in *this* town, surely!' 'It's such a woolly area – children themselves can be the abusers, acting very seductively and then crying when something happens'. One felt that 'the problem of playing the "sexual abuse" card, which can never be proven', was that this would lead to 'a universal absolution of all subsequent psychopathic behaviour' (Santi Ireson 1995: 17).

Doctors of course are not the only ones who do not want to hear. In one client's words: 'I remember where we were. My mother was doing the washing up when I told her. She didn't say anything, just kept on washing up. Years later when I told her again she said I had never told her before'. I have heard others with the same story. Much of the trauma resulting from sexual abuse could be averted by families offering belief, comfort, protection and love to the hurt child. Children living in such an atmosphere are more likely to be able to tell an adult.

As counsellors we may often be the first to hear a disclosure. Hearing and believing the truth of a particular person's story sounds easy. After all, we are now educated enough to know that sexual abuse of children happens. Believing children was one of the most important things that ChildLine thought it should do when it opened its phone lines (Rantzen 1986). As individuals we need to learn how to hear things that we may find very difficult. For instance when the abuser was a woman, when there was more than one abuser at a time, when someone was repeatedly abused in different circumstances, when ritualised abuse took place, when there were sacrifices, when the child went back for more or when the child enjoyed both the seemingly loving contact and the sex.

Touch: a warning!

When you have been a therapist for ten years, experienced substantial personal therapy with a therapist who touches and with one who does not, when you have thought about touch extensively, had hours of supervision and read as much as you can find from a range of theoretical perspectives; *only then* start to think about touching your clients. Take it to supervision every time and be vigilant to the response of your client. Make sure that grateful smile is not an automatic repetition of a learnt response, like those on the faces of 4-year-olds on catwalks or stages living up to their parents' ideals. This may seem an extreme position, particularly for those operating from within the humanistic traditions. It is a serious and under-explored area on many training courses.

Case example 4

Jenny, a counsellor in a GP practice, had been working for three months with Maxine, a single bisexual woman who had been sexually abused in childhood. As Jenny was showing her out of a session she noticed a clothes tag showing from Maxine's jumper. Spontaneously, Jenny moved to tuck in the label while saying what she was doing. At the touch of the hand by her neck Maxine moved across the room with her back to the wall, clutching her neck, looking terrified with shortened, gasping breath. Jenny, shocked at the violence of the reaction, fortunately kept her distance while staying in contact with Maxine until she felt calm enough to leave. In supervision we explored the issue of flashbacks and Jenny looked candidly at her desire to hold clients in an equal relationship and how she could manage this while maintaining tighter boundaries than she had been.

Therapists are generally people who care about what happens to others and it would be strange if, working with abused clients, we did not want to make things better. It is hard to stay with someone in a place which seems unrelenting. When we are with someone who is wounded it seems natural to want to wrap them up in our arms and protect them. Your hug is unlikely to do that, although it may well make *you* feel better. A good practitioner does not need to use touch to convey empathy. Think through the implications for any abused client. For someone of minority sexuality it becomes more complicated. Does it mirror the gender pattern of the abuse? If you are a heterosexual therapist, does it indicate that you are interested in exploring your sexual continuum? How does the abused client keep compliant and safe at the same time? As a practitioner you may say 'I am not an abuser' but how does the client know that? Most sexual abuse starts with the abuser being very warm, friendly, attentive and empathic – just like a counsellor or therapist may be.

Conclusions

A framework for working with lesbian, gay and bisexual clients who have been sexually abused has to incorporate the political in the personal of both issues. Child sexual abuse traumatically interrupts a person's psychosexual development. Coming out in a homophobic world disrupts the same development. Double whammy! The isolation felt means that these young people are more vulnerable to attacks within their original communities, including sexual assaults on both genders. Women are assaulted by men to make them 'see sense' and experience a 'real man'; men by women to point out the error of their ways. Heterosexual men assault gay men to humiliate them and show them they are not 'real men', and to act out hidden fantasies in an aggressive manner while ensuring their own reputations as full-blooded males.

Trust is always an issue in therapy, doubly so for someone from a sexual minority wanting to work on their sexual abuse. If you fear this work, or these client groups, it would be ethical to stop counselling. I hear of too many incidents of damaging practice to clients who bring these issues in good faith. At worst their counsellor, therapist, health or alternative practitioner has sexually assaulted them; at best abandoned them because of their own inadequacies. I am amazed at the capacity of people to keep searching for a safe practitioner and horrified at the damage that has been done to them. I am concerned about counsellors and psychotherapists leaving training establishments where neither issues of abuse nor of working cross-culturally are being addressed. It is surprising how many counsellors in training and supervision believe this is not a problem as long as one is empathic.

The preferred word for someone sexually abused in childhood is 'survivor'; it has become part of our everyday language. We do not know how many children die as a consequence of their abuse either at the hands of their abuser or their own. The numbers are probably more than we realise. 'Survivor' has a ring of optimism and resilience about it which can belie the fact that the person was once a victim. This must also be acknowledged, the story must be heard, and the pain witnessed. Concepts such as 'rewriting one's script' or 'it's never too late to have a happy childhood' have an uplifting quality which does not stay the course. They are used by therapists unable to stay with the reality of the victim's hell: making the switch into blaming the person for not 'getting better' can be a short step away.

Guidelines for good practice

- Don't underestimate how painful this area of work *can* be. Make sure you are qualified to do it. By this I mean you will have done enough of your own therapy to have a personal understanding of emotional terrors from which you believe there can be no escape.
- Be professionally well-supported while you are engaged in this work: use supervision, consultancy, training and reading.
- If you don't know about, or understand, something the client is talking about, don't make assumptions – check things out.
- Work hard at making a good, safe relationship. Be consistent, boundaried and trustworthy.
- Be aware of external oppression and of your own ability, and sometimes desire, to oppress.
- Be aware of your own delights and disgusts around sex and sexuality.
- Don't try to pull down or penetrate someone's defences: respect their value and functions.
- If you want to touch someone think about it three times before you do, and ask permission.

- Be willing to hear the unbearable.
- Stay steady under pressure; the client's internal abuser may well try to have a go at you. When this happens use your internal feelings to inform your work, not to blame your client.
- Do not abandon your client when the going gets tough. There are counsellors who dump their clients. Know when you need to refer on as you reach your own limits of competence and do this as gracefully as possible.
- Look through your caseload with your supervisor on a regular basis: burnout will not help you or your clients.
- Look after yourself. Make sure there is fun and laughter and lots of self-care in your life.

References

Altschuler, J. (1997) *Working with Chronic Illness*. London: Macmillan.

Angelou, M. (1971) *I Know Why The Caged Bird Sings*. New York: Bantam Books.

Bass, E. and Davis, L. (1988) *The Courage To Heal*. New York: Harper & Row.

Bennett, J. and Forgan, R. (eds) (1991) *There's Something About A Convent Girl*. London: Virago Press.

Blume, S.E. (1991) *Secret Survivors*. New York: Ballantine Books.

Bond, T. (1993) *Standards and Ethics for Counselling in Action*. London: Sage.

Caldon, W. (1989) Personal communication.

Campbell, B. (1988) *Unofficial Secrets. Child Sexual Abuse: The Cleveland Case*. London: Virago.

Corby, B. (1993) *Child Abuse: Towards a Knowledge Base*. Buckingham: Open University Press.

Davies, D. (1996a) Homophobia and heterosexism, in D. Davies and C. Neal (eds) *Pink Therapy: A Guide for Counsellors and Therapists Working with Lesbian, Gay and Bisexual Clients*. Buckingham: Open University Press.

Davies, D. (1996b) Working with young people, in D. Davies and C. Neal (eds) *Pink Therapy: A Guide for Counsellors and Therapists Working with Lesbian, Gay and Bisexual Clients*. Buckingham: Open University Press.

Davies, D. and Neal, C. (eds) (1996) *Pink Therapy: A Guide for Counsellors and Therapists Working with Lesbian, Gay and Bisexual Clients*. Buckingham: Open University Press.

Elliott, M. (ed.) (1993) *Female Sexual Abuse Of Children: The Ultimate Taboo*. Harlow: Longman.

Finkelhor D. (ed.) (1984) *Child Sexual Abuse: New Theory And Research*. New York: Free Press.

Fontes, L.A. (ed.) (1995) *Sexual Abuse In Nine North American Cultures: Treatment and Prevention*. Thousand Oaks, CA: Sage.

Gil, E. (1988) *Treatment of Adult Survivors Of Childhood Abuse*. New York: Launch Press.

Gomez, L. (1995) Satanist abuse. *Counselling*. 6(2): 116–20.

Gonsiorek, J.C. (1994a) Assessment of and treatment planning and individual psychotherapy for sexually abused adolescent males, in J.C. Gonsiorek, W.H. Bera and D. LeTourneau (eds) *Male Sexual Abuse: A Trilogy of Intervention Strategies*. Thousand Oaks, CA: Sage.

Gonsiorek, J.C. (1994b) A critique of current models in sexual abuse, in J.C. Gonsiorek, W.H. Bera and D. LeTourneau (eds) *Male Sexual Abuse: A Trilogy of Intervention Strategies*. Thousand Oaks, CA: Sage.

Gonsiorek, J.C. (1994c) Male victims of sexual abuse, in J.C. Gonsiorek, W.H. Bera and D. LeTourneau (eds) *Male Sexual Abuse: A Trilogy of Intervention Strategies*. Thousand Oaks, CA: Sage.

Gonsiorek, J.C. (1994d) Diagnosis and treatment of young adult and adolescent male victims: an individual psychotherapy model, in J.C. Gonsiorek, W.H. Bera and D. LeTourneau (eds) *Male Sexual Abuse: A Trilogy of Intervention Strategies*. Thousand Oaks, CA: Sage.

Gonsiorek, J.C., Bera, W.H. and LeTourneau, D. (1994) *Male Sexual Abuse: A Trilogy of Intervention Strategies*. Thousand Oaks, CA: Sage.

Herman, J.L. (1994) *Trauma and Recovery*. London: Pandora.

Isensee, R. (1997) *Reclaiming Your Life: The Gay Man's Guide To Love, Self-Acceptance and Trust*. Los Angeles: Alyson Books.

Jenkins, P. (1997) *Counselling, Psychotherapy and the Law*. London: Sage.

Johnson, J. (1993) 'The long-term impact of childhood sexual abuse on sexual functioning in lesbian women', unpublished master's thesis, Smith College School for Social Work, Massachusetts.

Keith, L. (ed.) (1994) *Mustn't Grumble*. London: The Women's Press.

Kempe, R.S. and Kempe C.H. (1978) *Child Abuse*. Shepton Mallet: Fontana Open Books and Open Books Publishing Ltd.

Kennedy, M. (1990) The deaf child who is sexually abused – is there a need for a dual specialist? *Child Abuse Review*, 4(2): 3–6.

Kennedy, M. (1996) Sexual abuse and disabled children, in J. Morris (ed.) *Encounters with Strangers: Feminism and Disability*. London: The Women's Press.

Lago, C. with Thompson, J. (1996) *Race, Culture and Counselling*. Buckingham: Open University Press.

Lew, M. (1990) *Victims No Longer*. New York: Harper Collins.

Loulan, J. (1987) *Lesbian Passion: Loving Ourselves and Each Other*. Minneapolis, MN: Spinsters Ink.

McMullen, R. (1990) *Male Rape*. London: GMP.

Purdie, F. (1991) Counselling children with disabilities who have been sexually abused. Paper given at Spastics Society (Scope) conference 'Child Abuse and Special Needs', Wallingford, Oxfordshire, 26 March.

Purdie, F. (1994) Changing words, changing hearts? Personal, sexual, relationship and family division of the *British Association for Counselling Newsletter*, March.

Queer Press Collective (eds) (1991) *Loving in Fear: An Anthology of Lesbian and Gay Survivors of Childhood Sexual Abuse*. Toronto: Queer Press Publishing.

Rantzen, E. (1986) Personal communication.

Rape Crisis Federation (1997) Policy statement, 'Rape crisis groups and men', 27 September.

Samuels, A. (1997) Gender, sexuality and the father in contemporary psychotherapy and counselling. Paper given at Second International Conference of British Association for Supervision Practice and Research, London, 26 July.

Sanford, L.T. (1991) *Strong at the Broken Places*. London: Virago.

Santi Ireson, S. (1995) 'The silent scream: an investigation undertaken in one GP practice of the somatic presentation of childhood sexual abuse to the doctor', unpublished postgraduate diploma, University of Bristol.

Shakespeare, T., Gillespie-Sells, K. and Davies, D. (1996) *The Sexual Politics Of Disability: Untold Desires.* London: Cassell.

Sinason, V. (1989) Uncovering and responding to sexual abuse in psychotherapeutic settings, in H. Brown and A. Craft (eds) *Thinking the Unthinkable: Papers on Sexual Abuse and People with Learning Difficulties.* London: FPA Education Unit.

Sinason, V. (ed.) (1994) *Treating Survivors of Satanist Abuse.* London: Routledge.

Spring, J. (1987) *Cry Hard and Swim.* London: Virago.

Vanaerschot, G. (1993) Empathy as releasing several micro-processes in the client, in D. Brazier (ed.) *Beyond Carl Rogers.* London: Constable.

Walker, M. (1992) *Surviving Secrets.* Buckingham: Open University Press.

Westcott, H. and Cross, M. (1996) *This Far and No Further: Working Towards Ending the Abuse of Disabled Children.* Birmingham: Venture Press.

Wilson, M. (1993) *Crossing the Boundary: Black Women Survive Incest.* London: Virago.

Zinschitz, E. (1998) The person-centred approach in work with disabled persons. *Counselling,* 9(3): 210–16.

Long-term consequences of bullying

Introduction

Bullying behaviour has been a feature of the school experiences of many people for a great many years. Until quite recently it was viewed as nothing more than a rite of passage: a process through which most children passed, experiencing the roles of victim, bystander and then 'bully' as they moved through the school system. Before the advent of anti-bullying initiatives, those who experienced victimisation at the hands of their peers were often told to stand up to 'bullies' and fight back. Alternatively, some were told not to make such a fuss, as their aggressors would soon move on to someone else. In this chapter I consider some of the research that has been conducted with young lesbians, gay men and bisexual men and women who have been bullied or victimised at school, and discuss some of the findings from my own study of bullying and its long-term effects.

Bullying at school: what do we know?

In a survey conducted with 7000 primary and secondary school children in the UK, it was found that 27 per cent of primary and 10 per cent of secondary school pupils were bullied 'sometimes' or more often; 10 per cent and 4 per cent respectively reported being bullied 'once a week' or more (Whitney and Smith 1993). In terms of the types of behaviour that occur in schools, young children are more likely to use physical aggression (e.g. hitting, kicking, pushing) when bullying others whereas teenagers have been found to use name-calling and social exclusion much more effectively than physical acts of aggression (Rivers and Smith 1994).

It has been suggested that around one in three lesbians, gay men and bisexuals are bullied or otherwise victimised in adolescence because of their actual or perceived sexual orientation (Rivers 1999). In a recent survey conducted by the political lobbying group *Stonewall*, according to participants under the age of 18 years, 40 per cent of all the violent attacks reported were found to take place at school with 50 per cent of those being perpetrated by peers (Mason and Palmer 1996). In the USA, Pilkington and D'Augelli (1995) found that 30 per cent of gay and bisexual young men, and 35 per cent of lesbian and bisexual women had been victimised by peers at school. Furthermore, they found that 7 per cent of their sample of 194 lesbian, gay and bisexual youths had been 'hurt' by a teacher. More recently, in my own study of bullying and its long-term effects for 190 lesbians, gay men and bisexuals living in the UK, I found that the average age when homophobic bullying began at school was 10 years, and its average duration was five years, although it is worth mentioning the average age when participants first knew they were lesbian, gay or bisexual was 13 years (Rivers 1999).

Although the long-term effects bullying can have are yet to be established fully, it is now believed that repeated exposure to violence or harassment can have detrimental effects upon psychological well-being. While one small-scale longitudinal study conducted in Norway with a sample of heterosexual men indicates no significant lasting effects other than a slightly increased risk of depression (Olweus 1993), anecdotal evidence suggests that women and men who experienced a great deal of harassment at school do continue to live with its effects well into adulthood. For example, Smith (1991) recalled one woman of 28 who reported having been bullied throughout middle school and, as an adult, continued to experience feelings of self-doubt, anxiety and fear when she met children.

For lesbian, gay and bisexual youths, Sharp and Cowie (1998: 107) have suggested that bullying at school can have 'serious psychological, educational and emotional consequences'. Yet, despite this recognition of the impact such behaviour can have, it seems that schools have allowed the victimisation to continue because they have been provided with little, if any, guidance on how to tackle this form of harassment. To a certain extent, the lack of support offered to these young people today is a consequence of the continued confusion over the application of Section 28 of the Local Government Act 1988 which prohibits the teaching in any maintained school of the acceptability of homosexuality as a pretended family relationship. But, as Warren (1984) demonstrated, youngsters from sexual minorities were being bullied at school long before the advent of Section 28. In his survey of lesbian, gay and bisexual youth growing up in London, Warren found that 39 per cent of the 416 people he and Lorraine Trenchard sampled had experienced problems at school. Of the 154 who specified the nature of those problems, 25 per cent said that they had felt isolated and had nothing in common with other pupils, 21 per cent said that they had been called names, 13 per cent had been teased, 12 per cent had been physically hurt by another pupil, 7 per cent had been ostracised, and another 7 per cent had been pressured by others to change their behaviour (Trenchard and Warren 1984).

Although Warren (1984) only alludes briefly to the fact that some of the young people in his study felt pressured by those around them to change their behaviour, for many bullying is a result of peers identifying traits or mannerisms which they perceive to be gender atypical. (This may explain why bullying begins three years before a young person self-identifies as lesbian, gay or bisexual.) For example, Rottnek (1999) has illustrated how much of the hostility a young lesbian, gay or bisexual person experiences at school is a consequence of gender inappropriate behaviour. In his own autobiographical account of moving to a new school in the USA, he recalls how he welcomed an opportunity to start over:

> I was excited to attend a much larger school with college-like facilities, where students wore ties and that was only a 20-minute commute from home. I felt like I was growing up. I also clearly remember hoping for this: a chance to start over, a chance to watch my behavior more closely – so I wouldn't be hated, wouldn't be pegged the faggot, pansy, homo, loser, wouldn't be the last pick of the team, wouldn't be spit at, laughed at, joked about – a chance to try harder.
>
> (Rottnek 1998: 115)

For those pupils who decide not to hide or deny their sexuality, the consequences of their actions can be severe as David, a young gay man from the North-west of England, recounted:

> On the first day at my new high school I was full of a kind of optimistic trepidation. I was very pleased that I had got this far, and I was happy to be surrounded by boys and girls who seemed just like me. Later in the first year I realised I was homosexual and I soon came to terms with it and in a way I was glad I was a little different from the rest – the others were all the same, but I was the one who stood out in the crowd. It [the bullying] started one morning in assembly. A boy in the same year group as me yelled out the word 'poofter' and, like a fool, I looked round. From that moment on I was the subject of beatings, verbal abuse and so-called 'queerbashing'. I received torrents of verbal abuse and I had things stolen from me not just by other boys, but also by girls. There was no way round it; I was being punished for being gay.
>
> The injuries I received were numerous: I had my left arm broken (the bullies said that I was lucky it wasn't my right arm), I was held down while cigarettes were stubbed out on the back of my neck, and I was kicked repeatedly by both boys and girls even when a teacher was

nearby. One teacher told me that my problems were my own fault because I refused to deny my sexuality.

(Rivers 1996: 5)

David's closing comments about the less than sympathetic attitude a teacher took when he was being assaulted are not unusual. As the following letter written by three school principals to the editor of the *Belfast Telegraph* demonstrates, there continues to be opposition to the introduction of a discussion of homosexuality in schools:

> All who accept the authority of the Bible acknowledge homosexuality to be not only a deviant form of behaviour but utterly depraved . . . While we are opposed to all types of bullying, it must be considered ironic that it is the gays who are attempting to bully the respectable people of this country into subjecting their children to instruction on sodomy.

(Rivers 1997a: 45)

As previously mentioned, Pilkington and D'Augelli (1995) found that 7 per cent of the young people in their survey reported that they had in fact been 'hurt' by a teacher. In my study, 28 per cent said that they had been bullied by a teacher because of their sexual orientation (Rivers 1998a: 188):

> One day I came into class with my clarinet case and he [the English teacher] latched onto the case and proclaimed it in front of the class as being the 'typically puffy [*sic*] case' that he would expect. He . . . he then began this play on words around the word 'puff' and started teaching the class about sentences such as 'the snow puffed against the window'. This was obviously meant to refer to me.

(Mark, aged 22)

Where bullying is perpetrated by teachers as well as by pupils it is not surprising to learn that their victims stay away from school. For example, in my study, of the 85 participants who answered questions about avoiding school, 74 per cent (63) said that they had either feigned illness or played truant to escape the bullies (Rivers 1998b).

According to Hunter and Schaecher (1987) school failure has been a common element in the lives of young lesbians, gay men and bisexuals. In the USA for example, educational programmes have been developed specifically for those young people who are in danger of dropping out of school. The Harvey Milk School in New York and the EAGLES (Emphasising Adolescent Gay and Lesbian Educational Services) Centre in California have been at the forefront of attempts by educators to ensure that youths from sexual minorities can stay in school and finish their education (Battey 1995). However, staying in school is sometimes only one of a number of battles they have to fight. As Trenchard and Warren (1984) reported, 20 per cent of those who decide to 'come out' in adolescence are thrown out of the family home. While some are fortunate enough to find accommodation through organisations such as the Albert Kennedy Trust, others are forced to live on the streets, and some eventually fall into prostitution. As one young man recalled, the step from repeated victimisation to commercial sex was not that great as the damage had already been done: 'I'd already had so much hurt I decided I wasn't going to feel any more. I didn't feel anything – good, bad, or indifferent. I turned off the emotions' (Owens 1998: 115).

In terms of school bullying there would seem to be little difference in whether a young person is 'out' or not: being, or being perceived to be, non-heterosexual do not seem to be poles apart in the minds of the bullies. For example, of the 190 lesbians, gay men and bisexuals who took part in my own study, 169 were 'out' as adults and the average age at which they 'came out' was 20 years (21 years for men and 17 years for women). Yet, 82 per cent recalled being called names at school (these included *AIDS victim, dyke, lemon, lessie, pervert, poof* and *queerboy*). Ridicule had been suffered by 71 per cent and 60 per cent had been hit by peers. In addition 59 per cent said that rumours had been spread about them and 58 per cent had been teased. 52 per cent reported having been frightened by a look or stare and 49 per cent had personal possessions stolen. Finally, 27 per cent said that peers had isolated them and 11 per cent reported having been sexually assaulted at school. The majority of these behaviours were not isolated incidents: 69 per cent said that they were bullied once a week or more (Rivers 1998a).

The impact such behaviour can have upon a young person can be seen readily in the following account taken from a letter written to me in 1996 by a young gay man (then aged 17 years):

> I never was your typical macho male and always stood out from the crowd but at the time I never knew what it was that made me different. At school I was tormented by taunts of 'pansy', 'faggot' etc. I never really understood what these meant but I realised that these people had a hatred of me.
>
> Although I did have a large circle of friends the majority of them were girls and even though I had male friends a lot of them kept their distance. At the time I didn't really care, it wasn't until I got into my senior year that things got bad. The hassle had increased drastically and my life was being made a misery at school. I dreaded going in every day wondering what would be said or done. There wasn't any real physical abuse it was mainly mental but in my belief this is the worst kind. Finally, in October of last year, I decided I could take no more and I tried to kill myself, luckily (although I thought unfortunately at the time) I didn't succeed.

It was this that made me decide things had to change. I changed schools and left behind all the misery. Finally, things started to look up for me. I was getting good grades and had fallen into a group of people whose company I fully enjoyed. One girl in the group whom I was extremely close with told me she was gay and by being in her and her fellow gay friends' company I finally started to accept my own sexuality. A month later I came out to my parents and close friends. At last I felt happy with myself and all my worries seemed to disappear. All this ended a couple of weeks later when I was jumped and bashed by three teenagers. Although I managed to run away I was left with two black eyes and a bust nose, but the mental scars were the worst and for ages afterwards I refused to walk about on my own. If it hadn't been for the support of the Rainbow Project I doubt I would be writing this letter today. I'm still coming to terms with what happened but I realise now I shouldn't let these people's ignorance get me down. Being 17 and gay isn't the easiest thing in the world but I don't regret 'coming out' or being gay and hopefully in years to come societies [*sic*] attitude will change.

(Rivers 1997a: 36)

Although this letter contains elements of great sadness and despair, towards the end it demonstrates a resilience that is not uncommon among former victims of bullying. In the following section I have described some of the key findings from my own study of long-term effects – the positive as well as the negative – in the hope that they provide some guidance for those working with clients from sexual minorities.

Bullying and its long-term effects: the Luton study

In February 1994 I began a study, by placing a series of advertisements in the gay press, that asked for volunteers to participate in a pilot project conducted at the University of Luton looking at bullying in schools and its long-term effects. Overall, 60 individuals (48 gay or bisexual men and 12 lesbian or bisexual women) were sent a brief questionnaire which asked them to describe their experiences of school. Thirty-seven gay or bisexual men and seven lesbian or bisexual women eventually returned 44 questionnaires. Over the following two years calls for volunteers were circulated via various lesbian and gay community groups, pen-pal associations, practitioner conferences and journals. By July 1997 190 men and women had completed questionnaires about their experiences of bullying in school, with 119 of those (63 per cent) also completing detailed life history questionnaires (Rivers 1997a; 1997b). Additionally, 16 participants agreed to be interviewed over a two and a half year period (this part of the study was funded by the Froebel Educational Institute). The major findings from the study are outlined below.

Self-destructive behaviour and suicidal ideation in the UK

Recently, one Australian researcher (Rigby 1997) argued that where a child or young person is bullied repeatedly at school they are at increased risk of engaging in self-harming or suicidal behaviour. This is a view shared by several researchers working with lesbian, gay and bisexual youth. For example, in the USA Hershberger and D'Augelli (1995) found that 42 per cent of their sample had attempted to take their own lives as a result of the hostility they had experienced towards their sexuality either at school or in their local community.

Fifty-three per cent of the lesbians, gay men and bisexuals who were surveyed as part of the Luton study had contemplated self-harming behaviour or suicide as a consequence of being bullied at school; 40 per cent had attempted suicide or self-harm at least once, and three quarters of those (30 per cent of the total sample) had attempted more than once.

Participants were asked two sets of questions relating to suicidal ideation: first of all they were asked to estimate the number of times they had contemplated (even briefly) self-destructive behaviour or suicide as a result of being bullied, and to record the number of times they had actually attempted such behaviour. They were then asked whether or not there were any other factors that could have influenced their desire to self-harm (e.g. problems coming to terms with their sexuality, general adolescent *angst*, difficulties in the home, etc.), and were asked to provide information on whether or not they had made attempts to hurt themselves (see Table 10.1).

Table 10.1 Self-destructive behaviour and suicidal ideation

Question	Percentage of participants contemplating/ attempting behaviour		
	Contemplated	1 attempt	2+ attempts
As a result of being bullied at school	53	40	30
For 'other' reasons	37	19	8

The results suggest that while few young lesbians, gay men and bisexuals are likely to attempt self-destructive behaviours because of their sexual orientation either once (19 per cent) or more than once (8 per cent), significantly more are likely to engage in multiple attempts if they have been bullied at school (30 per cent). It is worth noting here that the results for 'other' factors are very similar to those quoted by Warren (1984), and provide constructive validation for the belief that around one in five young lesbians, gay men and bisexuals self-harm.

Depression and anxiety

In the Luton study, participants were assessed for both depression and anxiety by comparing their scores on the Multiple Affect Adjective Check List (MAACL) (Zuckerman and Lubin 1965) to three other groups to determine the severity of long-term effects (see Table 10.2). These groups were: 109 heterosexual adults who had been bullied in school; 98 heterosexual adults who had not been bullied at school; and 116 lesbian, gay and bisexual adults who had not been bullied at school. As in a small-scale study conducted in Norway (Olweus 1993), participants were found to be much more likely to suffer from depression than both heterosexual or lesbian, gay and bisexual people not bullied at school, but were very similar to those heterosexuals who had been bullied.

Table 10.2   Depression and anxiety among bullied and non-bullied samples

	Affective state score	
	Depression	Anxiety
Heterosexual not bullied	13.4	7.1
Heterosexual bullied	19.0	9.2
LGB* not bullied	14.9	8.6
LGB bullied	18.6	9.5

*Lesbian, gay and bisexual

In terms of reported anxiety, scores were not found to differ between heterosexuals who had been bullied at school and lesbian, gay and bisexual participants who had not. Nevertheless, all three other groups were more likely to experience anxiety as adults than heterosexuals who were not bullied at school.

Self-esteem and self-perception

One of the most important factors in this study was to determine how participants felt about themselves and others, and how willing they were to disclose their sexual orientation to other people. Of the 119 who completed very detailed life histories, 105 said that they were open about their sexual orientation while the remaining 14 had not disclosed it to anyone. To assess the degree to which bullying had an effect upon self and general perceptions about being lesbian, gay or bisexual, and disclosure to others, participants' responses were compared to those of the sample of 116 lesbians, gay men and bisexuals who were not bullied.

Interestingly, participants were not found to differ from their non-bullied peers in terms of their self-perceptions, or their willingness to disclose their sexual orientation to another person. Significantly, they were much more positive about homosexuality than their non-bullied peers, which suggests that they may have reached a point in their lives where they had ceased to be concerned about the perceptions of others. This was demonstrated aptly by one woman (Susan, aged 30) who said of her work environment:

> It's [being a lesbian] something that the customers will stop and that they will try to use, but in some respects it's counter-productive because it's just about the least upsetting thing they could now pick. I would be far more upset being called a racist than I am now being called a lesbian. That doesn't bother me at all, and I'm likely to turn and say, 'Yes, well you've got that one right'.

Post-traumatic stress and bullying at school

Various studies have shown that exposure to extreme violence, or to experiences that fall outside those of the general population may result in the onset of post-traumatic stress disorder (PTSD). For example, Mauk and Rogers (1994) argued that symptoms often associated with PTSD can also be found among school-age populations where young people have experienced an unexpected bereavement of a peer as a result of accidental death or suicide.

Symptoms associated with PTSD were assessed using a new questionnaire (Rivers 1998a) based upon the criteria listed in the *Diagnostic and Statistical Manual of Mental Disorders* (American Psychiatric Association 1994). Participants were asked to rate the frequency of each symptom they had experienced on a scale of 1 (never) to 5 (always). They were also asked to estimate the duration of persistent symptoms on a second scale of 1 (zero to six months) to 5 (five years or more). As this is the first time PTSD has been associated with school bullying, each symptom is discussed below and figures are quoted for those who experienced negative effects regularly (from the questionnaire this is interpreted as 'often' or 'always'). Symptoms are clustered under three headings: persistent recollections of being bullied; current and persistent avoidance of bullying-associated stimuli, and a numbing of responsiveness; and current and persistent symptoms of arousal.

Recollections of school bullying

Approximately one quarter (26 per cent) of the 119 participants included in the study of long-term effects indicated that they had been or continued to be distressed regularly by recollections of bullying at school. The majority reported distressing or intrusive memories of those events (21 per cent) and indicated that they experienced psychological distress when in situations which reminded them of their school days and being bullied (26 per cent). Very few (only 4 per cent) reported having dreams or nightmares about being bullied at school. However, slightly more (9 per cent) recalled having experienced 'flashbacks' (illusions, hallucinations and disassociative episodes) or a feeling of reliving events while awake.

Avoidance/numbing of responsiveness

Forty-six per cent reported regularly feeling like an outsider in social situations and 34 per cent said that they regularly felt as if they had no real future (no prospect of having a partner, career or long life). Thirty-three per cent reported that they often or always found it difficult to show emotion to others while 23 per cent said that they actively avoided social situations which would (potentially) remind them of events at school. Nineteen per cent felt that they actively sought to avoid thoughts and feelings they associated with their school days on a regular basis, and 15 per cent often or always had difficulty recalling particular incidents associated with being bullied at school. Only 10 per cent regularly found it difficult to continue with any interests they had prior to being bullied, although this result was to be expected as interests/recreational activities/hobbies are likely to change with age.

Arousal

Irritability was the most commonly cited symptom (42 per cent) that participants reported experiencing on a regular basis, followed by symptoms such as a wariness of meeting new people or facing new situations (39 per cent). About one quarter often did not feel as if they were in control of their lives or said that they often had outbursts of anger. Seven per cent took alcohol regularly to help them cope with memories of being bullied while 5 per cent also took non-prescription drugs to help them cope. Finally, 4 per cent indicated that they were regularly prescribed drugs which helped them cope with memories of being bullied at school.

Overall, 20 participants (17 per cent) met the criteria for PTSD. This group were found to be more prone to depression, had lower levels of self-esteem and had more casual sexual partners (ratio of 4:1) than the other lesbians, gay men and bisexuals who were bullied at school. As one participant recalled, the effect bullying had upon his self-esteem did not diminish as soon as he left school, it persisted for some time afterwards:

I think by the time I'd got to nineteen, twenty or twenty-one, I realised that if I was going to have any future, I was going to have to tell someone I was gay and it all hung on that . . . everything hung on that. So, I told someone and then I told another person. The whole 'coming out' process took years, but I did it bit by bit by bit, but I had to go really low, sink to a very very low point when I was about – a bit older than I said – twenty-two when I did overdose on sleeping tablets accidentally. It wasn't an attempt to die, but I did overdose and that would be the lowest you would get – the absolute rock bottom – there was seriously something wrong.

(Matthew, aged 36)

Although stories such as Matthew's are not uncommon, while many people experience a great deal of hardship during adolescence and early adulthood, they often prove to be resilient and go on to lead very successful professional as well as personal lives.

Resilience: surviving bullying at school

In a recent review paper, Peter Fonagy and his colleagues (Fonagy *et al.* 1994) argued that there are a number of defining attributes of resilient children when compared to their vulnerable counterparts. Among these attributes Fonagy *et al.* cited things such as temperament, age at time of trauma, the absence of early separations or losses, a good relationship with at least one primary care giver, support from partner or family in adulthood, and a good network of informal relationships and formal social support through education or involvement in organised religious activity. In addition, they also suggested that there are a number of 'psychological' attributes such as good problem solving skills, a high sense of self-worth, interpersonal awareness and empathy, and a sense of humour.

Although not all of these factors were explored in the Luton study, both the long-term data and the small number of interviews I conducted did suggest that there were common 'elements' among those who had fared much better as adults. These 'elements' may be divided into two attributional categories: the 'social' and the 'psychological'.

At a social level resilient lesbians, gay men and bisexuals were:

- non-competitive as young people;
- not rejected by their families;
- not rejected by all their friends when they 'came out';
- willing to use voluntary organisations/agencies/switchboards to obtain advice;
- adults who were in an established long-term relationship.

At a psychological level resilient lesbians, gay men and bisexuals were:

- independent of mind;
- able to continue their education in adulthood;
- able to find career/job fulfilment by facing personal challenges/fears.

Both the interviews and the surveys suggested that support from family members and peers was an important buffer against long-term negative outcomes. Similarly, comments from interviewees demonstrated that the support they received from voluntary organisations and helplines had been very useful in assisting them take positive steps towards 'coming out'. The presence of a long-term partner had also given them a degree of confidence they felt would otherwise be absent.

In terms of educational experience and achievement very few participants (8 per cent) had no formal academic qualifications, and approximately one third (30 per cent) of all participants had gone on to study at university or college, some as mature students. In addition, 37 per cent had undertaken courses leading to professional qualifications and 28 per cent held or were studying for vocational qualifications. This suggests that bullying had not prohibited participants from continuing their studies in later years.

In terms of psychological functioning, participants shared the profile of the resilient person offered by Fonagy *et al.* (1994). Not only had they continued their education in adulthood and achieved various qualifications, they had also demonstrated an ability to overcome hardship and insecurity – factors which, it is argued, suggest a degree of determination and self-efficacy previously undiscovered among lesbian, gay and bisexual samples. Furthermore, given their resolve to put their experiences of school behind them, some participants had taken on occupational or voluntary roles which led them to face a number of personal challenges which not only demonstrated an independence of mind but also illustrated that they had not let their experiences get them down.

Summary and conclusions

Despite the high rate of reported self-harming behaviours, participants in the Luton study did not fit the typical victim mould. Many had overcome their negative experiences at school and gone on to have success in both their professional and personal lives. Indices of both depression and PTSD were found among a small group of participants who experienced particularly violent bullying both in the classroom and schoolyard. However, for most, while the memories of school remained vivid, early adulthood marked a period in their lives when anguish and insecurity subsided, and the process of healing began: 'Over the past year and a half, I've begun to find a lot of stability in my personality and I've begun to be an awful lot more confident and happy about myself. I feel this in myself and other people said that they've noticed a change' (Mark, aged 22).

References

American Psychiatric Association (1994) *The Diagnostic and Statistical Manual of Mental Disorders*, 4th edn. Washington, DC: American Psychiatric Association.

Battey, J. (1995) In their own words, in D. Deitcher (ed.) *Over the Rainbow: Lesbian and Gay Politics Since Stonewall*. London: Boxtree.

Fonagy, P., Steele, M., Steele, H., Higgitt, A. and Target, M. (1994) The theory and practice of resilience. *Journal of Child Psychology and Psychiatry*, 35(2): 231–57.

Hershberger, S.L. and D'Augelli, A.R. (1995) The impact of victimization on the mental health and suicidality of lesbian, gay, and bisexual youths. *Developmental Psychology*, 31(1): 65–74.

Hunter, J. and Schaecher, R. (1987) Stresses of gay and lesbian adolescents in schools. *Social Work in Education*, 9(2): 180–90.

Mason, A. and Palmer, A. (1996) *Queerbashing: A National Survey of Hate Crimes Against Lesbians and Gay Men*. London: Stonewall.

Mauk, G. and Rogers, P. (1994) Building bridges over troubled waters: school-based postvention with adolescent survivors or peer suicide. *Crisis Intervention Time Limited Treatment*, 1(2): 103–23.

Olweus, D. (1993) Victimization by peers: antecedents and long-term outcomes, in K.H. Rubin and J.B. Asendorf (eds) *Social Withdrawal, Inhibition and Shyness*. Hillsdale, NJ: Lawrence Erlbaum.

Owens, R.E. (1998) *Queer Kids: The Challenges and Promise for Lesbian, Gay, and Bisexual Youth*. New York: Harrington Park Press.

Pilkington, N.W. and D'Augelli, A.R. (1995) Victimization of lesbian, gay, and bisexual youth in community settings. *Journal of Community Psychology*, 23(1): 33–56.

Rigby, K. (1997) What children tell us about bullying in schools. *Children Australia*, 22(2): 28–34.

Rivers, I. (1996) *The victimization of lesbian, gay, and bisexual youths*. Conference paper, Pennsylvania State University conference series 'Research on Lesbian, Gay, and Bisexual Youths: Implications for Developmental Intervention', 7–9 June.

Rivers, I. (1997a) Violence against lesbian and gay youth and its impact, in M.S. Schneider (ed.) *Pride and Prejudice: Working with Lesbian, Gay and Bisexual Youth*. Toronto: Central Toronto Youth Services.

Rivers, I. (1997b) *The long-term impact of peer victimisation in adolescence upon the well-being of lesbian, gay and bisexual adults*. Conference paper, fifth European congress of psychology 'Dancing on the Edge', Dublin, 7–11 July.

Rivers, I. (1998a) 'The long-term consequences of peer victimisation for lesbian, gay and bisexual adults', unpublished report. University of Surrey, Roehampton Institute London.

Rivers, I. (1998b) *Bullying of gay and lesbian young people: messages from the research*. Conference paper, 'In From the Margins', London, 2 November.

Rivers, I. (1999) 'The psycho-social correlates and long-term implications of bullying at school for lesbians, gay men and bisexual men and women', unpublished PhD thesis. University of Surrey, Roehampton Institute London.

Rivers, I. and Smith, P.K. (1994) Types of bullying behavior and their correlates. *Aggressive Behavior*, 20(5): 359–68.

Rottnek, M.J. (1998) Esto vir, in K. Jennings (ed.) *Telling Tales Out of School: Gays, Lesbians, and Bisexuals Revisit Their School Days.* Los Angeles: Alyson.

Rottnek, M.J. (1999) *Sissies and Tomboys: Gender Nonconformity and Homosexual Childhood.* New York: New York University Press.

Sharp, S. and Cowie, H. (1998) *Counselling and Supporting Children in Distress.* London: Sage.

Smith, P.K. (1991) The silent nightmare: bullying and victimisation in school peer groups. *The Psychologist: Bulletin of the British Psychological Society*, 4(6): 243–8.

Trenchard, L. and Warren, H. (1984) *Something to Tell You.* London: London Gay Teenage Group.

Warren, H. (1984) *Talking About School.* London: London Gay Teenage Group.

Whitney, I. and Smith, P.K. (1993) A survey on the nature and extent of bully/victim problems in junior/middle and secondary schools. *Educational Research*, 35(1): 3–25.

Zuckerman, M. and Lubin, B. (1965) *Manual for the Multiple Affect Adjective Check List.* San Diego, CA: EdITS.

Gay men and sex: clinical issues

Introduction

Gay men are famous (some might say notorious) for their colourful and diverse sexual lives. Spurred on by the AIDS epidemic the media have paid a lot of attention to sensational aspects of gay sexuality, so a large audience has now been informed about the existence of, for example, backrooms, gay saunas, cruising places and leather parties. It's not quite clear how people react to this kind of information. For some, prejudices about gay men may be confirmed while others will adopt a more positive viewpoint based on the information now available. However, for a very long period in Western European cultures sex between men has been regarded as the worst imaginable sin or as a consequence of mental illness. I believe it is vital for therapists to understand how central the issue of sex (and, more precisely, the issue of anal sex between men) has been, and still is, in all forms of homophobia.

During a training session on therapists' attitudes towards homosexuality, a participant said: 'I consider myself to be a liberal person where sexuality is concerned. I firmly believe gays should be free to live the lives they choose. I have gay friends! But when I visualise two men having sex, I cannot help feeling disgusted'. His statement was both honest and revealing. The under-lying feeling about gay sex was shared by most of the therapists in the group.

Extremely negative feelings about gay sexuality are deeply rooted in our culture and are still common, although more often hidden under a thin layer of tolerance. One only has to think about the different reactions to publicly expressed feelings of affection between a man and a woman or between two men. As a female therapist expressed it: 'I don't like these new safe sex posters with two men kissing each other. What do I tell my children when they see these posters?' Obviously, the same woman had no objections about similar posters showing a man and a woman kissing.

In an environment characterised by an outright rejection of their sexuality, gay men have built their own sexual subculture, which was kept secret for a long time. The first section of this chapter describes developments within this subculture since it became possible to partly lift the secrecy, at least in the larger urban areas of Western Europe. Next, gay male sexual styles are described, followed by a discussion of body image. Finding a satisfying combination between sex and intimacy is a central issue for many gay clients, so some space is devoted to this topic. Finally, the role of the therapist is looked at in some detail, followed by some concluding remarks.

Sexuality and gay male subcultures

In order to understand the current role of sex within gay male subcultures it is necessary to go back into recent history. The social attitude towards homosexuality in the western world has been characterised by a strong, emotional rejection of sexual acts between members of the same sex. Not surprisingly, therefore, the gay movement in post-war Europe and the USA wanted more attention for the human beings behind these sexual acts and stressed the affective character of same-sex attraction. The introduction of the terms 'homophile' and 'gay' during this period should not only be understood as an attempt to break free from a diagnostic category, but also to move away from the focus on sex inherent in the word 'homosexual' (Tielman 1982).

The 1960s are usually seen as the start of the 'sexual revolution'. One aspect of this was that sex became a more private matter, suited for self-regulation. The state interfered less in the sexual lives of its citizens, provided that sex took place in private and between consenting adults. Thus the 1970s became a period of growing tolerance and freedom of movement for gay men as for others. Commercial nightlife flourished as never before and provided increasing possibilities for meeting sexual partners. The 1970s were also characterised by a new trend for gay men which reflected an important change in self-image and social image. Many were fed up with the stereotype of the effeminate homosexual and became adepts of the so-called 'macho trend'. Elegant bars changed into cowboy saloons and men started dressing in tight jeans, lumberjack shirts and leather jackets. Moustaches and crew cuts became the new symbols of their masculinity. Gay pornography changed along the same lines: erotic pictures of slim youths gave way to images of somewhat older, muscled guys. To some there was so much uniformity in the new outer appearance of many gays that they started calling them 'clones'.

Although the macho trend and a varied, promiscuous sex life are still popular, there was an influential countermovement, even before the onset of the HIV epidemic. Some younger men, who seemed to be taking the newly-found sexual liberties for granted, criticised the overemphasis on sexual aspects in the gay community and felt that all men above 30 looked alike. In my clinical practice I started noticing that younger gay men seemed fearful of the image of being oversexed, while they no longer seemed to share the fear of being seen as effeminate, which haunted the generation before them.

Of course the 1980s and 1990s saw major changes in sexual attitudes and behaviours among gay men, due to AIDS. The scope of this chapter makes it impossible to describe these changes in detail (see, for example, Ross 1995 and Chapter 4). Control over sexual behaviour was a major issue and monogamous relationships became more popular. Moralistic ideas and misconceptions about the interrelationship between the number of sex partners and the chance of becoming infected seem to have triggered a growing interest among therapists in the problem of *'compulsive sexuality'* in gay men (see, for example, Quadland 1983; Fontaine 1995). Having sex with a relatively large number of partners was supposed to be caused by a *'sex addiction'*. Out of fear of HIV infection some gay men, who previously enjoyed unrestrained sex, were apt to label themselves as *'sex addicts'*. Frequency and function (or meaning) of sexual behaviour are often mixed up in these kinds of self diagnosis (see Simon and Whitfield 2000). The fact that certain sexual techniques may be a health hazard is no reason to qualify the frequency of these behaviours as inherently pathological. Men who seek professional help for 'sex addiction' usually suffer from moral judgements about 'anonymous' sex at semi-public places like parks or backrooms in certain bars. These men often have problems accepting and appreciating their homosexuality, or their integration into the gay male subculture has been restricted to the commercial nightlife or cruising places only. Some express a dissatisfaction with the nature of sexual contacts, which are experienced as mechanical or unsatisfying. In these cases the central problem usually has to do with a fear of intimacy.

These kinds of problem should only be diagnosed as compulsive when the sexual behaviour has a clear function in avoiding overwhelming fear, depression or psychosis. The therapy is the same as with other compulsive behaviour or thoughts, and should be aimed at understanding the underlying mechanisms as well as at getting the symptoms under control.

Case example 1

Martin (44) had come to the conclusion that he was a 'sex addict'. During our first session he explained that he felt his 'obsession' with sex prevented him from forming meaningful and longer-lasting relationships with other men. Every Friday he would decide to stay home and have a quiet night in.

Around ten he would start feeling restless and go to one of the local 'cruising areas'. There he usually had sex, after which he returned home, often feeling depressed and lonely. The pattern was repeated on Saturday evenings. Martin wanted to stop going to the cruising areas altogether, but seemed unable to reach this goal by himself. He told me that he often enjoyed the cruising, as well as the sex itself, but started feeling bad after he had reached orgasm.

Martin appeared to have a negative image of men in general and gay men in particular. His mother had told him men only want 'one thing' and after she caught him masturbating, she kept telling him he was no better. Being a shy and insecure person, it had taken Martin time to accept the fact that he was gay. He had a lover for a few years, but after he found out his partner had sex with others he ended the relationship. It became clear that Martin expected to find a partner at the cruising areas, but all he got was sex. This confirmed his self-image and his image of other men. I explained to him it didn't seem helpful to label himself an addict who needs to stop the addictive behaviour once and for all, when in fact he seemed to suffer from internalised prejudices and fear of intimacy with other men. Giving up his cruising would mean a lack of contacts with other gay men, since he never went to any other activity in the gay community. I proposed he plan his cruising for Fridays and Saturdays (instead of planning something else, then cruising anyway) and change the way in which he made contact with the men he met. This was enough to make him feel less depressed and lonely afterwards, because he had given himself permission for the cruising and aimed at getting a little more intimacy, alongside the sex. He joined a gay therapy group to work on his fear of intimacy and, at a later stage, explored the other services and activities the gay community had to offer. About a year after our first session he told me he still went cruising about once a week. Sometimes he would feel great afterwards, sometimes bad, depending on what had happened. He had made a few gay friends and felt much less isolated and pessimistic about the future.

AIDS has changed the subjective experiencing of sexuality among gay men, as well as the nature and frequency of sexual problems (see Chapter 6). For some gay men it has reactivated the stigma, which has been attached to gay sex for ages and which, unavoidably, has been internalised by gay men themselves (see Chapter 4).

The liberal sex lives of a number of gay men have been admired and condemned. In the past few years new experiments with sexuality, at least in the larger urban areas, seem to be aimed at the deconstruction of the strict separation between sexualities, as witnessed by the popularity of so called 'kinky parties', which are being organised for men and women of all sexualities and which have contributed to the development of a whole new subcultural scene (see Chapter 2).

Sexual styles

It is not an easy task to describe the ways in which gay men express their sexuality and how they go about finding sexual partners. Some insight into these complicated issues can be gained by means of the concept of *'lovestyles'* (Lee 1988). Based on extensive research among gay men, Lee distinguishes five different styles, which represent a typology of contacts and relationships, not of persons. So one person may, depending on the circumstances, use different styles or combinations of style. Below, each style is illustrated by the text of a personal contact advertisement.

> Attr. boy (28) looking for muscled, blonde, well-hung guy. No spectacles; beard and/or moustache OK. Masculine type. Sex important, relationship possible.

This lovestyle is characterised by the value attached to *outward appearance*. The wish to find a certain physical type, with a specific hair colour, build, penis size, distribution of body hair et cetera, is central.

> Energetic, creative guy (35/1.85/76) seeks attractive guys with active lifestyles. Likes going out, travel, uncomplicated sex. No problematic types, please!

This advert illustrates a style used by men who are not looking for a specific type of person, but are mainly interested in the *playful aspects* of sexuality. Having pleasure and fun are important and relationships are only maintained as long as these desires are being fulfilled.

> Man (40) looking for pen pal, about same age. Goal: building friendship. Do not exclude relationship for the future.

This style is characterised by the wish to become *friends* before sexual contact is considered.

> Have you also been used and disappointed? Are you, like me, looking for the one and only? Honest, sensitive boy (23) seeks ditto for monogamous relationship. Do you really exist?

This style is characterised by a strong focus on finding *one partner*. Although the idealised object of love is unavailable, this doesn't stop the sometimes unrelenting search for the prince on a white horse.

> Am 38, looking for a man, interested in art, culture and travel. Graduate. I have a good job, nice house, car. I miss good conversation, going to the theatre and possibly more!

This text stresses the importance of *personal and social similarities* between partners on dimensions like education, income, religion and political beliefs.

The concept of '*lovestyles*' offers a quick diagnostic tool for the therapist confronted with gay clients who are dissatisfied with their love life. Many clients use one particular lovestyle persistently, even if it doesn't bring them what they expect from it. Finding out which is being used and why other styles do not feature in the person's repertoire will shed light on the nature of the underlying problems the client is dealing with. Informing the client about alternative styles may help him to develop more effective strategies in partner selection.

The examples above also indicate that not all gay men have participated in, or are happy with, the emphasis on sex of the commercial male subculture, such as cruise bars, saunas or cruising areas and sex on premises. This subculture caters mainly for men who use lovestyles emphasising the appearance of partners and the pleasurable, exciting aspects of sexuality. It is often disappointing for men who would like to make contacts in different ways. Therapists should be aware of the fact that, statistically, gay men as a group may have more sex and more partners compared to heterosexual men (Sandfort and de Vroome 1996), but that this generalisation may not apply (at all) to individual clients.

Sexual techniques used by gay men do not differ greatly from those used by heterosexual men. Masters and Johnson (1980) found only small differences between the sexual behaviour of their gay and straight subjects. They noted, however, that gay couples were less orgasm-oriented than straight couples. The gay men in this classic study played with lowering and intensifying sexual excitement and lingered in the plateau phase of the sexual response cycle. Straight couples, on the other hand, focused on getting 'the job done' (i.e. reaching orgasm), especially through intercourse.

Aversion or shame in gay clients is often triggered by anal contact. Penetration or stimulation of the anus are techniques to enhance sexual excitement. For many men (and women) the anus is an erogenous zone. The anus and the surrounding areas are rich in nerve-endings and a large proportion of these nerves and a number of muscles in this area are directly connected to the genitals (Agnew 1985). Gay men themselves attribute all kinds of meanings to anal sex. For some it is the ultimate form of sex, linked to feelings of intimacy, symbiosis or being at one with the partner. For others, feelings of lust are paramount in this form of sex. The receptive (or 'passive') role in anal sex can cause feelings of surrender and submission, while the penetrative (or 'active') role may be associated with power and domination. Research into the attribution of meaning to anal sex by gay men shows that anal sex is most often linked to trusting the partner. 'Before one can fuck or be fucked, there first has to be an atmosphere of trust', is the conclusion of researchers (van Kerkhof *et al.* 1995: 115). Some have a strong preference for the receptive role while others prefer the penetrative. Usually, however, the preference will change, depending on the partner and the circumstances and it is quite usual for partners to assume both roles intermittently during one sexual encounter.

Although the anal zone is always sensitive, not everyone will derive pleasure from it. Many people even show aversion to anal stimulation, usually because of the excretory function of this part of the body, combined with common myths that anal sex is 'unnatural', a 'terrible sin', or a sign of (mental) illness. Early in life, some gay men (just like many other people) learn that everything connected to the anal area is dirty and unnatural, and should remain hidden as much as possible. These learned aversions may be problematic with partners who do enjoy anal sex (again, see Chapter 6). Unprotected anal sex is a major risk factor in contracting HIV and other sexually transmitted diseases. This fact may, of course, intensify or reinforce feelings of aversion.

Case example 2

Joop and Hans have been together for two years. Joop likes anal sex very much, while Hans has strong reservations about it. They have tried anal contact and Hans has only felt aversion. Just thinking about the smell of faeces makes his sexual excitement disappear completely. Because they have always used a condom, he is not afraid of being contaminated with HIV. Hans stresses that he would like to learn to enjoy anal sex: he wants to pleasure his partner, and feels he's missing something important for himself as well. After we discussed the possible consequences if the desired goals were not achieved, I felt that Hans was motivated and that their relationship would not suffer unduly if Hans did not learn to appreciate anal contact.

I give both partners information about the anatomy of the anus and about cleaning the lower intestines using an anal douche or clisma. The first step is for Hans to get to know his own body better. He is to create a relaxed atmosphere, after which he will look at his anus by means of a hand mirror. Also, I ask him to notice the effects of anal self-stimulation, by inserting a lubricated finger. After Hans has learned to do these exercises in a completely relaxed state, Joop takes over the stimulation. They can stop if Hans feels any aversion, concentrating instead on relaxation and gentle mutual stroking or massage. When both are relaxed and feeling good, they can resume the anal stimulation. The anal contact is gradually made more intensive – I keep stressing the need for relaxation and discovery of pleasurable feelings with each new step taken. Finally, the couple tries penetration with Joop's penis (using a condom). After five sessions Hans' aversion has almost completely disappeared.

Body image

Obviously, the image one has of one's own body plays a central role in the way one experiences oneself and one's sexuality. This is true for most people, gay and straight. Nevertheless, in gay men and, more specifically, in gay clients presenting with sexual problems, the issue has some specific aspects related to scientific discourse on homosexuality, socio-cultural factors, and factors linked to gay identity development. Therapists may make mistakes in diagnosing gay clients with body image problems, gay clients themselves may have misconceptions about the importance of their physical appearance in socialising with other gays, and difficulties in accepting and appreciating their homosexuality may be expressed by some as dissatisfaction with physical appearance.

Scientific discourse

The way in which science has studied, explained and described homosexuality and gay men has had a profound influence on how gay men see themselves and how they are seen by others (Foucault 1984; Greenberg 1988). Traditional and modern psychoanalytic theories on the development of a gay preference have been very influential in shaping views of homosexuality (see Shelley 1998). This is particularly true for therapists, who have usually been exposed to the psychoanalytic discourse on homosexuality during their training. More traditional analysts in particular (for example Socarides 1989; Fenichel 1990) have claimed that the development of a homosexual preference is linked to narcissistic personality disorder. The idea that gay men are more narcissistic than others has become part of the cultural stereotype and has also been identified as an important internalised stereotype in gay men themselves (Schippers 1996). One of the consequences may be that therapists make mistakes in diagnosing (and thus in treating) such clients. A gay man who is insecure about the way he looks and who feels his appearance is to be blamed for his social isolation may easily be diagnosed as suffering from narcissistic personality disorder, when in fact he might be using a narcissistic defence mechanism based, for example, on rejections in his past, or simply be more focused on his body than most straight men. The few studies that have been conducted in this area indicate that there is no relationship between homosexuality and narcissism, but suggest gay men may use more narcissistic defence mechanisms because this offers one way of surviving in an anti-homosexual environment (Alexander and Nunno 1996). A danger for therapists is to label these differences as psychopathology.

Socio-cultural factors

As has been stressed before, part of the commercial gay subculture is structured in such a way that physical appearance seems to be a crucial factor, determining whether men will be successful in making contact with others, or not. Participation may thus lead to affirming experiences ('men look at me, flirt with me, so I must look good'). On the other hand, a negative body image may be reinforced when a man gets the feeling no one is interested in him. In my experience, quite a few clients blame their social problems or inadequacies on their physical appearance. Such a negative self-image, in combination with problems in making contact means meeting new friends and sexual partners is even more difficult, so the client may easily find himself in a vicious circle. Some feel under pressure in relation to their physical appearance. Their position may, in this respect, be comparable to heterosexual women, who are also pressurised to appear young and attractive because of centuries of sexual objectification. This may explain why gay men and heterosexual women are more vulnerable to body dissatisfaction and eating disorders (Herzog *et al.* 1991; Siever 1996). This situation may be changing, since heterosexual men are now presenting with body image difficulties as a result of being confronted with idealised male bodies in commercials and in the media. Presently, however, cultural norms and values of physical appearance are differently affecting straight and gay men. Some gay men, therefore, may seem to be 'preoccupied' with their bodies by frequently working out, by paying a lot of attention to the kind of clothes they wear or by decorating their bodies through body piercing and tattoos. Once again, therapists should not 'over-pathologise' this behaviour, which may be understood primarily as related to cultural differences rather than to personality problems.

Gay identity development

Gay identity development is usually described as a series of stages a gay man goes through in order to learn to accept and appreciate his homosexuality (see Davies 1996a; Schippers 1997). The first stages (a vague feeling of being different, sexual identity confusion and the struggle against sexual feelings for other men) are usually gone through in complete isolation out of fear of rejection. About one third of all gay men remember feeling different from other boys as early as the age of 3 or 4, while others report having first had these feelings when they were about 12 or 13 (Schippers 1996).

Especially during these periods in which being or becoming gay is an issue the person doesn't dare to talk about, rejection by other significant males may lead to a negative self-image. Gay boys may experience rejection by their own fathers (see Isay 1989) and by peers (for example, at school) (see Schippers 1996 and Chapter 10), especially when they have shown 'sissy boy' or gender atypical behaviour. Many tell their therapists they used to be bad at sports ('always the last to be selected for the soccer team'), preferred the games the girls were playing and got teased a lot by other boys. In my experience these early rejections by significant males are probably the main cause for the development of some 'narcissistic' defence mechanisms in gay boys and men, and may also play a major role in the development of a negative body image. These negative feelings may be overcome at a later age, when other achievements become more important for group status, or when the person finds there are lots of other men who do think they are attractive (see also Chapter 7). Others, however, try to feel better about themselves by overcompensating, showing a single-minded focus on the development of their body. In still others the problem persists in adult life: in these cases therapeutic attention for rejection by significant males during childhood is certainly warranted.

Sexuality and intimacy

When homosexuality was seen as an illness the professional literature paid no attention to the sexual problems gay men may have suffered. The definitions of sexual dysfunctions were heterosexually biased and stressed the inability to get or sustain an erection and reach orgasm (see Chapter 6). Today, many therapists are aware that male sexuality involves more than penetration and orgasm. Hardly any research is available, however, investigating the prevalence and nature of sexual disorders in gay men. One of the few exceptions is a study by Rosser *et al.* (1997) of a sample of 197 gay men who attended a health seminar. Almost all reported some sexual difficulties over their lifetime and more than half reported a current difficulty. Nevertheless the same men reported average to above average sexual satisfaction: 'Correlates of sexual satisfaction included more liberal attitudes toward human sexuality, greater comfort with men's sexual attraction to other men, lower levels of internalised homophobia, and greater satisfaction with one's relationship status' (Rosser *et al.* 1997: 61).

According to Paff (1985) the main causes of sexual dysfunctions in gay men are: achievement compulsion (the idea that one has to get an erection in all erotic situations); a negative attitude towards sexuality in general and homosexuality in particular; religious beliefs or background; letting the pleasure of one's partner take precedence over one's own; the (subjectively experienced) negative aspects of growing older; abuse of alcohol and drugs; lack of information; and severe psychopathology. Sexual problems may also play a role in efforts to hang onto a relationship. One of the partners may (secretly or subconsciously) wish for his partner to remain dysfunctional – for example out of fear of losing him. I feel the list of causes by Paff should be extended to include the possible consequences of sexual abuse or violence (including anti-gay violence), and the effects of the AIDS epidemic (fear of infection, guilt and anger, problems with safe sex, dysfunctions caused by physical illness and/or medication, and the consequences of multiple loss; see Ross 1995).

The sexual problem most frequently presented by gay male clients is, in my experience, a difficulty in finding the right balance between sexuality and intimacy. These kinds of problem are usually very complex and include intra-psychic factors (see Alexander 1997) as well as causes rooted in socialisation.

The traditional way in which boys are raised to become (heterosexual) men stimulates competition as well as cooperation with other males, but is much less focused on skills like self-disclosure, expression of emotions, caring and touching. There are indications that the way one has been brought up is related to the experiencing of intimacy within a gay relationship. Deenen (1992) found that younger gay men with steady partners were less satisfied with the level of intimacy with their partners when they labelled their parents as 'traditional'. The closer their contact with their father (or, curiously enough, with their mother in the case of older gays), the higher satisfaction with the level of intimacy within the relationship appeared to be. For younger gays Deenen also found that the experiencing of physical contact within a relationship tended to be more negative when the men concerned perceived their fathers as having stereotypical ideas about how males are supposed to relate to other males.

When the sexual problems of a client are characterised by difficulties with the balance between intimacy and sexuality a therapeutic approach aimed at solving the sexual problem (like erectile dysfunctions or inhibited orgasm) alone will usually not be effective. In my experience the quality of relationships with significant boys and men from the past plays an important role in the development of fear of intimacy combined with sexual problems (Schippers 1996).

Case example 3

Volker (28), raised in Austria, has a very expressive face and uses his hands and arms (and sometimes his whole body) to underscore emotion. He likes to laugh and seems open and friendly. Volker explains he has problems making friends and maintaining relationships. He doesn't like the sexualised atmosphere in gay bars and is afraid that men will abandon him once he has had sex with them. He finds it difficult to let go sexually, but also when he feels angry or hurt.

Volker is the youngest of three boys. His father and mother had been members of the Hitler *Jugend* and his mother had been incarcerated in a Russian camp just after the war. At home no one ever spoke about this traumatic period. Volker was an obedient child. His father, usually absent because of work, was strict and beat his sons when they had done something wrong. His mother is described as talkative, intelligent, theatrical and mean. The relationship with his brothers was problematic as he felt they abused their strength and oppressed him. At primary school he was teased because he wore spectacles and clothes discarded by his brothers, and played the violin. During secondary school things improved until Volker was about 14, when he started to have feelings of insecurity, isolation and depression. He felt he didn't belong because he was different. This feeling was strengthened when he started thinking he might be gay.

At home no one ever discussed sex. Volker felt extremely guilty about masturbation and his occasional wet dreams. When he was 18 he fell in love for the first time and enjoyed physical contact with his partner, who liked unhampered frequent sex. After a few weeks, however, Volker started to have problems maintaining his erection and was unable to reach orgasm. A vicious circle developed in which he tried to satisfy his partner's wishes, but increasingly failed. They broke up and Volker moved to the Netherlands. During later relationships the same pattern developed. Making love with a new partner he felt very excited at first, but this disappeared as soon as he found himself in a more 'passive' position (on his back). He also observed that his excitement disappeared completely when he was close to orgasm.

Volker's history is one of rejection by other males. He has developed a fear of bonding and feelings of 'not belonging'. His ambivalent attitude towards his brothers (admiration, aversion and fear) holds true for his feelings towards his peers. Fear of intimacy and sexuality seems to be based on a fear of males in general instead of internalised anti-gay feelings only.

In therapy it becomes clear that the pain, sadness, and anger caused by rejection in the past are repressed. Especially the awareness and expression of anger are problematic. Rejection triggers overwhelming feelings of shame: 'Now everyone who has witnessed this rejection can see for themselves that I'm nothing'. In order to avoid this shame, Volker avoids rejection by anticipating it and withdrawing from friendship and, interestingly, from ejaculating before the other man can find out who he really is.

During the last of three years of therapy Volker had a steady relationship. Fear of rejection and competition over getting attention played a role in this relationship too. However, sexual dysfunction slowly ameliorated and Volker shifted towards a more assertive, less fearful attitude.

With gay male clients having problems with sexuality and intimacy, it is important to gain insight into the history of the homosexual desires towards men and boys during childhood and puberty. Awareness and expression of consequent pain and anger are important steps towards healing. Male therapists especially must be aware of the different transference feelings that play a role during therapy. Volker, for example, usually behaved as an 'ideal client'. He experienced great difficulties in expressing criticism or aggression towards me. By continuously monitoring the way in which clients deal with these issues of distance and closeness between themselves and the therapist, much can be learned about the mechanisms that may play a role in their daily lives. In these cases the gay male therapist has a certain advantage over heterosexual or female therapists. Transference occurs, no matter what the gender or sexuality of the therapist, but the transference between gay male clients and therapists is often a direct reflection of the client's problems with intimacy in gay relationships. Therefore, the gay therapist can often use the transference as an example of how the client deals with feelings for other males. Countertransference merits specific attention as well, because it often unveils important information about the effects of the client's behaviour on men in his environment.

Guidelines for good practice

Therapists working with gay men who have sexual problems should be aware of a number of possible pitfalls and specific aspects which may influence the therapeutic process and outcome.

Most importantly, the therapist must be aware of his or her own attitude towards sex in general, gay men in general and sex between men in particular. Discussion of sexual issues can be difficult even for the most experienced and sophisticated therapists. When clients engage in sexual behaviours which the therapist feels are immoral, repugnant, or representative of a lifestyle with which the therapist is unfamiliar, countertransferential mistakes are easily made (Davies 1996b).

A liberal or tolerant attitude is certainly not enough when one is working with gay sexual problems. When a therapist has feelings of disgust, fear or rejection when visualising gay sex, he or she is not ready to work with this specific group. A therapist must feel comfortable discussing gay sexuality, including the more uncommon forms it may take. Being able to visualise gay sex without negative reactions or to talk openly about sexual techniques doesn't mean, of course, that the material would sexually excite therapists.

Most dangerous is the unconscious rejection of gay sex by the therapist, which will undoubtedly translate itself into an equally unconscious, and often subtle, rejection of the client himself and of the sexual behaviours that might be essential to his well-being, growth and healing. Such rejection may in fact jeopardise all three basic conditions for therapeutic work: unconditional positive regard, respect and congruence (Rogers 1990; Davies 1998).

A therapist working with gay clients needs knowledge about gay identity development, subcultures and their history, sexual styles and techniques, sexual problems (like pain during anal intercourse), the influence of AIDS and other sexually transmitted diseases, and gay relationships. Only part of this knowledge can be obtained by training and by professional reading (see Neal and Davies' Introduction to this volume). Also of benefit is the more impressionistic knowledge gained from visiting the gay scene, interacting with gay friends and reading gay literature. Most gay therapists have easier access to this personalised knowledge and thus may sometimes be better equipped to help gay therapy clients who present with sexual problems.

The therapist should be aware of a number of factors which may affect gay clients and which may, therefore, influence the therapeutic process in general and the working alliance in particular. As has been stressed, our society is very judgemental about gay sexuality. This situation has certainly not become any better since the AIDS epidemic. Because of this, clients may be reluctant to ask for help with sexual problems, or to discuss their sexual lives with their therapist. This is especially true when the client presumes or knows his therapist to be heterosexual. Through fear of rejection, other clients try to shock the therapist by giving detailed accounts of all kinds of sexual exploits. They are testing the limits of their therapist's tolerance, sometimes verbally and sometimes by coming to sessions in full leather or hardly dressed at all. Therapists may also be confronted with sexual transference expressed by seductive behaviour or by the client telling the therapist he has fallen in love with him. Therapists should be able to work with this transference without feeling threatened or flattered. Obviously, one should keep in mind that such behaviour may be rooted in sexual or physical violence in childhood. In these cases the client is not so much testing the limits of tolerance as the ability of the therapist to set limits. Outright rejection of the client's feelings or fantasies (for example, by saying: 'You know I'm not gay') may easily trigger pain about earlier rejections and thus endanger a positive outcome of therapy. In some cases, depending on the therapeutic strategy which has been chosen, the therapist should take the initiative in discussing positive or negative transference, especially when fear of intimacy is one of the client's problems.

Gay therapists may face some specific challenges, like a confrontation with their own internalised anti-homosexuality, sexual countertransference towards clients and encounters with clients in the gay subculture (see Chapter 3).

Concluding remarks

Sexuality is a difficult topic for therapists and clients. Many avoid the issue or are hesitant to ask direct questions about it. Some of my gay clients have been in therapy for years, but the issue of sexuality has never been addressed either by themselves or their previous therapists.

When gay sex is discussed in therapy, a number of pitfalls and gay-specific aspects may emerge as outlined in this chapter. The therapist's aversion to gay sex, deeply rooted in western cultures, may be a crucial factor in the avoidance of the issue or may lead to therapeutic mistakes, threatening process and outcome. An unbiased and positive attitude, as well as knowledge about the specific issues involved, is crucial in increasing the quality of professional help offered to gay therapy clients.

174 Jan Schippers

References

Agnew, J. (1985) Some anatomical and physiological aspects of anal sexual practices. *Journal of Homosexuality*, 12(1): 75–98.
Alexander, C.J. (1997) *Growth and Intimacy for Gay Men. A Workbook.* New York: Harrington Park Press.
Alexander, C.J. and Nunno, V.J. (1996) Narcissism and egocentricity in gay men, in C.J. Alexander (ed.) *Gay and Lesbian Mental Health. A Sourcebook for Practitioners.* New York: Harrington Park Press.
Davies, D. (1996a) Working with people coming out, in D. Davies and C. Neal (eds) *Pink Therapy: A Guide for Counsellors and Therapists Working with Lesbian, Gay and Bisexual Clients.* Buckingham: Open University Press.
Davies, D. (1996b) Towards a model of gay affirmative therapy, in D. Davies and C. Neal (eds) *Pink Therapy: A Guide for Counsellors and Therapists Working with Lesbian, Gay and Bisexual Clients.* Buckingham: Open University Press.
Davies, D. (1998) The six necessary and sufficient conditions applied to working with lesbian, gay and bisexual clients. *The Person-Centered Journal*, 5(2): 111–24.
Deenen, A. (1992) *Intimiteit en Seksualiteit in Homoseksuele Mannenrelaties [Intimacy and Sexuality in Gay Male Relationships].* Utrecht: Rijksuniversiteit Utrecht.
Fenichel, O. (1990) *The Psychoanalytic Theory of Neurosis.* London: Routledge.
Fontaine, M.M. (1995) Issues of isolation and intimacy for the HIV infected, sexually addicted gay male in group psychotherapy, in M.W. Ross (ed.) *HIV and Sexuality.* New York: Harrington Park Press.
Foucault, M. (1984) *Geschiedenis van de Seksualiteit [History of Sexuality].* Nijmegen: SUN.
Greenberg, D.F. (1988) *The Construction of Homosexuality.* Chicago: University of Chicago Press.
Herzog, D.B., Newman, K.L. and Warshaw, M. (1991) Body image dissatisfaction in homosexual and heterosexual males. *The Journal of Nervous and Mental Disease*, 179(6): 356–9.
Isay, R.A. (1989) *Being Homosexual: Gay Men and Their Development.* New York: Avon Books.
Lee, J.A. (1988) Forbidden colours of love: patterns of gay love and gay liberation, in J.P. De Cecco (ed.) *Gay Relationships.* New York: Harrington Park Press.
Masters, W.H., and Johnson, V.E. (1980) *Homoseksualiteit [Homosexuality in Perspective].* Deventer: Van Loghum Slaterus.
Paff, B.A. (1985) Sexual dysfunction in gay men requesting treatment. *Journal of Sex and Marital Therapy*, 11: 3–18.
Quadland, M.C. (1983) Homosexual men and compulsive sex. *New York Native*, 7: 20.
Rogers, C.R. (1990) The necessary and sufficient conditions of therapeutic personality change, in H. Kirschenbaum and V.L. Henderson (eds) *The Carl Rogers Reader.* London: Constable.
Ross, M.W. (1995) *HIV/AIDS and Sexuality.* New York: Harrington Park Press.
Rosser, B.R.S., Metz, M.E., Bockting, W.O. and Buroker, T. (1997) Sexual difficulties, concerns, and satisfaction in homosexual men: an empirical study with implications for HIV prevention. *Journal of Sex and Marital Therapy*, 23(1): 61–73.

Sandfort, T.G.M. and de Vroome, E.M.M. (1996) Homoseksualiteit in Nederland: een vergelijking tussen aselecte groepen homoseksuele en heteroseksuele mannen [Homosexuality in the Netherlands: a comparison between two aselect groups of homosexual and heterosexual men]. *Tijdschrift voor Seksuologie*, 20: 232–45.

Schippers, J. (1996) *Homoseksuele Identiteiten [Gay Identities]*. Amsterdam: Thesis Publishers.

Schippers, J. (1997) *Liever Mannen: Theorie en Praktijk van de Hulpverlening aan Homoseksuele Mannen [Preferring Men: Theory and Practice of Psychosocial Care for Gay Men]*. Amsterdam: Schorer/Thesis.

Shelley, C. (1998) *Contemporary Perspectives on Psychotherapy and Homosexualities*. London: Free Association Books.

Siever, M.D. (1996) The perils of sexual objectification: sexual orientation, gender, and socioculturally acquired vulnerability to body dissatisfaction and eating disorders, in C.J. Alexander (ed.) *Gay and Lesbian Mental Health. A Sourcebook for Practitioners*. New York: Harrington Park Press.

Simon, G. and Whitfield, G. (2000) Social constructionist and systemic therapy, in D. Davies and C. Neal (eds) *Therapeutic Perspectives on Working with Lesbian, Gay and Bisexual Clients*. Buckingham: Open University Press.

Socarides, C.W. (1989) *Homosexuality – Psychoanalytic Therapy*. Northvale/London: Jason Aronson Inc.

Tielman, R.A.P. (1982) *Homoseksualiteit in Nederland (Homosexuality in the Netherlands)* Meppel: Boom.

Van Kerkhof, M.P.N., de Zwart, O. and Sandfort, T.G.M. (1995) *Van Achteren Bezien: Anale Seks in Het Aidstijdperk [Seen from Behind: Anal Sex in the Era of AIDS]*. Amsterdam: Schorer.

Transgender issues in therapy

Introduction

The relationship between sexual orientation and transgender is an uneasy one. On the one hand the two are closely connected – a change of gender has implications for one's sexual orientation. On the other hand they seem to exclude each other, as the concepts of gay, lesbian or bisexual imply a dichotomy that becomes undermined by transgender. In principle, the straightforward idea of a same-sex relationship will, at least, be questioned when either or both partners is involved in transgender. The number of people to whom the transgression of gender applies includes diverse groups who have become visible and been analysed, distinguished and named, one group after another, hence generating assumptions that the issues and the people involved are so completely different that no common denominator exists. To avoid any association with other 'transgenders', separate groups have exaggerated the differences, and seen others as the 'real' deviants. Our inability to deal with social diversity creates the need for separate communities. The same inability causes resistance to diversity *within* groups.

The first occurrence of transgender in Europe, a form of cross-dressing, was usually understood as transvestism, based on appearance and role-play. However serious its intention, it was mostly considered as entertainment, either solely for the transvestite or, in a more 'theatrical' context, where its purpose was to be seen – for example, 'drag'. Gradually it became clear that, for an increasing number of people involved in cross-dressing, appearance and role-play were not enough. They felt they belonged to the 'opposite' sex and in the process of expressing their feelings on a social or professional level the description that eventually became accepted was that they were 'in the wrong body'. They were called transsexuals to distinguish them from transvestites. Social acceptance of transsexuality has been supported by general familiarity with the concept of two genders: this helped transsexual people to become a group that was seen as homogeneous, with clear-cut problems that could be solved in respectable, medical ways. However great the confusion caused by transsexuality and however strongly the results of the transformation were criticised, at least the aim of the change was adjustment to one gender identity, man or woman, and never anything ambiguously in between. The way transsexual people are perceived has evolved (as historically with gay men) from people who broke the law by their behaviour, to deviants with bizarre needs that were of interest to psychiatry (Lipsitz-Bem 1994: 82). Subsequently they became 'respectable' patients with predicaments that, at last, could be treated with the development of medical technology.

The emergence of 'transgender' – a departure from the strict definition of transsexuality, with people opting only for partial treatment or no treatment at all, who eventually were called transgenderist – reopened the discussion so that the laboriously reached consensus is now questioned again in very similar ways to those that have always surrounded homosexualities. 'Is transsexuality really a condition that cannot be ignored or do people have a choice?' Numerous transsexuals have claimed that the need for a gender reassignment is, in fact, a matter of life and death. It cannot be denied that a great number have committed suicide when they could not see a future in which they could be true to themselves, as with lesbians and gays (see Chapter 10). The fact that a transsexual person does not seem to have a choice is to some extent caused by a rigid concept of just two sexes. At the same time this dichotomy has become much of the justification for medical treatment. It is therefore understandable for many of those involved in transsexuality from early on, either personally or professionally, to maintain it should be considered something completely different from all other occurrences of transgender. The present state of science reflects the same interest by research, which attempts to show that the brains belonging to transsexuals are essentially different from those of other people – and possibly similar to those of gays and lesbians (Jiang-Ning *et al.* 1995).

When people found their way to gender clinics asking for treatment according to how they experienced themselves, and not to the concept of a particular gender, the medical world became aware of the growing number of people with varying transgender identities and needs. It is important to observe that this development coincides, and is connected, with increasing diversity in sexual orientation. More people feel they are not simply either a man or a woman, or simply straight, gay or bisexual. Separate genders imply mixed genders just as sexual orientations enable people to go between. The very existence of boundaries enables people to cross over. Although these variations have always existed they have recently become more visible, partly due to the fact that more and more people find the courage to make them known. I refrain from giving examples in order to avoid any unnecessary classification: whereas 'variations' present themselves to us in a particular person and on a personal and therapeutic level, the main importance is in the interaction with that particular person.

Queer gender

As previously stated, the connection between transgender and sexual orientation is an uneasy one, varying from denial or avoidance to cultivation. A common example of friction we see is the irritation caused by questions about a gay couple, such as: 'Who is the woman and who is the man?' Such ideas were reflected in the femme-butch patterns widely enjoyed in lesbian circles of the 1950s, until questioned by feminism because they were considered carbon copies of heterosexual roles. In all responses, whether positive or negative, the key question is to what degree stereotyping or diversity is going to be tolerated or encouraged. Although forms of transgender have always existed within gay and lesbian communities there has been – in spite of the obvious overlap – a great deal of antagonism and lack of recognition between subgroups.

In the Stonewall riots of 1969 a great number of gays and transvestites took part together. Or should we say: gay transvestites or gay transgenderists? At any rate, 'Stonewall', the gay rights group named after the event, has produced a manifesto: *Equality 2000* (Stonewall 1997) in which transgender is not included or even mentioned.

On a historical level, a clear example of overlap between transgender and sexual orientation is found in Radclyffe Hall, who has always been claimed by the lesbian community. However if gender reassignment had been available in the 1920s, she might very well have been recorded in history as a female to male transsexual.

What kind of relationship did Chopin and George Sand have? Can it be called femme-butch? Was it a gay relationship? Or lesbian? What were their respective genders, in spite of possible physical evidence? All possible variations and overlap of transgender and sexual orientation have always existed but since the visibility of lifestyles is increasing we can no longer ignore the diversity.

Along with the visibility, the availability of role models increases, such as Boy George, Julian Clary, K.D. Lang, Eddie Izzard, Quentin Crisp, Diana Torr and Peggy Shaw. This is a development that is distinctly irritating to some, but encouraging to many. The emergence of new identities, in spite of initial resistance, are stimulating and reinforcing each other.

Acknowledging common ground between those who define themselves as transsexual, transgender, gay, lesbian and bisexual people has resulted in the need for a more inclusive term which refers to all possible variations and combinations and puts an end to infinite classification that creates more confusion than it solves. So far, the familiar name 'queer' has been introduced and attempts have been made to develop a queer theory. That this has not yet been embraced widely shows in the approach of this series of 'Pink Therapy' texts (Davies and Neal 1996, 2000 and this present volume) where extensive discussion of transgender is restricted to this chapter.

The concept of 'queer' gives all variations of transgender, gay and lesbian identities recognition, considering them ordinary, everyday life options that do not need to be classified as pathologies or otherwise. This collective approach could free us from hidden, judgemental and homo/transphobic concepts, held by many clients and therapists (see Neal 1998). It takes care of the ever-recurring temptation of clients and professionals to see the ability 'to make up one's mind' (e.g. be either male or female, gay/lesbian or bisexual, transsexual or transgenderist) as a desirable symptom of 'normality.'

Queer Studies (Beemyn and Eliason 1996: 5), states that the concept 'queer' 'leaves room for all people who are attracted to others of the same sex or whose bodies or sexual desires do not fit dominant standards of gender'.

I am in favour of this approach in respect of affirmative and empowering therapy as it offers a creative validation of ambiguity. Whereas gay and lesbian communities have reacted against the oppressive standards of hetero-sexuality, they have often felt uncomfortable with pluriformity within their own ranks. Bisexuals have often been thought to be unreliable (see Chapter 8). Lesbians who did not reject sex with men, although they would not call themselves bisexual, had to hide this from the lesbian community in order not to be 'excommunicated'. Lesbians who used make-up were, during the 1970s, considered not 'the real thing'. About ten years later the contrary occurred: since then lesbians have been 'allowed', or even encouraged to look 'feminine'. Shaving one's legs has become fashionable recently, when it used to be denounced as 'giving in to male expectations'.

Transgenderists are often dismissed because they are not 'real' men or women, not real transsexual people and not real gays or lesbians either! One of therapy's main aims is to help clients learn to deal with and enjoy ambiguity. Transgender offers the ultimate ambiguity that has often been denied recognition by sexist attitudes. Affirmative therapy has an import-ant task in this respect to help clients free themselves from internalised trans- and homo-, phobia and sexism, in order to gain creativity and self-esteem.

The irony and power of the term 'queer' is that, after it's pejorative history, it means a return to the collective term 'invert' without the patho-logical and negative implications (see Figure 12.1).

In developing my professional attitude as a gender therapist it has been extremely inspiring to associate the ambiguity of transgender with the

Figure 12.1 Terminology in historical perspective: from 'inverts' to 'queer'

```
        ⎧ Homosexuals                                                    ⎫
Inverts ⎨                                                                ⎬
        ⎩ Cross-dressers   Transvestites, drag queens                   ⎬ Queer
                           Transsexual people  ⎫                        ⎬
                           Intersexual people  ⎬ transgender people     ⎬
                           Transgenderists     ⎭ or transpeople         ⎭
```

concept of 'migration'. This allows me to interpret transgender as a psycho-social and cultural process that takes place on two levels: within the individual and within society – both becoming genuinely 'multicultural'. This acknowledges that creative learning takes place in individual people and within social interaction: learning new forms of expression, 'languages', physical dynamics and so on while in search of personal identity. It should be remembered that the essence of identity is self-presentation: the expression of the way someone wants to be seen, named and treated. As the ultimate expression of 'self', this should never be decided by others.

Professional interest

It will be clear that I do not view transgender as one of a number of sundry 'further client issues'. Transgender concerns all of us in varying degrees and while most therapists will be dealing with issues of sexism, this is fundamental where transgender is concerned.

The recognition of transgender is generally blurred by the notion of only two sexes, exclusively based on physical appearance: a male or female body. Present practice suggests that we have to review our ideas and professional attitudes. One of the most poignant examples is the fact that an increasing number of *intersexuals* (who have a combination of male and female genitals and who have been operated on, shortly after birth, towards a body regarded as either male or female, whatever is deemed physically 'most appropriate') later feel that they have been robbed of an ambiguity they consider to be an essential part of themselves (*Hermaphrodites Speak* 1996).

I believe transgender issues should be viewed in a far wider perspective and that we shall find them becoming more and more important in affirmative and queer therapy.

Common clinical presentations

When transgender is meant in the widest sense therapists may see clients who express themselves to some extent in terms of an 'opposite' or alternative gender, experimenting with a range of 'femme' and 'butch' identities.

Some of them may eventually turn to a partial sex reassignment, pursuing only hormone treatment or both hormones and 'top surgery' (male to female breast augmentation, female to male mastectomy).

Another aspect of transgender clients is that most, at some stage of their lives, have considered the possibility of being gay or lesbian, even to the extent of trying to live these identities and taking part in gay or lesbian communities and lifestyles. Although they took refuge in the overlapping areas of, for example, butch lesbians (in the case of female to male) or gays and drag queens (in the case of male to female transgender people), these never felt 'quite right'. It is important that therapists learn to see through this confusion and help clients to find some clarity.

A third group of clients with specific needs are those transsexual people who do not change their sexual orientation after the transformation, thus becoming 'gay' or 'lesbian' in the strict sense, although a number of them may not identify as such.

Finally there are gay transvestites who express a sense of guilt about being gay that seems to be lessened by cross-dressing. I particularly want to mention this because, unfortunately, the characterisation of these feelings has caused some researchers to conclude that *all* transvestites are closeted gays! I want to stress that in all transgender occurrences it is of great importance to approach every client as an individual and to avoid generalisation into categories. This may seem a trivial remark, but transgender in particular shows us the infinity of variations.

Unnecessary categorising is a risky business, resulting in incorrect conclusions. Academics, in their eagerness to search for conclusive classifications, are being heard to call not only all transvestites closeted gays, but also all male to female transsexual people, and vice versa, gay. In therapy, where identity development is crucial, this kind of intrusion should be avoided in every possible way.

Professional guidelines

Gender could be defined as the sum of a person's non-physical and non-biological characteristics that determine their sense of being male, female or neither or any combination. Rather than 'being', the feeling is more in terms of 'belonging to'. Having said that gender concerns non-physical entities, it is remarkable that transgender is so heavily related to appearance, medical treatment and physical reassignment. These are however means to the ends of self-expression and self-presentation, which are the essence of identity: showing the world who and what we are and hopefully convincing others. Gender also concerns mental and emotional aspects like a sense of belonging and the way a body is being experienced in comparison to the way it is actually seen. Understandably, a change of body and appearance are fundamental contributions to a transformation, but the process is essentially a cognitive and emotional one.

Some of the emotions that determine the course of a transformation to a great extent are: fear, guilt and shame. Unavoidably these feelings will often be at the centre of gender therapy. Fear is mostly of the risk of rejection by significant others, of losing them and of social disapproval. Guilt mostly concerns the fact that some transgender people feel there is no option other than a transformation, and go ahead in spite of the consequences. Shame (for example, although seldom expressed openly) can concern the often fiercely criticised 'result' of a transition and also the alleged 'intrusion' into the world of the other sex. All three emotions are connected to pressure from the outside world based on the verdict that, considering the disturbance caused by a transformation, the result 'better be good'! Transgender people seem to have an obligation to be a success; their choice has to be 'worth it'! This, together with a transperson's own sexism, often makes 'passing' into a burden and may spoil the creative possibilities along with the fun it has to offer.

In my experience, transpeople tend to become much more comfortable in their lives when they stop focusing on 'passing', realising that even passing convincingly is no guarantee for qualifying as a man or a woman. They may still have to deal with endless confrontations about why they are not 'genuinely' male or female – for example 'because they cannot have children'. There are a great variety of transgender people who in some stereotypical view may not 'pass', but who feel so thoroughly at ease within themselves that nobody is going to argue. They may not 'pass' but they do 'convince'! The issue is not primarily one of 'being' male, female or neither but of being considered, respected and treated as whatever one experiences oneself to be. That is, in my opinion, what gender therapy is about!

If transgender should not be considered a separate client issue then why would there be a need for specialised gender therapists such as myself? What is the role of 'affirmative' or 'queer' therapy in respect to transgender?

At best a specialised therapist should be temporary and ideally any general therapist should, in principle, be able to deal with issues in respect of sex and gender, integrated into the therapy of choice. The same could be said about gay affirmative therapy: such integration could be the ultimate demystification of homosexuality and transgender, acknowledging the fact that anybody can at some stage experience homosexual or transgender feelings. This would oppose the current approach of reserving these feelings to a specific group of rather bizarre people, in need of specialised medical and psychological 'treatments' (see the introduction to this volume).

The sooner transgender is considered to be an everyday life issue the better. However, so far, clients involved in transgender seeing general therapists have experienced a lack of factual knowledge or too much fascination from the therapist, as well as a lack of recognition of transgender as an ordinary human characteristic that the therapist can relate to. At the other extreme, every other issue brought up has been interpreted in view of the client's transgender. Many clients seeing general therapists felt they were educating *them*, while paying for inadequate help.

The process of transgender becoming integrated into our lives is hindered in several ways. On the one hand some transgender people feel the need to justify and excuse themselves for who they are by emphasising transgender as a medical condition. On the other hand there is sexism in all of us, and in the structure of society, which needs to be addressed if people are to be enabled to be different. Even capitalism plays its role – for example, when transpeople find themselves losing their jobs, with managers stating: 'It's nothing personal, but I have to think of my clients!' Large-scale change can never be achieved without individual change.

Specialised gender therapy's main aim is to help clients integrate their transgender in the widest possible sense and to find their own identity at the same time. The present situation shows that more and more gay, lesbian and transpeople wish to belong openly to two communities at least: the one they were born into (their families, etc.) and the community they 'emigrate' into – not solely as a place to hide but as a second culture to be developed and enjoyed. The second community also appears to be pluriform and the diversity is still growing.

Therefore, affirmative therapists should be able to approach transgender issues and gender therapists should feel comfortable with bisexual, gay or lesbian identities and lifestyles. In this respect it is important to remember that, when gender reassignment was carried out by gender clinics in the 1970s and 1980s, transsexual people were only considered suitable for treatment when their sexual orientation was heterosexual. The result was a great deal of pretence from people who, again, could not openly be what they were and the help on offer reinforced the feeling that it was wrong to be bisexual, gay or lesbian.

The close connection and overlap between transgender and gay and lesbian issues shows in the following example.

Case example 1

In 1997 a married woman came to see me. She had recently discovered her attraction to women. When she fell in love with another woman she could not validate and accept her own experience and, watching a programme on television about transsexual people, decided that she was probably 'one of those'. Women loving women was not an option for her as that did not seem 'natural' and transsexuality made it 'right': she had to be a man. Eventually she found great relief in the fact that she could be herself as a lesbian without going through a long and demanding process of transformation. In this instance it was not a matter of resisting the option of lesbianism out of repulsion (she was rather open-minded), but heterosexuality was her only frame of reference.

It often occurs that conventional transsexual people (i.e. those who prefer to be transsexual and heterosexual rather than gay) are initially disappointed when, after the transformation, they find that their sexual orientation has not changed as well. This is why a great number of male to female transsexual people have relationships that, in one sense, are 'lesbian'. Sometimes that term is avoided out of homophobia, sometimes it is embraced because it is felt to confirm, or even 'prove', the transsexual person's 'femininity'.

Although transsexual people with partners often separate before or during the transition, recently more couples have been staying together. Consequently issues of sexual orientation will have to be addressed by two people who appeared to be heterosexual and are now in a same-sex relationship, or two people who appeared to be in a same-sex relationship who are now in a heterosexual one. Whether a couple will be able to rebuild and maintain their relationship depends on: the extent to which the transsexual person is able to develop their femininity or masculinity in the presence of their partner; the way partners deal with the challenges resulting from the loss of their male or female partner; their ability to redefine their sexual relationship together; and whether both partners feel comfortable with any remaining gender characteristics noticeable in the transsexual person's appearance, attitudes or behaviours. All four aspects depend to a great extent on the degrees of homophobia and heterosexism involved in the relationship.

In every possible variation it is important (in the context of affirmative therapy with its aim of empowerment) that a therapist helps to validate the client's experience. There are two distinct aspects in this process of validation and affirmation: helping someone to own their experience individually and, at the same time, to share experience as part of a greater, social representation. There are four ways to describe this, as follows.

Demystification

Any form of transgender has mostly been treated as an incomprehensible inclination, inspiring ever-recurring questions about its cause. Why does somebody want to engage in any of a variety of changes concerning gender role, lifestyle, dress code, sexual orientation and even physical appearance? The answer could be a simple one: because the binary construction of two sexes, based on biological and genetic characteristics does not fit everybody. There appear to be people who feel they are not in the category that suits their gender experience and people who feel they do not fit either category and want to be between or left out completely. (See also Neal 1998)

It seems rather unrealistic, when distinguishing categories and designating boundaries, to be surprised when the scheme does not apply to everybody.

All categories have exceptions and when there are boundaries there will always be people who want to cross them for whatever reason. In spite of the various explanations of transgender it is still commonly considered as a 'mystery'. All forms of human curiosity – from everyday life to scientific research – deal with this mystery and each conclusion has its own political implications. While most people take their own sex for granted there seems to be a need to keep looking for explanations when other people question it.

In Western European cultures, when there are no answers available, people become curiosities and subsequently become excluded and isolated, or persecuted. Turning people into a never-ending source for research and media reports we have not learned to view exceptions in a positive and spiritual way, with interest and respect. It is not in the nature of western culture to value difference. We usually find it threatening and treat it accordingly. Therefore it is important to help clients to free themselves from the gloom, the heaviness, from the burden of their 'mystery' and review it as one of their remarkable and enriching characteristics that they can embrace and reclaim as their own.

De-pathologising

The fact that many transsexual people feel they have no other option than a complete gender reassignment and the subsequent involvement of the medical establishment has medicalised transgender to a great extent. In order to achieve their aim transsexual people have often hoped that science would provide a watertight 'proof' for the cause of their predicament and that they would thereby gain acceptance. If only it was proven that they 'could not help it' and therefore had 'no choice'. Or, rather, had one choice only, about which they presently often feel guilt, because it mostly causes so much upheaval and pain to others about whom they care.

This is where transsexual people and other transpeople themselves mystify and pathologise their issue as a way of justifying their choice. This view can have great impact on every area of life. It may pathologise everything else as well or create a split existence: pathological in one sense and desperately trying to be more than 'normal' in every other way.

The medical model as constructed by Harry Benjamin (Benjamin 1966) may seem attractive at first but it carries a risk of stigmatising and limiting life. As in any other therapy, it is important that affirmative – or gender – therapy helps clients to realise that, whatever the cause of a condition or characteristic they will always have choices, which are their own responsibility, and no one ever has to justify who or what they are.

Affirmative and empowering therapy can only de-pathologise transgender when the issue is not seen as a problem in itself. Therefore I avoid any descriptions of gender therapy as dealing with *'gender problems'*. Gender therapy's concern is primarily gender identity development. Any problems with respect to transgender are mostly part of a 'survival strategy' that was adequate in the client's past but is no longer relevant, or has become limiting and harmful and is usually discarded in the course of successful therapy. Important in gender therapy is the timing: at a time of profound change such as a gender transformation, all aspects of somebody's life become visible and need redefining: relationships, sexuality, work, etc. There is no better time to go into 'ordinary' therapy to approach general issues as well as how particular issues of transgender are handled in certain, personal ways. The combination of these two perspectives offers new possibilities for someone to come to terms with, and value, their past and a future where they can be themselves.

De-medicalisation

When cross-gender was no longer solely seen as a criminal offence and more thought was given to the possible causes of such 'deviant' behaviour it became the interest of mental health and psychiatry (Lipsitz-Bem 1994). As in previous efforts to change gays and lesbians, attempts were made to 'cure' the condition by means of therapy which, apart from rare 'success stories' that were never critically evaluated, was not successful. Even people highly motivated to 'adjust', due to all the social and relational misery they had to cope with, could not give up their true experience. When conversion therapy did not seem to be able to change a client's mind or behaviour, the next logical step was to try to change the body or, rather, adjust it to how someone experienced their gender. This has been a tremendous relief to a great number of people.

However important the availability of gender reassignment is, it is unfortunate that a great part of the professional field of transgender seems to be dominated by medical technology and those who are involved in its practice. It is a distinct advantage to clients when the view of transgender is not restricted to interest in its causes and the availability and development of medical technology.

Because treatment is mainly a medical matter, many transgender people become 'patients' for some considerable time and this can easily rule their lives. Neither concern about the cause of transgender nor the treatment should take over people's lives, attitude and identity. A number of my clients are considered to have been through a medically successful treatment. However, at the end of the physical transformation they felt at a loss about almost everything: their emotions, their past, their relationships and their sexuality. Transformation is a mental, social and cultural process: from my viewpoint a process of migration. It goes far beyond the physical adjustment and, seen in the widest sense, it is not essentially different from the process of growth that many biological men and women go through. It is in fact life itself, and in no way restricted to a medically-oriented period of gender reassignment which like all other medical provisions is only a means to an end.

Counselling and therapy have so far mainly been confined to the diagnostic process to determine whether someone is transsexual and will benefit sufficiently from gender reassignment to justify the treatment. I want to emphasise the need for, and importance of, independent, accessible therapy at every stage for anyone involved – including relatives. This must not be part of the diagnostic process, where the client is depending on the practitioner's permission for treatment, because this is not compatible with the essence of therapy: a non-judgemental relationship where clients can say anything without the risk of losing access to treatment. Guidance offered by gender clinics should never be called, or considered to be, therapy. An independent therapist is in a much better position to help the client discover whether medical treatment is the sole option, or even the best choice for change, in their particular case.

De-colonising

When understanding transgender in respect of culture and migration it is useful to consider the terms 'colonising' and 'appropriation'. They are connected but work in opposite directions. Any culture has a tendency towards either incorporating the immigrant or rejecting those who refuse to adjust. At the same time there is an attempt to 'normalise' individual, 'foreign' characteristics that are appropriate or useful to a particular culture by modifying them almost out of recognition. These two processes will have a strong influence on individuals who try to develop and maintain their own identity. Critical awareness will be necessary to safeguard one's own choices and boundaries (see also Chapter 1).

As previously mentioned, more and more individuals who are 'different' express the wish to belong openly to more than one community, keeping their roots intact, while migrating into newly-discovered territory. De-colonising the process of developing one's identity without adjusting involuntarily to the dominant culture means freeing oneself from many ideas that go unquestioned: the preconceptions and expectations that surround any process of change. Anyone with whatever expression of transgender can easily get caught in a series of painful self-examinations and interrogate whether they are a 'real' transsexual person and (after the change) a 'real' man or woman. Additionally, there will be the burgeoning issue about whether or not someone is 'passing' satisfactorily in their new role. All this is comparable to questioning whether someone is truly gay, lesbian or bisexual. Change into another stereotype seems at first most easily accepted. For example, being gay is more tolerable to a majority of heterosexuals when those concerned are in a monogamous, lasting relationship. Being a transgender person is more acceptable when the result is somebody who at least tries to suit the new role of being a 'real' man or woman, rather than someone who feels comfortable in between, or prefers switching according to mood.

Transgenderists get the same kind of criticism as bisexuals: not being able, or refusing, to 'make up their minds'. The most scathing comment that trans and gay people share is the complaint that they are not *'real'*. Not real men or women. Gays with moustaches rather than handbags were a great surprise to homophobes. Lesbians have always had a difficult time claiming their femininity, whether butch or not. Even recently, I came across an article that mentioned 'women and lesbians'! This was meant in general and not about particular people. While gender crossing was always meant to increase our freedom there is a real risk that we will finish up even more oppressed than before. I'm aware that some transsexual people will respond that they would rather be oppressed in their new identity than not change at all. This is, of course, understandable, but it means they are still left with a deep longing for a full life, which they should be able to achieve as they endeavour to become who they really want to be. Spending the rest of one's life and energy on trying to live up to what is expected is similar to the situation that made transpeople want to change in the first place.

Counselling and therapy can contribute in many ways by:

- helping clients deal and live with ambiguity and confusion;
- helping clients make the most of their choices and decisions;
- helping open up a new reality where the client can feel at home, without being confined to it and losing touch with their background;
- helping clients deal with pain, minimise unavoidable losses and make this whole hard and demanding process lighter, enjoyable and worthwhile.

Guidelines for good practice

- One of the pitfalls to be avoided is being constrained by the 'consistency' of a classification of transgender. The approach in therapy should always be based on congruity of the client's own experience, needs and wishes.
- Gender therapy is principally 'ordinary' therapy, where the main focus is (like all therapy) the way clients deal with the important matters in their lives, transgender being one of them.
- Assuming that all therapists working affirmatively with gay and transgender clients have confronted their own homo/transphobia, therapy should help clients to deal with feelings of self-hate, repulsion and low self-esteem caused by their situation and experiences. This is a vital step towards facing up to intolerance and discrimination.
- One countertransferential aspect of gender therapy in particular needs to be acknowledged. Whereas change is generally the goal of therapy, that which possibly occurs in gender therapy could be the ultimate change a

therapist may witness. It is most important that this does not cause a therapist to get 'carried away' or try to win a client's trust by appearing exceptionally 'open-minded'. A number of my clients have experienced 'over-encouragement' towards transformation and treatment from general therapists who, by the time they have become better informed, tried to slow down the process. Neither encouragement nor discouragement are adequate therapeutic responses: only support for choices made by clients themselves.

Recommended further reading

Bornstein, K. (1997) *Gender Outlaw: Men, Women and the Rest of Us*. New York: Routledge.
Bornstein, K. (1998) *My Gender Workbook*. New York: Routledge.
Davies, D. and Neal, C. (eds) (2000) *Therapeutic Perspectives on Working with Lesbian, Gay and Bisexual Clients*. Buckingham: Open University Press.
Dreger, A.D. (1998) *Hermaphrodites and the Medical Invention of Sex*. London: Harvard University Press.
Hausman, B. (1995) *Changing Sex: Transsexualism, Technology and the Idea of Gender*. London: Duke University Press.
Herdt, G. (1994) *Third Sex, Third Gender*. New York: Zone Books.
Jasso, N. (1981) *The Intersex Child: Pediatric and Adolescent Endocrinology*. New York: S. Karger.
Kessler, S.J. (1998) *Lessons from the Intersexed*. New Brunswick, NJ: Rutgers University Press.
Morris, J. (1974) *Conundrum: An Extraordinary Narrative of Transsexualism*. New York: Henry Holt.
Stoller, R.J. (1975) *Sex and Gender, Vol. II: The Transsexual Experiment*. New York: Jason Aronson.

References

Beemyn, B. and Eliason, M. (1996) *Queer Studies*. New York: New York University Press.
Benjamin, H. (1966) *The Transsexual Phenomenon*. New York: The Julian Press.
Hermaphrodites Speak (1996) Video (Pal available). Intersex Society of North America, http://www.isna.org: NTSC.
Jiang-Ning, Z., Hoffman, M.A., Gooren, L.J.G. and Swaab, D.F. (1995) A sex difference in the human brain and its relation to transsexuality. *Nature*, 378(2): 68–90.
Lipsitz-Bem, S. (1994) *The Lenses of Gender: Transforming the Debate on Sexual Inequality*. New Haven, CT: Yale University Press.
Neal, C. (1998) Queer therapy, past and future. *Counselling News*, 4: 20–3.
Stonewall (1997) *Equality 2000*. London: Stonewall.

Index

abandonment, fear of (HIV/AIDS),
    59–60
abuse
    childhood sexual, 2, 29, 89, 93,
        128–43
    cycle of, 134, 135
    see also bullying
acculturation process, 11–12, 17
Achilles Heel Collective, The, 107
acting-out, 16, 42, 51, 106
Adam (case example), 97
Adams, Naomi, 4
addiction, 4, 108, 162–3
    alcohol problems, 89, 95
adversity, lack of (lesbian
    relationships), 90
advertisements, 164
affection, 106, 138
affirmative therapy, 1, 4, 8–9, 20, 29,
    74, 102
    transgender issues, 179–80, 182–5
African cultures, 13, 17
age of consent, 110
ageism, 108
aggression, 64, 171
    see also bullying; childhood sexual
        abuse
Agnew, J., 165
AIDS, *see* HIV/AIDS

Airey, C., 60
Akkerman, A., 88
Albert Kennedy Trust, 150
alcohol problems, 89, 95
Alcorn, Keith, 22–3, 31
Alexander, C.J., 167, 170
alienation, fear of (HIV/AIDS), 59–60
Allen, J., 116
Altschuler, J., 139
American Motorsport Clubs
    Confederation (AMCC), 27
American Psychiatric Association, 24,
    38–9, 84–5, 154
anal sex, 160
    anodyspareunia, 86, 91, 97, 98
    aversion to, 3, 91, 165–6
Anderson, S.K., 36
Angelou, M., 128
anger, 64, 105, 155
    expression of, 88, 92, 96, 106, 171
    management, 110
    rituals, 111
anodyspareunia, 86, 91, 97, 98
anonymous sex, 98, 162
anorgasmia, 84, 85
anti-discriminatory clauses, 39
anti-oppressive approach, 7, 8, 39, 125
'anti touch' society, 74
anxiety, 108, 140

bullying and, 153
  performance (sexual), 88, 91, 92,
    94–5, 98
  psychosexual problems, 88, 91–5, 98
appearance, 176
  body image, 3, 13, 167–9
archetypes, 78
Armstrong, S., 19
Arni (case example), 10–11
arousal (bullying symptoms), 154,
    155–6
arousal problems, 84, 85, 90–1, 94
art/art form, 68–9, 70–2, 75–80
Asian cultures, 13–14, 16
Association for Lesbian, Gay and
    Bisexual Psychologies UK (ALGBP
    UK), 1
association, fear of, 69, 81
attitudes (mainstream professional
    influences), 38–9
attraction, fear of, 69
autonomy (ethical dilemmas), 39, 40,
    44
avoidance of responsiveness (bullying),
    154, 155
Awareness (Stevens), 106, 107
awareness, 106, 107, 108–9, 171

Bancroft, J., 84
Barbarin, D.A., 18
Barrows, P.A., 60
Bass, E., 128
Battey, J., 149–50
Bebbington, A.C., 63
Bebko, C., 90
Becker, J., 89, 93
Beemyn, B., 179
Belfast Telegraph, 149
belief systems, 7, 13, 62, 128
Bell, A.P., 94
Bena (case example), 13–14
beneficence (ethical dilemmas), 39, 40,
    43, 44
Benjamin, Harry, 185
Bennett, J., 135
bereavement, 56–7, 65
Berhrendt, A., 90
Berman, J.S., 18, 36
Betan, E.J., 44
Bhugra, D., 91, 93

Biller, R., 56
biphobia, 15, 18, 19, 118, 121
Bisexual Horizons, 120
bisexuality
  blackness and, 8, 9–10, 14–20
  causes (myths), 132
  child sexual abuse and, 132, 134–5,
    141
  definitions, 116–18
  psychosexual problems (heterosexual
    paradigm challenged), 4, 83–4
  therapy and, 3, 115–26
  transgender and, 176, 177, 178–9,
    188
black clients/blackness, 9–20
Blasingame, B.M., 118
blood-letting (*minution*), 25
Blue Peter creations, 76–7
Blume, Sue E., 128, 129
Blumstein, P., 86
Blunkett, D., 119
Bodella, D., 74
body
  fascism, 108
  hatred, 109
  image, 3, 13, 167–9
  movement, 70, 71–4
  ownership of, 25–6
  therapy, 74
Bond, T., 36, 39, 41, 130
bondage, 22
Borys, D.S., 36
boundary management, 3, 32, 35,
    37–8, 39, 41–2, 43, 47, 48
boundary rider, 37, 47, 51
Boy George, 178
Boyle, M., 85
brachioproctal penetration, 22, 26
Brandes, D., 107
branding, 22, 28
Brauner, Rita, 3
breath control, 26
Brehony, K., 86
Bridoux, Denis, 3
Brindley, G.S., 95
British Association for Counselling, 2,
    39, 40, 42–3, 46–9
British Psychological Society, 2
British Social Attitudes survey, 60
Britton, P.J., 58, 61–2

Brook, L., 60
Brown, L.S., 37, 38
Browning, C., 37
bullying, 11, 59–60, 108
  long-term consequences, 2, 146–73
Bulmer, M., 60
Burgess, N., 37
burn out, 64, 65
'butch-femme' roles, 88, 178, 180

Caldon, W., 134
Cameron, J., 111
Campbell, B., 133
capitalism, 183
Carl, D., 84
case examples (use of), 5
casual sex, 47, 49–50, 90, 92, 98, 162
celibacy, 93
Center for Energetic Studies
  (California), 111
Center for Practice of Zen Buddhist
  Meditation, 111
Chan, C., 16
chastity games, 22
Child Abuse (Kempe and Kempe), 129
Child Watch (TV programme), 131
childhood sexual abuse, 2, 29, 89, 93,
  128, 142–3
  definitions, 129–30
  history, 129
  myths, 131–5
  political context, 130–1
  practice issues, 135–41
ChildLine, 140
children
  bullying (long-term consequences), 2,
    146–73
  sexual abuse of, *see* childhood sexual
    abuse
  with disabilities, 139
Chopin, Frédéric, 178
Christian tradition/beliefs, 25, 59
Ciso (case example), 15–16
Clark, D., 74, 105
Clarkson, P., 36, 51
Clary, Julian, 178
clay work, 77
Cleveland case, 133
client-centred psychotherapy, 69–70
client-counsellor dialogues, 50–1

client-therapist relationship, 5
  differences (culture/race), 3, 7–20
  ethics of dual relationships, 3,
    35–52
  model of the world, 30
clinical presentations (transgender),
  180–1
*Codes of Ethics and Practice for
  Counsellors* (BAC), 39, 42–3,
  46–9
cognitive dissonance, 91
Coleman, E., 87, 92, 93
collective unconscious, 72
colonialism, 7, 9, 11
colour, use of, 70, 71, 72, 74–5
'Coming Home' group, 103
'coming out'
  attitudes to, 94
  as bisexual, 119
  groupwork, 102–3, 104, 109
  intercultural perspectives, 16–18
'Coming Out and Coming In' groups,
  102–3, 109
community care, 60
compensation (pressures on gay men),
  92
compulsive sexuality, 92, 109, 162
condoms, 93, 166
confidentiality, 31, 42, 44, 79, 105
conflict resolution, 36
congruence, 172
consciousness, 71
consensual activity, 27–8, 33
contact abuse, 129
contagion, fear of, 69
containment, 42, 44
conversion therapy, 186
Cooper, Terry, 103
Cope, R., 12
coping strategies, 11, 62–3
Corby, B., 129
corporal punishment, 22
cottaging, 109
countertransference, 42, 44, 172, 173,
  188–9
couples therapy, 84
Cowie, H., 147
Coyle, A., 38–9
creative connection model, 70–4,
  80

Creative Connections: Expressive Arts as Healing, The, (Rogers), 70–4, 80
creative techniques/creativity, 2, 31, 68–82
crisis management, 42, 52
Crisp, Quentin, 178
Cross, M., 128, 139
cross-dressing, 176, 180, 181
Crowe, M., 84
cruising, 109, 160, 162, 163, 165
culture
    differences (addressing/embracing), 3, 7–20
    transgender, 180, 187
Curry, A.E., 9
cycle of abuse, 134, 135

daily temperature reading, 111
Daines, B., 85
Dan (case example), 137
dancing, 68, 69, 73, 74
D'Augelli, A.R., 147, 149, 152
Davidson, 79
Davies, Dominic, 3, 5, 8, 29, 38, 70, 74, 84, 91, 98, 102, 118, 131–2, 137, 168, 172, 179
Davis, L., 128
de Vroome, E.M.M., 165
de-colonising (transgender), 187–8
de-medicalisation (transgender), 186–7
de-pathologising (transgender), 185–6
death
    fears of, 58
    suicide, 137, 140, 150–1, 152–3, 177
decision making, ethical (dual relationships), 39–50
Deenen, A., 170
defence mechanisms, 65, 167, 169
demystification (of transgender), 182, 184–5
denial, 16, 51, 109, 136
depression, 12, 57, 58, 93, 109, 140
    bullying and, 153, 155, 157
desire discrepancy, 86–92, 94, 96–7
Diagnostic and Statistical Manual of Mental Disorders (DSM-IV), 24–5, 28, 84–5, 154

difference
    cultural (addressing/embracing), 3, 7–20
    lack of (lesbian relationships), 89–90
dildos, 88
'dispiritation', 108
distress, 12, 13
Donny/Emir (case example), 17–18
drag queens, 176, 180, 181
drawing, 68, 69, 75–6
dream work, 111
dreams (after bullying), 155
dressing up, 68, 69, 78
drug treatments (for HIV/AIDS), 57
drug use (illegal drugs), 58–9, 95, 155
dual relationships (ethical dilemmas), 3, 35–52
dual roles, 41, 42, 43, 48, 51–2
Duberman, M., 104
Dutroux, Mark, 27
Dworkin, S.H., 37
dyspareunia, 84, 85

EAGLES Centre (in California), 149
eating disorders, 168
ecology (of SM lifestyle), 30–1
educational achievement (of bullies), 157
Edward Carpenter Community Gay Men's Weeks, 110
ego development, 44
'ego-dystonic homosexuality', 83
ejaculation (premature/delayed), 84, 85, 90, 97
Eliason, M., 179
Elliott, M., 128, 130
Emerging Woman: A Decade of Mid Life Transitions (Rogers), 70
Emir/Donny (case example), 17–18
empathy/empathic process, 10, 136, 141–2
empowerment, 19, 38, 184, 185
endorphins, 22–3, 25
enemas, 22
Epstein, R.S., 38
equal opportunities, 39
Equality 2000 (Stonewall), 178
erectile dysfunction, 84, 85, 90, 93, 94–6, 97, 169, 170, 171

erotic desire, difference and, 90
erotic transference, 45, 49–50
erotophobia, 47, 109
Essence (magazine), 116
ethical dilemmas (in dual
relationships), 3, 35–52
ethics, codes of, 39, 42–3, 46–9
ethnicity/ethnic identity, 3, 7–20
European Association for Lesbian, Gay
and Bisexual Psychologists, 1, 3
European Confederation of Motorsport
Clubs (ECMC), 27
European Court of Human Rights, 28,
31
European cultures, 13, 160, 185
Evans, B.A., 55
exclusion, 104, 107
social (bullying), 146
existentialism, 111
expressive therapy, 2, 68–82

face paints, 78
Fadiman, J., 70
faeces (scat), 22, 26
'fallout' impulses, 42
false memory syndrome, 131, 133,
137
family
gay men in groups, 3, 102–13
of HIV patients, 61–263
fantasies, 22, 27, 32, 88, 106, 141
Farber, B., 70
Fascism, 11
Fatinilehin, I., 11
fear, 108, 182
of association, 69, 81
of attraction, 69
of contagion, 69
Federation of United Kingdom Clubs
(FUKC), 27
fellatio, 91
femininity, 91, 117, 184, 188
feminism, 26, 38, 130, 178
feminist model (of sexual abuse), 133,
134
femme-butch roles, 88, 178, 180
Fenichel, O., 167
fetishism, 22, 24
fidelity (ethical dilemmas), 39, 40, 44,
46

Finkelhor, D., 134
fisting, 22, 26
flagellation, 25
flashbacks (after bullying), 155
Fonagy, Peter, 156–7
Fontaine, M.M., 162
Fontes, L.A., 128
Forgan, R., 135
Foucault, Michel, 167
Frager, R., 70
Freud, Sigmund, 117, 133
Froebel Educational Institute, 152
Fryer, P., 11
fusion/merger, 89–90, 92

Gabbard, G.O., 37
Gabriel, Lynne, 3, 37, 41–2
Garber, Marjorie, 116
Gareth (case example), 59–60
Gartrell, N.K., 37, 38
Gatter, P.N., 63
gay affirmative therapy, 1, 3–5, 8–9,
20, 29, 74, 102, 125
gay identity development, 3, 168–9,
181
gay men
blackness and, 7, 8, 9–13, 14–20
clinical issues, 3, 160–73
group work, 3, 102–13
liberation movement, 26, 161
psychological problems (heterosexist
paradigm challenged), 4, 83–99
subcultures, 3, 161–3
transgender and, 176, 177, 178–9,
181, 183–4, 188
Gay Men's Weeks (Edward Carpenter
Community), 110
'gay positive' theories, 1
Gay Pride carnival, 105, 110
'Gay-Related Immune Deficiency'
(GRID), 55
gay rights (Stonewall), 147, 178
gender
identity development, 185–6
reassignment, 181, 183, 185,
186–7
roles, 16–17, 69, 91
social constructions of, 117
transgender issues, 3, 176–89
George, H., 94

George, K., 90
George, Sue, 116, 117
Gestalt therapy, 107, 111
Getzel, G.S., 61
Gil, E., 128
Gill, D.N., 55
Glunt, E.K., 60
golden showers, 22, 26
Gomez, L., 128
Gonsiorek, J.C., 38, 128, 130, 133,
    134, 139
Gordon, L.H., 111
GPs, sexual abuse reported to,
    139–40
Grahn, J., 104
Green, J., 90
Green, M., 19
Greenberg, D.F., 167
Greene, B., 14, 17
grief, 56–7, 64, 65, 105
Grof, Stanislaw, 29
Grothe, T., 57
'grounding' skill, 64
group work (with gay men), 3, 102–13
guilt, 19, 48, 58, 88, 93, 109, 181,
    182, 185
Guinan, J.J., 63–4
Gutheil, T.G., 37
Gutierrez, F., 37

Halgin, R.P., 60
Hall, M., 89
Hall, Radclyffe, 178
Hancock, 81
'hand dancing', 74
'Hankie Code', 27, 31
Hans/Joop (case example), 166
Harrison, J., 81
Hart, G., 55, 60
Harvey Milk School (New York), 149
Hatfield, E., 90
Hay, H., 102
Hays, R.B., 58
health
    history of (SM practices), 26–8
    HIV/AIDS counselling, 2, 15–16, 26,
        55–65
Henry, C., 39
hepatitis B/A, 26
Herek, G.M., 60

Herman, J.L., 128, 129
Hermaphrodites Speak, 180
Hershberger, S.L., 152
Herzog, D.B., 168
heterosexism, 3, 10, 11, 15, 19
heterosexuality
    experience of lesbian women, 83
    paradigm challenged, 4, 83–99
    passing, 58–9, 109
    values/norms (gay rejection of), 94
Heyward, Carl, 38
'hidden creativity', 68–9, 70–1, 76,
    81
Hilliard, R., 57
HIV/AIDS, 15–16, 26
    bisexuality and, 119
    clinical issues, 162–3, 166, 169,
        172–3
    counselling issues, 2, 55–65
    psychosexual problems, 93, 95
Hobfoll, S.E., 58
Holocaust, 7, 11
homework exercises (group work),
    105, 106, 110
homophile, 161
homophobia, 4–5, 7, 38–9, 88, 90,
    108, 160, 184, 188
    bullying and, 2, 11, 146–51
    creativity arrested/hidden by, 68–9
    HIV/AIDS and, 2, 59–60
    internalised, 7, 69, 91–2, 93, 97,
        139, 179
    racism and, 11, 12, 15, 17, 18–19
    self-destructive outcomes, 106
homosexuality
    attitudes (effect of AIDS), 59–60
    declassified as mental illness, 38–9
    Section 28 (Local Government Act),
        147–8
    transgender and, 176–80
    see also gay men; lesbian women
hormone treatment, 181
House of Lords, 28, 110
Houston, G., 104
humanistic approach, 8, 26, 69, 103,
    111, 140
humanistic expressive therapy, 69
Hunter, J., 149
hyperactive sexual desire, 92
hypoactive sexual desire, 85, 92

identity development
  gay, 3, 168–9, 181
  gender, 185–6
identity disorders (gay men), 92
image
  body, 3, 13, 167–9
  self-, 19, 119–20, 161, 163, 168
incest, 129
inclusion, 107
indecent exposure, 129
individuation, loss of, 89
informal carers (of HIV patient), 63
informed consent, 44, 129
inhibitions, 71, 72, 86, 170
inner codes, 46
inner self, 68, 71, 73
integrative psychotherapy, 8–9
intercultural therapy, 3, 7–20
internal knowledge, 136
'internal supervisor', 42
internal truth, 128
internalised homophobia, 7, 69, 91–2,
  93, 97, 139, 179
internalised oppression, 11, 15–16, 81,
  105, 108
International Drummer, 24
*International Journal of STD and
  AIDS,* 95
interpersonal factors (psychosexual
  problems), 94
interpersonal problems (following child
  abuse), 140
intersexuals, 180
intimacy, 107, 108
  avoidance (lesbian relationships), 89
  problems (gay men), 92
  sexuality and (in gay men), 3, 162,
  169–72
  value of, 78
intracavernosal injections, 95
inverts (terminology), 179–80
irritability symptom (after bullying),
  155
Isay, R.A., 168
Isensee, R., 106, 108, 128
Ivey, A., 70
Izzard, Eddie, 178

Jamieson, A., 38
Jason/Kayode (case example), 61–2

Jenkins, P., 130
Jenny/Maxine (case example), 141
Jiang-Ning, 2, 177
Jo/Nina (case example), 137–8
'Johari window', 76
Johnson, A.M., 55
Johnson, J., 134, 137, 138
Johnson, V., 84, 86, 90, 165
Jonathan/Olu (case example), 60–1
Joop/Hans (case example), 166
Jowell, R., 60
justice (ethical dilemmas), 39, 40, 41,
  44, 46

Kanellakis, Pavlo, 2
Kaplan, H.S., 84
Kareem, J., 8
Karen (case example), 132–3
Karpman, S., 111
Kayode/Jason (case example), 61–2
Keith, L., 139
Keleman, Stanley, 74, 111
Kempe, C.H., 129
Kempe, R.S., 129
Kennedy, M., 128, 129, 139
Khambatta, A., 9
King, M., 85
kink sex/therapy, 3, 22–34
'kinky parties', 163
Kinsey report (1947), 116, 117
Kitchener, K.S., 36, 39, 44
Kitzinger, C., 38
Klein, F., 118
knowledge, 13, 136
Kowszun, G., 89, 95
Krestan, J., 90

Labour government, 2
Lago, C., 10, 12–13, 39, 139
Lang, K.D., 178
Langs, R., 38
Lauren (case example), 96
leather parties, 160
Lee, J.A., 164
legal implications (SM lifestyle),
  31
Leigh, B., 87
lesbian women, 26
  blackness and, 7, 8, 9–10, 13–20
  causes (myths), 132

childhood sexual abuse and, 132, 134–5, 137–8
  heterosexual experience, 89
  'lesbian bed death', 86, 90
  psychosexual problems (heterosexist paradigm challenged), 4, 83–99
  transgender and, 176, 177, 178–9, 181, 183–4, 188
Lew, M., 128, 130
libertarian education, 111
'life maps', 111
Lipsitz-Bem, S., 177, 186
Little Hans case (Freud), 117
Local Government Act 1988 (Section 28), 147–8
Lolita (film), 134
London Black Lesbian and Gay Centre, 9
London, P., 58
London Society for the Protection of Children, 129
Lopez, D.J., 61
loss, 56–8, 105
Loulan, J., 85, 86, 88–9, 134, 138
Lourea, D.N., 125
Loveday, C., 55
lovestyles, sexual, 3, 164–6
Lowen, A., 74
Lubin, B., 153
Luca (case example), 58–9
Lucius, Clare A., 3, 116
Luton study, 2, 151–4, 156, 157
Lyn, L., 37

McCann, K., 63
McFarlane, L., 124
McGettigan, 138
McGovern, D., 12
McGrath, G., 39
macho trend, 161–2
McKusick, L., 57
McLeod, J., 39
McMichael, Timothy, 2
McMullen, R., 128
McNally, Ian, 4
McWhirter, D., 90
make-up, 78, 179
Malley, M., 89, 95
Margolies, L., 38
Martin (case example), 162–3

masculinity, 91, 107, 117, 133
masochism, 22, 24, 88
  see also sado-masochism
Mason, A., 147
Mason-John, V., 9
Masters, W., 84, 86, 90, 165
masturbation, 108, 109, 163, 171
Mattison, A., 90
Mauk, G., 154
Maxine/Jenny (case example), 141
Maylon, A., 8
Meara, N.M., 39
medical treatments (gay men's sexual problems), 95–6
medical model, 185
men
  masculinity, 91, 107, 117, 133
  relating to women, 108
  see also bisexuality; gay men
'Men for Men' groups, 103
mental health/problems, 12, 13, 24–6
merger/fusion, 89–90, 92
migration process (transgender), 179–80, 186, 187
Millen, L., 36
Miller, D., 90, 94–5
Milton, M.J., 38, 111
minution (blood letting), 25
model of the world (client/therapists), 30
modelling behaviour, 44, 47
monogamy, 87, 94, 98, 162, 187
monosexuals, 119
moral principles, 39, 40–1, 44
morals (mainstream influences), 38–9
Moreno, J., 111
mother-daughter bond (lesbian replication), 89
motivation for creativity, 70
movement, body, 70, 71–4
Multiple Affect Adjective Check List (MAACL), 153
multiple losses (to HIV/AIDS), 56–8
multiple roles, 41, 42
myths of childhood sexual abuse, 131–5

NAFSIYAT (intercultural therapy centre), 8
name-calling, 60, 146, 148, 149, 150

narcissistic defence mechanism, 167, 169
narratives, relevance of, 79
National Health Service, 83
National Society for the Prevention of Cruelty to Children (NSPCC), 139
Nazism, 7, 11, 28
National Vocational Qualifications (NVQs), 39
Neal, Charles, 3, 5, 29, 38, 91, 92, 98, 102, 106, 125, 132, 172, 179
Neuro-Linguistic Psychology reframing, 111
Nichols, M., 86
nightlife, commercial, 161, 162, 165
Nina/Jo (case example), 137–8
non-contact abuse, 129
non-maleficence (ethical dilemmas), 39, 40, 43, 46
Norway study, 147, 153
Nunno, V.J., 167

object relations theory, 43–4
objectification, 108
obscene phone calls, 129
Olu/Jonathan (case example), 60–1
Olweus, D., 147, 153
oppression, 5, 11, 15, 18–19, 102, 139, 188
    anti-oppressive approach, 7, 8, 39, 125
    homophobic, 2, 59–60
    internalised, 11, 15–16, 81, 105, 108
oral sex, 26, 86
organic factors (gay men's sexual problems), 93
organismic self, 68, 71, 73
orgasm, 87, 88, 165, 169, 170, 171
orgasmic disorders, 84, 85–6
overlapping connections, 37–8, 41–2, 50–2
Owens, R.E., 150
Oxley, Elizabeth, 3

Paedophile Information Exchange (PIE), 133–4
paedophilia
    myths, 131–5
    see also childhood sexual abuse

Paff, B.A., 90, 91, 169
pain, 171
    HIV/AIDS patients, 58–9, 62
    SM/kink (lifestyle), 3, 22–34
painting, 68, 75
Palmer, A., 147
panic, 58–9, 109
'passing', 106, 109, 120, 182, 187
patriarchy, 134
Paul, J.P., 117
Pearson, B., 36
pederasty, 129
penetrative sex, 88
    anal, 3, 86, 91, 97, 98, 160, 165–6
penile prosthesis, 95
performance anxiety, 88, 91, 92, 94–5, 98
Perlman, G., 111
Perls, F., 111
person affirmative (terminology), 5
personal issues (dual relationship), 45, 48
personal support networks (HIV/AIDS), 57, 58
Peterson, M.R., 37, 38
Phillips, H., 107
philosophies (mainstream professional influences), 38–9
phobias, 91
phone lines, 109, 140
physical activity/expression, 68, 70, 71–4
Piazza, N., 36
piercing, 22, 26, 168
Pilkington, N.W., 147, 149
Pink Therapy, 29, 91, 98, 118, 179
pipe cleaners (as art media), 77–8
piss (golden showers), 22, 26
Pivar, I., 62
political context (childhood sexual abuse), 130–1, 137
Pope, K.S., 36
pornography, 88, 109, 161
post-traumatic stress disorder (PTSD), bullying and, 154–6, 157
power, 44, 107
    child sexual abuse and, 129, 130, 133, 134, 136, 137
    kink sex and, 3, 22–34
pre-transference, 9

Prevention of Cruelty to Animals Act (1822), 129
Prevention of Cruelty to Children Act (1889), 129
pro-family model (sexual abuse), 133
pro-paedophile model (sexual abuse), 133–4
problem solving models, 3, 35, 39–50
process model (ethical problem solving), 39–50, 51
professional codes (dual relationships), 39, 42–3, 44, 46–9
professional influences, mainstream, 38–9
professional issues and responses (dual relationships), 45, 48
professional perspectives (expressive therapy), 70–1
Project for Advice, Counselling and Education (PACE), 124
promiscuity, 162
    see also casual sex
prostitution, 93, 150
psychoanalysis, 111, 133, 167
psychodrama, 69, 111
psychological consequences (bisexuality), 118–22
psychological problems, creativity and, 31
psychosexual problems/dysfunctions, 4
    definitions/treatment, 84–6
    gay men, 83–4, 90–6, 97–9
    lesbians, 83–4, 86–90, 96, 97–9
psychotherapy, client-centred, 69–70
Public Health Laboratory Service (PHLS), 55
publicity (ethical problem solving), 41
punishment, 25, 59
puppetry, 74
Purdie, Fiona, 2, 139

Quadland, M.C., 162
queer gender, 178–80
Queer Press Collective, 128
Queer Studies (Beemyn and Eliason), 179
queer therapy, 182

race, sexuality and, 3, 7–20
racism, 7, 8, 9–11, 12, 15, 17, 18–19, 108, 139
Rack, P., 12, 19
Rainbow Project, 151
Ramer, A., 109
Rantzen, E., 140
rape, 130, 131
Rape Crisis Federation, 130
reality, fantasy and, 32
recollections, persistent (of bullying), 154–5
Reece, R., 90, 91, 92, 93
rejection
    fear of, 171, 173, 182
    of gay sex (by therapist), 172
religious traditions/beliefs, 25, 26, 59, 129
resilience (surviving school bullying), 156–7
resistance to movement/physical activity, 73–4
respect, 30, 172
responsiveness, avoidance/numbing (after bullying), 154, 155
Rice, S., 56
Ridley, J., 84
Rigby, K., 152
rimming (oral-anal contact), 26
ritual, 28
ritualised abuse, 140
Rivers, Ian, 2, 108, 146–7, 149, 150–1, 154
Robinson, Anne, 135
Rogers, Carl, 18, 69–70, 172
Rogers, Natalie, 70–4, 80
Rogers, P., 154
role conflicts, 51
'role fluency', 36, 51–2
role models, 7, 58, 88, 90, 139, 178
role-play, 22, 23, 28, 176
Roll, S., 36
Rolland, J.S., 62
Roscoe, W., 109
Rosenblatt, Daniel, 111
Ross, M.W., 117, 162, 169
Rosser, B., 86, 91, 169
rota system, 44, 51
Roth, Jenner, 103
Rothblum, E., 86

Rottnek, M.J., 148
Royal Society of Medicine, 95
Rubinstein, Maggi, 116
Rudolph, J., 124

Sade, Marquis de, 24
sadism, 22, 24, 88
sadness, 171
sado-masochism, 22–4, 25, 26–7
safer sex, 26, 93, 95, 109
Samuels, A., 132
Sand, George, 178
Sanders, P., 76
Sandfort, T.G.M., 165
Sanford, L.T., 128
Santi Ireson, S., 139–40
saunas, 47–50, 160, 165
scat (faeces), 22, 26
Schaecher, R., 149
Schippers, Jan, 3, 167, 168, 170
Schmidt, L.D., 39
school, bullying at (long-term
    consequences), 2, 146–73
Schover, L., 95
Schreurs, K., 87
Schwartz, P., 86
scientific discourse (body image of
    gays), 167
Section 28 (Local Government Act
    1988), 147–8
self
    creative/expressive, 2, 68–82
    external, 68
    organismic (inner), 68, 71, 73
self-actualisation, 2
self-awareness, 1, 108–9
'self box', 76–7
self-concepts, 19, 71
self-determination, 19
self-disclosure, 19–20, 170
self-empowerment, 38
self-esteem, 2, 11, 12, 19, 32, 71, 89,
    91–2, 97, 153–4, 155, 179
self-exclusion, 104
self-expression, 68–9
self-harm, 64, 140, 152–3, 157
self-help strategies, 19
self-image, 19, 119–20, 161, 163, 168
self-knowledge, 13
self-perception, 153–4

self-presentation, 180, 181
self-regulation, 161
self-worth, 13
sex
    as bridging process, 90
    casual, 47, 49–50, 90, 92, 98, 162
    safe, 26, 93, 95, 109
    unsafe, 108, 166
sexism, 4–5, 69, 88, 108, 179–80,
    183, 184
sexual abuse, childhood, see childhood
    sexual abuse
sexual addiction, 4, 108, 162–3
sexual aversion, 85
sexual confidence, 89
sexual desire (discrepancy), 86–92, 94,
    96–7
sexual dysfunction, 171
    classification (DSM), 24–5, 28,
        84–5, 154
    definitions/approaches, 84–6, 169
    psychosexual issues, 4, 83–99
sexual language (inappropriate), 129
sexual 'lovestyles', 3, 164–6
sexual politics, 88, 94
sexual problems, 169–70, 172
    psychosexual issues, 4, 83–99
sexual response cycle, 84, 85, 95, 165
'sexual revolution', 161
sexual styles, gay male, 3, 164–6
sexuality
    bisexuality, 3, 115–26
    compulsive, 92, 109, 162
    definitions, 5
    ethnicity/race and, 3, 7–20
    gay (clinical issues), 3, 160–73
    intimacy and (gay men), 3, 162,
        169–72
    SM/kink lifestyle, 3, 22–34
    transgender, 3, 176–89
    see also gay men; heterosexuality;
        lesbian women; transgender
sexually transmitted diseases, 59, 93,
    166, 172
    see also HIV/AIDS
Shakespeare, T., 139
shame, 13, 15, 16, 48, 50, 109, 165,
    171, 182
Sharp, S., 147
shaving, 22

Shaw, Peggy, 178
Shelley, C., 167
Shires, A., 94–5
Siever, M.D., 168
Sildenafil (Viagra), 96
Sim, J., 41
Simon, G., 84, 97, 98, 162
Simon, R.I., 38
Sinason, V., 128, 139
Sketchley, J., 118
slavery, 7, 11, 12
sM (slave/Master relationship), 22, 25
SM sexual lifestyle, 3, 22–34, 98
Smith, A., 16, 17
Smith, P.K., 146, 147
Socarides, C.W., 167
social exclusion, 146
social support networks
    for bullying victims, 156–7
    HIV/AIDS, 57, 58
social systems, 10
socio-cultural factors
    gay body image, 167–8
    gay psychosexual problems, 94–5
Soho pub bombing incident, 110
somagrams, 111
somatic presentation (childhood
    abuse), 139–40
somatic psychology, 111
sound, 70, 71, 72, 79–80
Sowell, R.L., 62
'Spanner' case, 28–9, 31
Spectrum, 103, 110
Spring, J., 128
stereotypes, 26
    bisexual, 15, 18, 118
    ethnic minorities, 12, 15, 18
    gay men, 15, 18, 69, 91, 105, 108,
        161, 167
    lesbian, 15, 18, 69, 90
    transgender, 178, 187
Stevens, John, 106, 107
stigmatisation, 13, 25, 26, 88, 137
    HIV/AIDS, 60–1, 163
    of kinky sexual practices, 245
Stoltenberg, J., 108
stomach-ache (symptom of abuse),
    139
Stonewall, 147, 178
storytelling, 69, 78–9

stress, 32, 92, 97
    management, 42
subcultures, gay male, 3, 161–3
substance abuse, 58–9, 89, 95
suicide/suicidal ideation, 137, 140,
    150–1, 152–3, 177
Sumpter Forman, S., 118
supervision, 98, 140
    in dilemma management, 47, 48
support systems, 57, 58, 63–5, 156–7
surgery (gender reassignment), 181,
    183, 185, 186–7
survival strategies (transgender), 185–6
systems theory, 30–1

taboos (religious/social), 25, 26, 129
tattooing, 22, 168
teachers, bullying by, 149
Temoshok, L., 62
theories (mainstream professional
    influences), 38–9
therapeutic relationship, 5, 18
    dual (ethical dilemmas), 3, 35–52
therapists
    cultural values, 98
    embracing difference, 3, 7–20
    ethical dilemmas (in dual
        relationships), 3, 35–52
    rejection by, 172, 173
    self-disclosure, 19–20
    training/development, 4–5, 99
    working with SM clients, 29–32
therapy
    bisexuality and, 3, 115–26
    expressive, 2, 68–82
    intercultural, 3, 7–20
    terminology, 5
    transgender issues, 3, 176–89
Thompson, J., 10, 12–13, 39, 139
Thompson, M., 109
Tielman, R.A.P., 161
tit play, 22
Tobey, L.A., 58
Todor, N., 86
'top surgery', 181
Torr, Diana, 178
torture, 28
touch, 37–8, 140–1
    therapeutic value of, 74, 78
'Tracey Island', 76

transactional analysis, 11
transference, 9, 42, 44, 45, 49–50,
  171–2, 173
transformation process, 181–2, 186,
  189
transgender, 3
  clinical presentations, 180–1
  definitions/emergence, 176–7
  professional guidelines, 181–9
  queer gender, 178–80
transpersonal psychology, 29
transsexuality, 177–81, 183–4, 185,
  187, 188
transvestism, 176, 177, 178, 180, 181
traumatic early experiences (gay men),
  93
Trenchard, Lorraine, 147–8, 150
triple combination therapies, 57
trust, 105, 106, 137, 142, 165
truth (of sexual abuse), 128, 135–6,
  137, 140
Tucker, Naomi, 120
Turner, S., 19

Udis-Kessler, A., 118
unconditional positive regard, 172
unconscious, 71, 72
United Kingdom Council for
  Psychotherapy, 2
universality (ethical problem solving),
  40
unsafe sex, 108, 166
urinary tract infections, 140
Ussher, J., 83, 85

vacuum pump device, 95
vaginismus, 84, 85, 86
value systems, 11, 13, 14, 62
van Kerkhof, M.P.N., 165
Vanaerschot, G., 136
Vasquez, M.J.T., 44
Viagra (Sildenafil), 96
vibrators, 88
Vice Versa (Garber), 116

Vidal, Gore, 116, 125
Volker (case example), 170–1
volunteers (HIV social care), 63–4
von Sacher-Masoch, Leopold, 24

Wadsworth, E., 63
Walker, M., 109, 128
Walster, G., 90
Warren, H., 147–8, 150, 153
Webb, S.R., 37–8
Weinberg, M.S., 94
Wenner, 70
Westcott, H., 128, 139
Western European culture, 13, 160,
  185
Whitfield, G., 97, 98, 162
Whitman, Walt, 112
Whitney, I., 146
Wild Dance events, 107
'willingness model', 85
Wilson, M., 128, 139
women
  child sexual abuse by, 130, 131, 140
  femininity, 91, 117, 184, 188
  how men relate to, 108
  oppression of/power assertion by,
    25–6
  see also bisexuality; lesbian women
Women and Bisexuality (George), 116
'worthlessness', 12
Wright, B., 91, 93
writing, 70, 71, 72, 78–9
Wyatt, 139

xenophobia, 7

Young, V., 39

Zandvliet, Tony, 3
Zen Buddhism, 111
Zilbergeld, B., 91
Zinschitz, E., 139
'zones of awareness' exercises, 107
Zuckerman, M., 153

PINK THERAPY
A GUIDE FOR COUNSELLORS AND THERAPISTS WORKING WITH LESBIAN, GAY AND BISEXUAL CLIENTS

Dominic Davies and Charles Neal (eds)

Pink Therapy is the first British guide for counsellors and therapists working with people who are lesbian, gay or bisexual. It provides a much needed overview of lesbian, gay and bisexual psychology, and examines some of the differences between lesbians, gays and bisexuals, and heterosexuals. *Pink Therapy* proposes a model of gay affirmative therapy, which challenges the prevailing pathologizing models. It will help to provide answers to pressing questions such as:

• What is different about lesbian, gay and bisexual psychologies?
• How can I improve my work with lesbian, gay and bisexual clients?
• What are the key clinical issues that this work raises?

The contributors draw on their wide range of practical experience to provide – in an accessible style – information about the contemporary experience of living as a lesbian, gay or bisexual person, and to explore some of the common difficulties.

Pink Therapy will be important reading for students and practitioners of counselling and psychotherapy, and will also be of value to anyone involved in helping people with a lesbian, gay or bisexual orientation.

Reviews of *Pink Therapy* . . .

'A comprehensive British volume on lesbian and gay affirmative psychotherapy has been a while coming. *Pink Therapy*, however, has arrived, amply fills this gap, and is well worth the wait . . . A deft editorial hand is evident in the unusual consistency across chapters, the uniformly crisp, helpful chapter summaries, and the practical appendices, generous resources lists and well organized bibliographies.

I particularly liked the contributors' subtle appreciation of theoretical nuance, genuine open-mindedness to diversity of ideas, and willingness to synthesize in a pragmatic and client-oriented manner.'

John C. Gonsiorek, Past President, Society for the Psychological Study of Lesbian and Gay Issues, (Division 44 of the American Psychological Association)

'It is all too easy for the liberal heterosexual therapist to imagine he or she has it all sewn up as far as attitudes to homosexuality are concerned. This book shows that even the politically correct, have so much to learn not just about being gay, lesbian or bisexual, but also about research into sexuality, attitudes amongst therapists, and on training courses, as well as in the development of psychotherapy and counselling.'

Michael Jacobs, Director of the Psychotherapy and Counselling Certificate Programme, University of Leicester

'This book equips heterosexual therapists for gay affirmative work . . . It gave me much more knowledge and insight into being gay in our society. Extremely well researched, numerous tracks for further investigations, guidelines on relevant reading . . . the language and tone make it accessible to all except the most defensive . . . I recommend it strongly.'

Dave Mearns, Reader in Counselling and Director of the Counselling Unit, University of Strathclyde

Contents
Introduction – Part 1: Fundamental issues – An historical overview of homosexuality and therapy – Towards a model of gay affirmative therapy – Homophobia and heterosexism – Working with people coming out – Part 2: Working with particular issues – Working with single people – Working with people in relationships – Lesbian and gay parenting issues – Working with young people – Working with older lesbians – Working with older gay men – Alcohol and substance misues – Partner abuse – Religious and spirituality conflicts – Appendix 1: Resources – Appendix 2: Community resources – Appendix 3: Books for clients and counsellors – References – Index.

Contributors
Dominic Davies, Helena Hargaden, Graz Kowszun, Sara Llewellin, Dr Bernard Lynch, Maeve Malley, Lyndsey Moon, Charles Neal, Dr Bernard Ratigan, Gail Simon, Fran Walsh, Val Young.

256pp   0 335 19145 2   (Paperback)   0 335 19657 8   (Hardback)

THERAPEUTIC PERSPECTIVES ON WORKING WITH LESBIAN, GAY AND BISEXUAL CLIENTS

Dominic Davies and Charles Neal (eds)

Following the success of *Pink Therapy* (1996 Open University Press) as a practical guide for therapists, counsellors and others in related professions working with lesbian, gay and bisexual clients in affirmative ways, this volume is the first to address how this can be approached from ten of the major therapeutic perspectives. Each approach is discussed with regard to its historical and theoretical relationship to these client groups and how the approach can be beneficial or negative. Guidelines for using the perspective supportively or practically are given, along with references for further study. The volume marks an important step in the dialogue between theoretical approaches and in the future development of, and debate about, these increasingly important fields in contemporary therapy.

Contents

Introduction – Analytical psychology – Cognitive-behavioural therapy – Existential-phenomenological therapy – Gay, lesbian and bisexual therapy and its supervision – Neuro-linguistic programming – Person-centred therapy – Psychoanalytic therapy – Psychosynthesis – Social constructionist and systemic therapy – Transactional analysis – Index.

224pp   0 335 20333 7   (paperback)   0 335 20334 5   (hardback)